COMEDY

This new edition of Andrew Stott's *Comedy* examines the significance of comic 'events' through the study of various theoretical methodologies, including deconstruction, psychoanalysis, and gender theory. It provides case studies of a number of themes, ranging from the drag act to the simplicity of slipping on a banana skin. This new edition features:

- updates to reflect new research in the field
- new chapters on women in comedy, race and ethnicity and queer comedy
- a broader range of literary and cultural examples.

Written in a clear and accessible style, this book is an ideal introduction to comedy for students studying literature and culture.

Andrew Stott is Professor of English at the University of Buffalo, SUNY, USA.

THE NEW CRITICAL IDIOM

SERIES EDITOR: JOHN DRAKAKIS, UNIVERSITY OF STIRLING

The New Critical Idiom is an invaluable series of introductory guides to today's critical terminology. Each book:

- provides a handy, explanatory guide to the use (and abuse) of the term;
- offers an original and distinctive overview by a leading literary and cultural critic;
- relates the term to the larger field of cultural representation.

With a strong emphasis on clarity, lively debate and the widest possible breadth of examples, *The New Critical Idiom* is an indispensable approach to key topics in literary studies.

COMEDY

Second edition

Andrew Stott

LONDON AND NEW YORK

First published 2005, this edition published 2014
by Routledge
2 Park Square, Milton Park, Abingdon, Oxon OX14 4RN

and by Routledge
711 Third Avenue, New York, NY 10017

Routledge is an imprint of the Taylor & Francis Group, an informa business

British Library Cataloguing in Publication Data
A catalogue record for this book is available from the British Library

Library of Congress Cataloging in Publication Data
Stott, Andrew McConnell, 1969-
Comedy / Andrew Stott. -- 2nd edition.
pages cm. -- (The new critical idiom)
Summary: "This new edition of Comedy builds on themes presented in the first edition such as focusing on the significance of comic events through study of various theoretical methodologies, including deconstruction, psychoanalysis and gender theory, and provides case studies of a number of themes, ranging from the drag act to the simplicity of slipping on a banana skin. This new edition features: updates to reflect new research in the field, new chapters on Women in Comedy and Race and Ethnicity, a broader range of literary and cultural examples. Written in a clear and accessible style, this book is an ideal introduction to comedy for students studying literature and culture."--Provided by publisher.
Includes bibliographical references and index.
1. Comedy. I. Title.
PN1922.S78 2014
809'.917--dc23
2013049968

ISBN: 978-0-415-85418-4 (hbk)
ISBN: 978-0-415-85419-1 (pbk)
ISBN: 978-0-203-79589-7 (ebk)

Typeset in Garamond by Taylor & Francis Books

Printed and bound in Great Britain by
TJ International Ltd, Padstow, Cornwall

CONTENTS

SERIES EDITOR'S PREFACE

The New Critical Idiom is a series of introductory books which seeks to extend the lexicon of literary terms, in order to address the radical changes which have taken place in the study of literature during the last decades of the twentieth century. The aim is to provide clear, well-illustrated accounts of the full range of terminology currently in use, and to evolve histories of its changing usage.

The current state of the discipline of literary studies is one where there is considerable debate concerning basic questions of terminology. This involves, among other things, the boundaries which distinguish the literary from the non-literary; the position of literature within the larger sphere of culture; the relationship between literatures of different cultures; and questions concerning the relation of literary to other cultural forms within the context of interdisciplinary studies.

It is clear that the field of literary criticism and theory is a dynamic and heterogeneous one. The present need is for individual volumes on terms which combine clarity of exposition with an adventurousness of perspective and a breadth of application. Each volume will contain as part of its apparatus some indication of the direction in which the definition of particular terms is likely to move, as well as expanding the disciplinary boundaries within which some of these terms have been traditionally contained. This will involve some re-situation of terms within the larger field of cultural representation, and will introduce examples from the area of film and the modern media in addition to examples from a variety of literary texts.

Acknowledgements

In keeping with the communal spirit of comedy, this book is the product of a number of good-natured interactions and has benefited greatly from the assistance of the following people: Keith Hindle and Nigel Mapp were kind enough to comment extensively on drafts, and without the profit of their rigorous and generous readings, this work would be much impaired. Monica Kendall also furnished excellent comments on my final draft. Terry Hawkes graciously allowed me to borrow a bit on Simon Forman I heard him deliver at a meeting of the London Shakespeare Seminar in 2002. Liz Thompson at Routledge is to be thanked for giving me the opportunity to write the book in the first place, and for retaining always the virtue of patient and good-humoured correspondence while I moved countries and generally didn't get down to it. John Drakakis has offered consistently supportive and authoritative editorial advice from first to last, and I am delighted to appear in his series. The final and most outstanding debt of gratitude is owed to Josie Stott, the funniest person I know, whose love, encouragement and support make everything worth doing. For this, and everything else, I love you.

ACKNOWLEDGEMENTS TO THE SECOND EDITION

Warm thanks are due to my research assistant, Farhana Hasan, for her help compiling materials; to John Drakakis for further editorial insights; and to Ruth Moody and Elizabeth Levine for their support of this edition.

INTRODUCTION

Tragedy is when I cut my finger. Comedy is when you fall down an open sewer and die.

Mel Brooks

Answering the question 'what is comedy?' is not so easy. On the one hand, comedy is a relatively stable literary form with a lengthy history, a form that Alexander Leggatt has called our most consistent genre, 'surviving centuries of cultural change with its basic conventions stubbornly intact' (Leggatt, 1998: 1). Understood this way, comedy is a type of drama that uses stock characters in scenarios that require some kind of problem to be resolved. These plays end happily, often concluding with a communal celebration like a feast or a marriage, and the characters generally manage to resolve their differences without anyone being killed. Yet even the most cursory glance at how we apply the term in the present day tells us that such a simple definition falls far short of describing all that comedy can be. Of course 'comedy' applies to a type of drama, but it can also refer to a range of styles as diverse as they are numerous, including traditional categories such as pastoral, farce, burlesque, pantomime, satire, and the comedy of manners, but also many modern sub-divisions: cartoons, sitcom, sketch comedy, slapstick, stand-up, panel shows, game shows, impressionists, caricatures, drag acts, even silly walks.

Perhaps comedy is best defined not by its formal qualities but by its ability to induce laughter, surely the most obvious barom-eter of its success or failure. But even laughter does not belong to comedy uniquely, as not only do comedies regularly fail to rouse a laugh, but many have succumbed to laughter at moments of guilt, fear, or embarrassment, or as a result of having their feet tickled or being stupefied by laughing gas. As any definition that allowed for all these considerations would have to be so broad as to be meaningless, is 'comedy' even definable at all? Certainly, 'the comic' is a notoriously elusive quantity, one that evades scrutiny and has a tendency to bolt the moment critical attention is turned towards it. As the American philosopher and poet Max Eastman once wrote, 'the correct explanation of a joke not only does not sound funny, it does not sound like a correct explanation' (quoted in Holt, 2008: 119).

So why a book about comedy at all? Because comedy permeates every aspect of human life and is as common to living as breathing. As such, it is better understood as a tonal quality rather than a structural one, something related to narrative, character and plot, but also independent of them. Considered this way, comedy is a mood, viewpoint, or sentiment capable of manifesting itself in many places and at any time, irrespective of genre. Frequently it appears in a series of themes that seek to question the things that we take for granted. Like water in rocks, comedy has a particular talent for finding the cracks in the world and amplifying them to the point of absurdity, rendering life, in the words of John Bruns, 'strange and open' (Bruns, 2009: xv). Common comic themes include social inversion, the 'world-turned-upside-down' scenario where slave governs master or man bites dog; the ridiculing of foo-lishness, narrow-mindedness, and the rigid insistence on inflexible systems of living; and comic transfigurations that permit the inves-tigation of alternative identities or the suspension of laws governing the body. Even the matter-of-fact ability of language to more-or-less describe the world is brought into question by comic contortions and linguistic non-sequiturs that create parallel or nonsensical forms of meaning. In all of these examples, irrespective of when and where they appear, a notion of 'comedy' is at work. For the purposes of this book, then, 'comedy' is a term that can refer equally to a genre, a tone, or a series of themes that manifest themselves in diverse environments. As such, it will require us to think of comedy multi-laterally, as at once a literary tradition with identifiable structural qualities, and a way of describing isolated events or passages within other types of work.

THE ROOTS OF COMEDY

What we know of the historical development of comedy appears to confirm the idea of it as a permeable form that has adapted to suit the demands of the day. Cordatus, the moderator of Ben Jonson's play *Every Man Out of His Humour* (1600), offers us this potted account of its development from its origins in ancient ritual:

> 'tis extant, that that which we call *Comoedia*, was at first nothing but a simple and continued Satyre, sung by one only person, till *Susario* invented a second, after him, *Epicharmus* a third; *Phormus* and *Chionides* devised to have foure actors, with a *Prologue* and *Chorus*; to which *Cratinus* (long after), added a fifth and sixt; *Eupolis*, more, *Aristophanes*, more than they: every man in the dignity of his spirit and judgment, supplied something: and (though that in him this kind of Poeme appeared absolute, and fully perfected) yet how is the face of it chang'd since, in *Menander, Philemon, Cecilius, Plautus*, and the rest; who have utterly excluded the *Chorus*, altered the property of the persons, their names, and natures, and augmented it with all libertie, according to the elegancie and disposition of those times wherein they wrote?
>
> (Jonson, 1920: Induction, 261–275)

In this version, comedy begins as a simple song for a lone voice gradually accumulating interlocutors as each authorial generation adds to the form. In so doing, Jonson, whose own comedies were innovative and markedly different from those that preceded him, suggests that comedy is by definition open to continual adaptation, and as such offers greater opportunities for freedom of expression:

> I see not then, but we should enjoy the same *Licentia*, or free power to illustrate and heighten our invention, as they did; and not be tied to those strict and regular forms which the niceness of a fewe (who are nothing but Forme), would thrust upon us.
>
> (Jonson, 1920: Induction, 275–279)

Our knowledge of the origins and development of comedy has not advanced far beyond Jonson's. A clue to its beginnings may be found in the etymology of the word itself, which is generally agreed to be derived from an amalgamation of the Greek words '*kômos*' or '*kômai*', and '*oda*', words that reflect comedy's roots in the Greek peninsula. '*Kômos*' translates as 'revel', while '*kômai*' comes from the word for 'village'. Aristotle (c.384–322 BC) preferred this second definition, remarking that the Dorians 'call outlying villages *kômai* … the assumption being that comedians were so-called not from the revel or *kômos*, but because they toured the villages when expelled from the town in disgrace' (Aristotle, 1996: 6). '*Oda*' is uncontroversially translated as 'song', and so comedy is either a hymn of celebration or, as the poet Dante Alighieri (1265–1321) styled it, 'a rustic song' (Dante, 1984: 31).

Most critics and historians agree that comedy appears to be the product of a rural environment rather than an urban one, and to have come into being in association with seasonal agrarian fertility rites. At some stage, comedy also began a long association with the god Dionysus, whose divine characteristics and patronage are clearly impressed upon the form. Dionysus, the son of Zeus and Semele, was originally a god of the fertility of nature, a vegetation-spirit who died and was reborn yearly. His cult reached Greece from either Thrace or Phrygia at around 1000 BC, and was particularly notable for its devotional use of wine and the orgiastic revels of its votaries, especially women, who withdrew into the wild to make contact with nature. Dionysus was often described as having a minor god, Phales, as his companion, of whom little is known except his obvious association with the word 'phallus'. By the fourth century BC Dionysus had outgrown his association with organic fertility to become a sponsor of human sexual behaviour. The temperament and qualities of Dionysus and the nature of his worship appear, then, to have exerted a significant degree of influence on the principles of festivity, inversion, sexual freedom, and travesty that we find in comedy. Also significant is the removal from the city he encourages, placing him at the fringes of the civic environment and drawing his followers away from urban jurisdiction and inducing them into conduct that would be unacceptable in the city. Echoes of these Dionysial themes can still be heard much later on, as in the libidity, rusticity, and altered consciousness of William Shakespeare's *A Midsummer Night's Dream* (1595).

Dionysus's most important function in terms of the performance of comedy was as the divine patron of both the Lenaea and the 'Great Dionysia', annual Athenian theatrical festivals at which prizes were awarded to the best dramatists. Initially, the Dionysia, the more important of the two, was for tragedians only, with comedies performed only at the winter Lenaea. From around 486 BC, a comedy competition was initiated at the Dionysia, the point at which we may say that comedy is institutionalised as a significant literary form. We can say this because the Dionysia appears to have played an important role as a civic gathering and statement of national identity aside from the presentation of theatrics, a platform wherein the achievements of the state might be annually reiterated, honours granted to citizens of distinction, and the lines of social division and hierarchy be graphically represented in terms of seating and participation. A sense of collective involvement in the issues of city and government might also be raised through the debates aired in plays (Palmer, 1994: 31–32).

THE USES OF COMEDY

The organised, civic dimension of Athenian comedy then begs a further question: what purpose does comedy serve, and what, if anything, is its social function or philosophical value, aside from giving pleasure? Whereas the comedy of Aristophanes (c.448–380 BC) engaged in an overt political and satirical commentary, comic drama was encouraged to move away from current affairs at an early stage in its development. Aristotle tells us that it was Crates (active 450 BC) who 'first abandoned the form of a lampoon and began to construct universalised stories and plots'; and by the time of Menander (c.342–c.291 BC) nearly a century later, comedy had ceased to intervene in the issues of government, at least explicitly (Aristotle, 1996: 9). Instead, comedy was commended for its realistic representation of the human condition, famously moving the early Alexandrine scholar Aristophanes of Byzantium to ask, 'O Menander and Life / Which of you is imitating which?' (Segal, 2001: 153). By the fourth century AD, literary theorists thought of comedy as a primarily instructive form, as in the work of the Roman grammarian Donatus, who wrote enormously influential remarks on the comedies of Terence, works he would have never seen performed and would have only known as texts. Under these sterile conditions, Donatus declared comedy to be essentially didactic, mirroring everyday life and schooling us in practical ethics. He also emphasised the academic qualities of comedy, arguing that good comedy should be built according to sound rhetorical principles (Herrick, 1950: 65). Donatus's scholarly and moralistic method fortified comedy with some of the technical respectability of tragedy, and the principal arguments of comic theory from the Renaissance onwards are based on his ideas. That its primary function is corrective is argued in 1698, for example, by William Congreve in response to the clergyman Jeremy Collier's attack on him in particular and theatre in general. 'Men are to be laughed out of their vices in comedy', wrote Congreve. 'The business of comedy is to delight as well as to instruct; and as vicious people are made ashamed of their follies and faults by seeing them exposed in a ridiculous manner, so are good people at once both warned and diverted at their expense' (Congreve, 1997a: 515). Two centuries later, in his 'Essay on Comedy' (1877), the playwright George Meredith made a similar point, although metaphysically enlarging it by personifying comedy as a benign spirit monitoring human behaviour. 'Whenever they wax out of proportion, overblown, affected, pretentious, bombastical, hypocritical, pedantic, fantastically delicate', he writes,

> whenever it sees them self-deceived or hoodwinked, given to run riot in idolatries, drifting into vanities, congregating in absurdities, planning

short-sightedly, plotting dementedly; whenever they are at variance with their professions, and violate the unwritten but perceptible laws binding them in consideration one to another; whenever they offend sound reason, fair justice; are false in humility or mined with conceit ... the Spirit overhead will look humanely malign, and cast an oblique light on them, followed by volleys of silvery laughter. That is the Comic Spirit.

(Meredith, 1980: 48)

In the twentieth century, critics have been less keen to subscribe to comedy's didacticism. Some, like Maurice Charney, see a central lack of agreement in modern discussions of the form that leaves us with 'no common assumptions and no set of conventions by which we could agree on how to speak about comedy' (Charney, 1978: vii–viii). More assertive critics, like Harry Levin, see comedy as a conflict between the emotions of joviality and sobriety, a 'perennial war of the laughers against the non-laughers', of playboys against killjoys, 'locked in an eternal battle of world views' (Levin, 1987: 40). For Erich Segal, the history of Western comedy plots a long line of descent from the euphoric highs of 'Aristophanic triumph' to the resignation of the 'theatre of inadequacy', represented by the work of Samuel Beckett. According to this thesis, vigorous expressions of life begin to fade and become more complicated and contingent as history and experience instruct us in cynicism to the point that once boisterous, optimistic comedies are rendered increasingly untenable. Samuel Beckett's play *Waiting for Godot* (1953) epitomises comedy's fate:

The drama will have no happy ending. Indeed, it will have no ending at all. There will be no revel, renewal, or rejuvenation. For whatever Godot may represent, whether salvation or erotic rebirth, one thing is clear. The traditional happy ending is no longer possible – because comedy is dead.

(Segal, 2001: 452)

Rather than proposing narratives of comic function that are intended to hold true in all times and places, some critics, especially those with an interest in poststructuralist theory, are drawn to its apparent ambiguity and resistance to definition. Andrew Horton claims that 'like language, and like "texts" in general, the comic is plural, unfinalized, disseminative, dependent on *context* and the intertextuality of creator, text, and contemplator' (Horton, 1991: 9). Kirby Olson adopts a similar approach, reading comic fiction through the work of French philosophers Jean-François Lyotard and Gilles Deleuze, and finding in comedy an affront to rationality and meta-narratives that attempt to exhaustively explain or incorporate all aspects of the world:

> Comedy is an immanent form that does not make us look into the heavens or to God for answers to questions ... Comic theory traces a larger discourse over politics of the body and, within that discourse, between orthodoxy and heresy. Like desire, laughter is strangely fluid and cannot be contained by rational thought.
>
> (Olson, 2001: 5)

For Olson, the slippery problem of defining comedy and comic action satisfactorily is evidence of its postmodern virtues: 'Comedy is precisely *a certain freedom from definition*' (Olson, 2001: 6).

Perhaps the only formulation that remains appropriate is also one of the vaguest. In 1900, the French metaphysician Henri Bergson (of whom more in Chapter 1) argued that 'the comic does not exist outside the pale of what is strictly *human*', a statement that maintains that in all instances, events must at some point intersect with human consciousness to become comic (Bergson, 1980: 62). The humanness of comedy was noted by Aristotle who observed that we are the only creatures who feel compelled to laugh. Comedy is certainly a social activity first and foremost, conceived of always with some kind of audience in mind, and everywhere produced from the matter of dominant cultural assumptions and commonplaces. The question of *how* or *why* things come to be funny is similarly determined by culture. Even though comedy often seems to be suspending, inverting, or abandoning dominant norms, these inversions are produced in relation to the cultural orthodoxies from which they must always begin. It should there-fore be possible to trace comic events back to the significations they have transformed. In this way, the comic can be thought of as a means of opening up the possibility of multiple perspectives, as each concept culturally established as orthodox simultaneously presents itself for the possibility of comic subversion, a silent but parallel conversation that might erupt at any moment. Take the traditional story of the Greek poet Philomon, who, we are told, died laughing after he saw a donkey eating figs. The lethal quality of this scene was the perceived incongruity of a beast eating what was categorised as human food. What killed Philomon, therefore, was an event that violated certain pre-fabricated categories of decorum and appropriateness applicable to figs and donkeys, coupled with his ability to perceive that violation as ludicrous and culminating in dangerously high levels of amusement. We can understand this as an experience of division within the poet that allowed him to interpret multiple layers of significance instantaneously and simultaneously. For Bergson, the division between the perceived and the actual, and the possibility of reading situations in a number of different ways, was a phenomenon he isolated as one of the three principal triggers of laughter. What he labelled 'the reciprocal interference of series' is a scenario that 'belongs simultaneously to two altogether independent series of events and is capable of being interpreted in two entirely different meanings at the same time' (Bergson, 1980: 122). Examples would include Oliver Goldsmith's play *She Stoops to Conquer* (1773), where Marlow mistakes the Hardcastles' house for an inn, or Monty Python's film *Life of Brian* (1979), where Brian's life so parallels that of Jesus Christ that he is mistaken for the son of God. What is amusing is the tension caused by the co-existence and interplay between 'the double fact of coincidence and interference' (Bergson, 1980: 124), such as Brian's unwittingly amassing a devout following while his mother insists that 'he's not the messiah, he's a very naughty boy'. That both Brian's followers and his mother should be confirmed in their contrasting beliefs is made plausible by the setting and the action of the film, and thus *Life of Brian* demonstrates a continual awareness of the possibility of reading a scenario in two different ways, of a division in comprehension and the co-existence of parallel ideas.

The theme of comedy as a divided and doubled experience is even embodied for us in the double-act, a staple of comic performance since the appearance of Dionysus and his servant Xanthias in Aristophanes's *Frogs* (405 BC). Double acts present a perfect embodiment of the uneasy doubling and bi-focal perceptions of comedy. Similarly, we might look to the disparity between place and self that is continually used in comedy, stories in which people are geographically, linguistically, or in some profoundly existential way misplaced, 'fish out of water' comedies like Molière's *Le Bourgeois Gentilhomme* (1670), Buster Keaton's *The General* (1926), Eddie Murphy's *Trading Places* (1983), or Simon Pegg's *Shaun of the Dead* (2004). Another stock situation presents a discrepancy between the way a character presents him- or herself and the substance of their actions, as is the case with Shakespeare's pompous Falstaff, or the hypocritical devout in Molière's *Tartuffe* (1664), or David Brent/Michael Scott in the UK and US versions of *The Office*. A recurring technique of the comedy team Monty Python (1969–1974) was the discussion of quotidian topics in an elevated register, exploiting discontinuity between form and content, as in this sports report that blends philosophy with soccer:

> Last night in ... Jarrow, we witnessed the resuscitation of a great footballing tradition, when Jarrow United came of age, in a European sense, with an almost Proustian display of modern existentialist football. Virtually annihilating by midfield moral argument the now surely obsolescent catennachio defensive philosophy of Signor Alberto Fanfrino. Bologna indeed were a side intellectually out argued by a Jarrow team thrusting and bursting with aggressive Kantian positivism ...
>
> (Chapman et al., 1998, vol. 1: 139)

All these examples utilise some form of incongruity, and rely upon a culturally defined sense of incompatible orders, such as the displacement of people or discourses, to produce ambiguity and the feeling that normality has been momentarily decentred for pleasurable ends. This has been studied by Mary Douglas in her work on joking relationships in traditional cultures. Douglas argues that a joke cannot simply jump from nowhere, but derives from a sense of reality that pre-exists it, and which it seeks to distort:

a joke is seen and allowed when it offers a symbolic pattern of a social pattern occurring at the same time ... all jokes are expressive of the social situations in which they occur. The one social condition necessary for a joke to be enjoyed is that the social group in which it is received should develop the formal characteristics of a 'told' joke: that is a dominant pattern of relation is challenged by another. If there is no joke in the social structure, no other joking can appear.

(Douglas, 1975: 98)

Jokes therefore emerge from within the social framework and necessarily express the nature of their environment, which means that all jokes are necessarily produced in a relative relationship to the dominant structures of understanding and the epistemological order. Despite the violation of the social order implied by joking, the joker enjoys a kind of immunity through the belief that his or her wit represents insight into a different type of consciousness:

The joker's own immunity can be derived philosophically from his apparent access to other reality than that mediated by the relevant structure. Such access is implied in the contrast of forms in which he deals. His jokes expose the inadequacy of realist structurings of experience and so release the pent-up power of the imagination.

(Douglas, 1975: 108)

Douglas's conclusions suggest that joking is an imaginative exploration of alternative social formulations, and a recognition of lack in the 'realist structurings of experience' that usually represent it. Through joking, the joker appears to gain privileged insight beyond the social construct where its meanings are neither exhaustive nor absolute, but are simply choices. Joking reveals the practical limits of cultural structures; for all systemic choices, other choices might equally have been made.

Joking is quite different in Freudian psychoanalysis, but nevertheless similarly revealing of an underside to socially constructed 'reason'. For Sigmund Freud, a joke is an example of 'parapraxis', an act like a mistake or slip of the tongue that exposes something of the repressed thoughts hidden in the unconscious. Like dreams, jokes contain significant information about unconscious thoughts and the nature of inhibition, where the production of a joke is a means of negotiating the psychological barrier between the conscious and unconscious mind. Freud points out that jokes have a tendency to spring from nowhere, suddenly appearing like little emissaries of the unconscious. 'A joke', he writes,

> has quite outstandingly the characteristic of being a notion that has occurred to us 'involuntarily'. What happens is not that we know a moment beforehand what joke we are going to make, and that all it then needs is to be clothed in words. We have an indefinable feeling, rather, which I can best compare with an *'absence'*, a sudden release of intellectual tension, and then all at once the joke is there – as a rule ready clothed in words.
>
> (Freud [1905], 2001: 167)

Making jokes is an almost involuntary act; they come across the joker in an instant, fully formed and with no explanation as to how they were made. In Freud's analysis, joking is symptomatic of the division in the psyche that characterises human beings. Once again, the comic acts as a parallel conversation, tracking reason and subverting it.

COMEDY AND ECCENTRICITY

So what does this strange ability to at once recognise the social order and subvert it amount to? Existential philosopher Helmuth Plessner cites the perception of the comic as evidence that human beings are intrinsically *'eccentric'*, as they are the only animals with the capacity to reflect on their thoughts and experiences. Plessner argues that our experience of the world is a result of information mediated through the purposeful management of our speech, thoughts, and control of our limbs, all of which, organised around a coherent sense of self, leads us to believe in our mastery of the immediate environment. The world outside, however, is unconcerned with the individual ego, and treats the human body as yet more matter. Thus we are at once convinced of our control of the environment, but simultaneously aware that we are subject to disinterested nature:

Just as the world and my own body are revealed to me, and can be controlled by me, only insofar as they appear in relation to me as a central 'I', so, on the other hand, they retain their ascendancy over their subjection in this perspective as an order indifferent to me and including me in a nexus of mutual neighbourhoods.

(Plessner, 1970: 36)

The subject, then, comes to reflect upon itself as both ego and matter, and is divided in this knowledge. As Simon Critchley puts it, 'the human being has a reflective attitude towards its experiences and towards itself', living 'beyond the limits set for them by nature by taking up a distance from their immediate experience' (Critchley, 2002: 28). The title of Plessner's work is *Laughing and Crying*, because these effects, both largely involuntary, involve moments when the bodily intrudes into the sense of self and overruns it, disturbing the conscious mind. Human eccentricity is the product, therefore, of discontinuity between the world in our head and the world outside. 'In this respect', says Plessner, 'man is inferior to the animal since the animal does not experience itself as shut off from its physical existence, as an inner self or I, and in consequence does not have to overcome a break between itself and itself, itself and its physical existence' (Plessner, 1970: 37). We could attribute to this phenomenon of being 'shut off' the often remarked-upon cruelty of comedy, which requires a certain degree of desensitisation. If it is generically appropriate for tragedy to ask us to be sensible of human suffering, then comedy, as Mel Brooks's quote shows, allows us to stand back and look upon human misfortune from an emotional distance, sometimes even deriving great pleasure from it.

In a discussion of irony in a 1969 essay entitled 'The Rhetoric of Temporality', the literary theorist Paul de Man (1919–1983) develops a further idea of the discontinuity between what we might understand as material nature and human consciousness. In this essay, de Man explains that Baudelaire's notion of irony is not an intersubjective concept, something produced between people, but an internalised relationship, a 'relationship, within consciousness, between two selves' (de Man, 1983: 212). Where comic relationships often imply positions of superiority and inferiority, there are no proper 'selves' within the internalised ironic relationship to occupy those spaces, and so it is not possible to think of one as 'superior' or more knowledgeable than another. Therefore, says de Man, irony 'merely designates the *distance* constitutive of all acts of reflection. Superiority and inferiority ... become merely spatial metaphors to indicate a discontinuity and a plurality of levels within a subject that comes to know itself by an increasing differentiation from what it is not' (de Man, 1983: 213). This is especially pronounced when a human being differentiates him- or herself from the non-human world. When a person falls over, for example, the inauthentic nature of the relationship of identity to its surroundings is exposed:

> The Fall, in the literal as well as the theological sense, reminds him of the purely instrumental, reified character of his relationship to nature. Nature can at all times treat him as if he were a thing and remind him of his factitiousness, whereas he is quite powerless to convert even the smallest particle of nature into something human.
>
> (de Man, 1983: 214)

Human beings, prone to treat the world around them as if it were a thing that they can control (de Man uses the word 'reified', to suggest that nature is incorrectly perceived as a malleable commodity), find themselves made into a thing by nature. De Man continues by adding that humans largely know the world as a 'language-determined' experience, in which everything is perceived through a linguistic framework. Ironic language, the language of the fall, is language that expresses the 'inauthentic' nature of the subject's relationship to the world:

> The ironic language splits the subject into an empirical self that exists in a state of inauthenticity and a self that exists only in the form of a language that asserts the knowledge of this inauthenticity. This does not, however, make it into an authentic language, for to know authenticity is not the same as to be authentic.
>
> (de Man, 1983: 214)

Thus in irony, the subject is divided into an inauthentic self, and a self that knows itself to be inauthentic. In a different but similar vein, the Slovenian psychoanalyst and critic Alenka Zupančič argues that comedy works not because it punctures our illusions and reduces us to our basic animal essence, but because it reveals the lengths we go to to perpetuate our delusions, even in the face of the evidence that reveals them as illusions. 'If humans were only human,' she writes, 'there would be no comedy' (Zupančič, 2008: 49). For Zupančič, the principal mode of comedy is excess, asserting itself through hyperbole, grotesqueries, surprise, and exaggeration, and the pairing of illogical or contradictory ideas. As such, it brings opposing ideas together and holds them in tension, refusing to reduce them to a logical singularity.

Take, for example, the notion of an aristocrat slipping on a banana peel or repeatedly falling into a muddy puddle. A traditional view might see this as evidence that comedy can level even the loftiest among us to their core humanity. According to Zupančič, however, to concentrate on the fall itself is to mischaracterise what has happened. Instead, she notes the endless resilience of comedy figures, who, like Buster Keaton, Wile E. Coyote, or the unfortunate Kenny in *South Park,* are able to endure any number of violent accidents or traumatic affronts and keep moving, pursuing their objectives regardless of the setbacks. In the example of an aristocrat who falls into one muddy puddle after another, Zupančič claims that the force of comedy lies not in the fact that he falls, but in the fact that he gets back up completely unchanged, as convinced of his rank and status as he ever was. The fall, therefore, *reduces* the baron to nothing, but rather highlights the *excess* of identity and the persistence of an ideology that allows aristocracy to exist in the first place. Another important aspect of the fall for Zupančič is the fact that it exists as an instant outside narrative. Comedy, she argues, does not unfold like a story, but is rather explosive and terroristic. 'Things that really concern us,' she writes, 'things that concern the very kernel of our being, can be watched and performed only as comedy, as an impersonal play with the object' (Zupančič, 2008: 182).

In various ways, all of the ideas discussed above suggest that in some experience of the comic there is a division of consciousness that enables the subject to see the world with bifurcated vision. Instances of humour, joking, or irony invoke a separation between 'authorised', egocentric, or rational versions of the world and their revealed alternatives, commenting on established conventions as they go. This does not mean that joking opens up a path to 'truth', or even that it has the ability to cut through untruths, as it generally does not provide coherent counter-arguments and its efficacy as a platform for change is questionable. Indeed, we would have to say that the duality enabled in joking and comic scenarios opposes any univocal interpretation of the world. Given this principle, this book will not attempt to explain comedy in accordance with a single methodological framework or narrative of literary development. Instead, we shall approach comedy thematically, accepting what appears to be its bifurcated nature by treating it as a multi-faceted and diverse series of events, rather than a generic totality, and evoking particular theories or concepts only whenever they might usefully help us to better understand comic ideas.

1

COMEDY IN THE ACADEMY

And this book – considering comedy a wondrous medicine, with its satire and mime, which would produce the purification of the passions through the enactment of defect, fault, weakness – would induce false scholars to try to redeem the lofty with a diabolical reversal: through the acceptance of the base ... this is what we cannot and must not have.

Umberto Eco, *The Name of the Rose*

Umberto Eco's novel imagines a book on comedy, Aristotle's lost sequel to *Poetics*. The book is at the heart of a monastic conspiracy to keep humour out of religion by suppressing the Aristotelian authority that lends comedy intellectual legitimacy, thus preventing 'the operation of the belly' from becoming 'an operation of the mind' (Eco, 1983: 474). Eco's conspirators fear that if comedy were to be rehabilitated within a respectable context, the conceptual order of things would be radically altered and with it the social fabric that draws on its hierarchies, as 'on the day when the Philosopher's word would justify the marginal jests of the debauched imagination, or when what has been marginal would leap to the center, every trace of the center would be lost' (Eco, 1983: 475).

To preserve the status quo, the pages of the book are infused with a poison that kills those who read it.

While Eco's conspiracy is entirely fictional, it is certainly true that comedy has enjoyed less prominence within the academy, especially in comparison to tragedy. While this is due in part to the absence of an important critical treatment of it in the classical tradition, comedy has also been perceived as ephemeral and lacking in intellectual weight, or, as in the protests of those who claim that explaining a joke kills it, as a kind of communication that is closed to study and interrogation. While earlier writers like Congreve and Meredith had stood up for the corrective merits of comedy, it is only in the twentieth century that we meet critics who are prepared to 'redeem' it as a culturally rich and critically significant form within a rigorous intellectual context. This chapter will consider some of the reasons for the place of comedy in the academy, and the work of some of its most important critics.

PLATO AND ARISTOTLE

The generic codification of drama in ancient Greece laid the foundations for the subsequent disparagement of comedy in relation to tragedy. In Hellenic philosophy, comedy was thought to belong to the lower human instincts, and, as such, was to be avoided by the man of reason. Indeed, it became one of the measures against which a rational identity could be formed. The contaminating qualities of comedy are first asserted in Plato's *Republic* (c.370 BC):

> If there are amusing things which you'd be ashamed to do yourself, but which give you a great deal of pleasure when you see them in a comic representation or hear about them in private company – when you don't find them loathsome or repulsive – then isn't this exactly the same kind of behaviour as we uncovered when talking about feeling sad? There's a part of you which wants to make people laugh, but your reason restrains it, because you're afraid of being thought a vulgar clown. Nevertheless, you let it have its way on those other occasions, and you don't realize that the almost inevitable result of giving it energy in this other context is that you become a comedian in your own life.
>
> (Plato, 1994: 360)

Here, Plato establishes an historically dogged distinction that opposes the vulgarity of laughter and clowning with the sovereignty of reason. Comedy is a force outside the guiding authority of reason that exerts a powerful anti-rational allure. Prolonged exposure to such thoughts or performances can result in the transformation of the subject into a comedian, as we 'irrigate and tend to those things when they should be left to wither, and ... [make] them our rulers when they should be our subjects' (Plato, 1994: 360). Plato's denigration of comedy in *Republic* exists within the context of his broader project to categorise and index subjectivity for the purposes of cultivating the ideal person in the ideal state. Unhealthy or counter-productive thoughts, emotions, and behaviours are restrained by an act of will and reason is promoted above all other things.

Whereas Plato creates a distinction between comedy and reason as a means of policing the self, Aristotle's *Poetics* (c.330 BC) establishes the fundamental structure through which the literary distinction between comedy and tragedy has been made. *Poetics*, the most influential work of literary theory in Western culture, implicitly establishes the idea that comedy is a type of drama with specific rules, character types, and outcomes. Both comedy and tragedy, Aristotle argues, seek to represent the world as it truly is, but whereas tragedy 'is an imitation of an action that is admirable, complete and possesses magnitude' (Aristotle, 1996: 10) set among people of substance, comedy deals with people who are 'low' by nature:

> Comedy is (as we have said) an imitation of inferior people – not, however, with respect to every kind of defect: the laughable is a species of what is disgraceful. The laughable is an error or disgrace that does not involve pain or destruction: for example, a comic mask is ugly and distorted, but does not involve pain.
>
> (Aristotle, 1996: 9)

For Aristotle, comedy is the imitation of the ridiculous or unworthy aspects of human behaviour, where little of real significance passes on stage and 'inferiority' amounts to a failure to uphold moral virtues. Ideally, tragedy depicts the decline in fortune of an individual which 'is not due to any moral defect or depravity, but to an error of some kind' that inevitably leads to a death or to the experience of 'something terrible' (Aristotle, 1996: 21). Comedy, on the other hand, ends happily and conflicts are resolved: 'In comedy even people who are the bitterest enemies in the story … go off reconciled in the end, and no one gets killed by anybody' (Aristotle, 1996: 22). The brief discussion of comedy in *Poetics* is not intended as a dismissal, but as a counterpoint to tragedy in the contrast between genres, the one form representing 'high' ideals, the other 'low', for the purposes of producing a symmetrical literary system that reflects a conception of humanity as an amalgamation of two competing facets of character.

It is widely assumed that Aristotle intended, or had already written, a companion volume to *Poetics* that concentrated on comedy, but this text, if it ever existed, is now lost. A brief document entitled the *Tractatus Coislinianus*, which outlines the construction of jokes and catalogues types of comic character, may offer an insight into its content, but its own provenance is uncertain, being 'variously hailed as the key to Aristotle's views on comedy and denounced as a sorry Byzantine fabrication' (Janko, 1984: 1). To what extent the existence of a comic *Poetics* would have improved the reputation of comedy in academic or scholarly circles is impossible to know, but as it is, Aristotle's passing remarks have shaped generic thinking to a degree that is difficult to overstate: 'On this Aristotelian basis,' writes M. S. Silk, 'all subsequent Western theory has been founded, most explicitly in the shape of a series of syntheses, late Greek, Graeco-Roman or Renaissance, but explicitly or implicitly in all ages' (Silk, 2000: 54).

GENRE TROUBLE

While comedy may have been of a lower order, in the ancient world, at least, it was relatively well defined. The Roman comedies of Plautus (c.254–184 BC) and Terence (c.190 or 180–159 BC), commonly known as 'New Comedy', consisted of a series of recurring characters and plots that were so similar that for modern readers the genre seems narrow and formulaic. From another perspective, however, this tells us how coherent and specialised the concept of comedy was at this time. During the medieval period, for example, the identity of comedy became far more confused and its boundaries blurred. The drama that conformed to Aristotle's formulae or directly emulated the writers of classical antiquity had disappeared from literary culture with the fall of the Roman Empire and the depletion of the theatres, not to re-emerge until the fifteenth century. Aristotle's definitions were kept alive by generations of medieval grammarians who used them to annotate the texts of Greek and Roman authors, while the distinctions between comedy and tragedy were upheld in commentaries and treatises by writers such as Diomedes, Evanthius, and Donatus. Yet all this was done in a vacuum, since while these authors continued to transmit Hellenic ideas about comedy, they had little or no first-hand experience of what they were writing about. And so two parallel streams emerged: the classical definition of comedy maintained in medieval scholarship, and actual comedic practice.

In the medieval period, comedy, which had previously been conceived solely as a type of drama, began to appear in both prose and verse as a distinguishable mode or tone rather than a specific genre. As Paul G. Ruggiers writes, 'the forms of tragedy and comedy inherited from classical antiquity had no real impact upon the like modes of experience ... in the Middle Ages', resulting in considerable diversity and discontinuity amongst comic forms (Ruggiers, 1977: 7; Shanzer, 2002: 25). Amongst other things, there developed alternative prose types to which 'were attached the considerations of their serious and non-serious biases, and of the subject matter and vocabulary once reserved for the dramatic forms, but now applied inadvertently to the narrative fictions' (Ruggiers, 1977: 7). This is the ultimate source of the problems of definition and confusion that inevitably arise in discussions of comedy, where 'comedy' can describe at once a dramatic genre, a literary mode, or instances of humour real or fictional. Both Boccaccio (1313–1375) and Chaucer (c.1343–1400) were interested in the textures and possibilities of comedy and tragedy, yet neither was a dramatist. The clearest example of the broadening of the term in the medieval period is the title of Dante's *Divine Comedy* (begun c.1314), a poem that, for the most part, contains little that may be described as humorous. Structurally, however, Dante's poem, like Greek and Roman comedy before it, moves out of ignorance to understanding and towards a happy conclusion, or in terms of its theological framework, from despair to eternal life. In a letter to his friend Can Grande, Dante further explains his choice of title by indicating that it is written in what he calls 'an unstudied and low style' (Dante, 1984: 31). Medieval mystery and morality plays similarly incorporated comic elements in accordance with these principles, where 'comedy' represents a condition of ignorance prior to eventual salvation. The Vice figure of the drama was often intentionally humorous, an inversion of the ideal qualities of humanity presented in the didacticism of the principal narrative.

With the rise of Humanism, the Renaissance educational movement that devoted itself to the study of classical authors and the pursuit of pure literary style, Aristotelian standards of generic difference were reintroduced to literature. Humanist scholars returned to their sources in Greek and Roman texts, the reputation of these volumes having flourished since the fall of Constantinople in 1453 and the re-introduction of otherwise overlooked authors that this event occasioned in Western Europe, and sought to emulate their language, plots, and structures. Nicholas Udall's *Ralph Roister Doister* (1552), for example, widely recognised as the first comic drama in English, proudly proclaimed its classical heritage:

> The wyse poets long time heretofore,
> Under merrie Comedies secretes did declare,
> Wherein was contained very virtuous lore,
> With mysteries and forewarnings very rare.
> Such to write neither Plautus nor Terence dyd spare,
> Which among the learned at this day beares the bell;
> These with such other therein dyd excel.
> (Udall, 1984: Prologue, ll.15–21)

Udall, headmaster at Eton, saw his play as an Anglicised Latin comedy, affording it both academic and moral integrity. When, in 1588, Maurice Kyffin translated Terence's *Andria* in a version principally to be used in schools, he prefaced the text with praise of Terence's style, clearly revealing the influence of the comic theory of Donatus:

> Among all the Romane writers, there is none (by the judgement of the learned) so much available to be read and studied, for the true knowledge and purity of the Latin tong, as *Pub. Terentius*: for, sith the cheefest matter in speech, is to speak properly and aptly, and that we have not a more conning Craft-master of apt and proper speech than Terence, well worthy is he then, even will all ease and diligence, to be both taught and learned before any other.
>
> (Kyffin, 1588: sig. A1, Recto)

As early-modern scholarship favoured classical models for the purity of their form and style, Sir Philip Sidney, in his *Defence of Poetry* (1579–1580), complained of the disregard theatre practitioners had for generic boundaries, particularly taking them to task for their

> Gross absurdities, how all their plays be neither right tragedies, nor right comedies, mingling kings and clowns, not because the matter so carrieth it, but thrust in the clown by head and shoulders to play a part in majestical matters with neither decency nor discretion, so as neither the admiration and commiseration, nor the right sportfulness, is by their mongrel tragic-comedy obtained.
>
> (Sidney, 1991: 67)

Sidney's exasperation with mixed modes stems from a desire to impose conformity and uniformity on the drama of the Elizabethan stage, and to lend it some order and legitimacy. Yet, as Stephen Orgel tells us, comedy was not 'simply the opposite of tragedy, but ... the largest condition of drama' during this period (Orgel, 1994: 36). There is some anecdotal evidence that the comic aspects of Renaissance drama may have been amongst the most prominent for contemporary audiences. London doctor and astrologer Simon Forman, for example, records his presence at a performance of *The Winter's Tale* on 15 May 1611. His report differs considerably from modern readings of the play as it concentrates almost exclusively on the clown character of Autolycus, which leads him to conclude that the play is about 'feigned beggars or fawning fellows' (Rowse, 1976: 310). Similarly, the Swiss tourist Thomas Platter, in the playhouse for a performance of Shakespeare's *Julius Caesar* at the Globe in 1599, mentions little about the tragedy aside from the 'jig' that followed it, which was performed 'exceedingly gracefully, according to their custom, two in each group dressed in men's and two in women's apparel' (quoted in Shakespeare, 1998: 1).

Throughout the medieval and Renaissance periods, therefore, it seems that a scholarly definition of comedy, loyal to the Aristotelian blueprint, existed separately from popular plays, poems, and other vehicles for humour. The academy's apparent distance from popular culture is confirmed in the nineteenth and twentieth centuries and is concomitant with the rise of professional English literary studies. Inspired by the Victorian poet and critic Matthew Arnold (1822–1888), and largely concerned with what Chris Baldick calls 'questions of literature's social function' (Baldick, 1987: 18), the view of comedy in the universities at this time is best summed up by a footnote in F. R. Leavis's study of the novel, *The Great Tradition* (1972 [1948]), that calls the work of eighteenth-century satirist Laurence Sterne 'irresponsible', 'nasty', and 'trifling' (Leavis, 1972: 10). As Baldick says elsewhere, critical opinion held that 'the author's quality of mind [was] reflected in the quality of the literary work: to speak of the maturity or integrity of one is to commend the other' (Baldick, 1996: 164). Comic themes were thought to be parochial and vulgar, antithetical to a vision of art that believed in its ability to communicate beyond the specific moment of its creation. A passage from A. C. Bradley's prestigious British Academy lecture of 1912 expresses this idea. 'Most of the great tragedies', he writes,

> leave a certain imaginative impression of the highest value … What we witness is not the passion and doom of mere individuals. The forces that meet in tragedy stretch far beyond the little group of figures and the tiny tract of space and time in which they appear. The darkness that covers the scene, and the light that strikes across it, are more than our common night and day.
>
> (Bradley, 1929: 75)

It was the view of the literary establishment that comedy did not belong in such profound and cultured company, and that 'Comedy and satire should be kept in their proper place, like the moral standards and social classes which they symbolize' (Frye, 1990: 22).

FERTILITY AND THE '*ÉLAN VITAL*': CORNFORD, BERGSON, LANGER

'The history of literary criticism is also the history of attempts to make an honest creature, as it were, of comedy', writes David Daniell (1997: 102). The first significant modern attempt to make comedy a 'serious' object of study appeared in 1914, written by a scholar of Ancient Greece. Francis Macdonald Cornford's *The Origin of Attic Comedy* is a combination of literary criticism and anthropology that attempts to reconstruct the sources and forms of the original comic entertainments. Cornford was part of a Cambridge-based movement of anthropological classicists known as the 'Cambridge Ritualists', a group of scholars who examined the ceremonies and beliefs of primitive communities in an effort to see their influence on modern thinking and social organisation. Like James George Frazer's famous anthropological survey *The Golden Bough* (1890–1915), Cornford's *Origin of Attic Comedy* is interested in the ceremonial, seasonal, and ritual roots that lie at the heart of Greek Old Comedy, and his text argues for an aboriginal relationship between comedy and the religiously sanctioned revel and fertility beliefs that stemmed from Dionysiac and Phallic ritual (Cornford, 1914: 3). The study describes how agrarian rituals, beginning with simple work-chants and songs, developed in form and complexity until they had become invested with significance that led to prepared and stylised activities growing up around them. A characteristic ritual of this type was the phallic procession, a parade of phallic symbols that used profanity and sexual and scatological imagery as a kind of benevolent magic to protect the community. As he writes,

> Besides the distribution of benign influence ... these processions have also the converse magical intent of defeating and driving away bad

> influences of every kind. The phallus itself is no less a negative charm
> against evil spirits than a positive agent of fertilisation. But the sim-
> plest of all methods of expelling malign influences of any kind is to
> abuse them with the most violent language ... There can be no doubt
> that the element of invective and personal satire which distinguishes
> the Old Comedy is directly descended from the magical abuse of the
> phallic procession, just as its obscenity is due to sexual magic.
>
> (Cornford, 1914: 49–50)

Comedy was now an identifiable form that retained its characteristics from ancient folk practices long after the beliefs that nurtured
them had either become obsolete or been subsumed into the
secular aspects of the performance. While the exact nature of this
transformation is not entirely clear, Cornford argues that the reason that the forms of the fertility songs and dances were preserved
after their religious significance had evaporated was because they
were, essentially, funny:

> The ... double intent of stimulating fertility and averting bad influences
> lies at the root of many forms of festival dance, which, when the ser-
> ious purpose has died out of them, are kept under the sanction of old
> customs, and partly for the sake of pleasurable obscenity.
>
> (Cornford, 1914: 50)

Comedy now had well-defined structural components: the *agon*, in
which the hero-protagonist struggles with an adversary and wins;
the enjoyment of the victory, celebrated by feast and sacrifice; and
a final victory procession, the *komos*, followed by marriage or some
kind of resurrection.

The relationship of comedy to agrarian fertility-rituals can be
clearly seen in Aristophanes's play *The Archarnians* (425 BC), the
oldest comedy in existence. Having been drinking, the farmer
Dikaiopolis mounts a phallus on a pole and celebrates his 'Country Dionysia' by making offerings of cake and asking the god to
bless his sexual adventures with the neighbour's slave: 'For now is
the time to be merry, with pleasure for one and / all' (Aristophanes,
1973: 61). Comedy, then, is a secularised version of a ritual that

was a source of pleasure was so entertaining that it could not be allowed to die out.

Cornford's text, with its emphasis on ritual and cultural significance, represented a new direction in academic treatments of comedy. Studies like his provided comedy with a credibility that it did not possess in the qualitative analyses and exclusions of English Literature departments by providing it with ancient roots. Cornford's study was also a product of its time, because for all its experimentalism, the literary culture of modernism was similarly fascinated by the distant myths of pre-Christian Europe. A recurrent fear of modernism was the idea that the industrial world was in danger of losing touch with its fundamental humanity, leading to enthused attempts to compile and analyse myths and other popular or 'folk' images of the past. The high visibility of texts such as *The Golden Bough* and Jessie Weston's *From Ritual to Romance* in the footnotes of T. S. Eliot's *The Waste Land* (1922), for example, indicates that the themes of modern fragmentation in the poem hope to find anchors in the mythic past. In Britain, there was concern that colonising the world had meant losing a sense of self, and so the founding of institutions such as Cecil Sharp's English Folk-Dance Society in 1911 worked to allay fears about the loss of indigenous culture by collecting songs and dances from a provincial and predominantly oral tradition. And so comedy, understood in Cornford's analysis as an authentic and enduring expression of the human life-force and its communal identity, took on renewed credibility.

When conceiving of comedy as a manifestation of human vitality, Cornford may have also been influenced by the philosophy of Henri Bergson (1859–1941). Key to Bergson's thought is the dynamic energy of intuition and impulse that he terms the '*élan vital*', those creative and demanding life-forces that reveal themselves to us continually and through which all social interaction is mediated. Bergson's famous essay 'Laughter' (1900) claims that humour is born in moments where the life-force is momentarily usurped or eclipsed by an involuntary manifestation of automatism or reduction of the body to a lifeless machine, what Bergson calls 'something mechanical encrusted upon the living' (Bergson, 1980: 84). The fullest articulation of comedy as vitalism appears in Susanne

Langer's study of aesthetics, *Feeling and Form*, which also calls Bergson 'pre-eminently the artists' philosopher' (Langer, 1953: 114). For Langer, art is an intuitive and essentially creative process driven by the need to be alive. Comedy is:

> an art form that arises naturally wherever people are gathered to cele-
> brate life, in spring festivals, triumphs, birthdays, weddings, or initiations.
> For it expresses the elementary strains and resolutions of animate
> nature, the animal drives that persist even in human nature, the delight
> man takes in his special mental gifts that make him the lord of crea-
> tion; it is an image of human vitality holding its own in the world
> amid the surprises of unplanned coincidence.
>
> (Langer, 1953: 331)

This version of the comic exists in the routine obscenity surrounding marriage celebrations, in the jubilant nick-naming of genitalia, or in bouts of celebratory bingeing that follow a triumph, however minor. What is important, emphasises Langer, is that the comic spirit constitutes an essential element of being human, and more importantly, being alive. This definition is potentially complicated by the very full tradition of morbid black humour that exists in Western culture, and which is prevalent in both literature and social interaction. Jokes about death or the fear of death can be devastatingly funny, but do not seem to conform to Langer's model unless morbid reflection itself constitutes a triumphant acknowledgement that one is yet breathing. But what is important about the work of Bergson and Langer is that it positions comedy at the ontological centre of human existence. In claiming for comedy a close relationship to fertility ritual, rites of passage, and reproductive events, these writers reintroduced comedy into the academic mainstream as a genre in which the fundamental imprint of human existence is as evident as in its tragic counterpart. However, in doing so they also reproduce the terms of the argument that elevate tragedy and denigrate comedy: even though comedy has been shown to be an object worthy of significant study, it is simultaneously shown to be closer to nature than art, and closer, therefore, to the body than the soul.

SPRINGTIME AND FESTIVAL: FRYE AND BARBER

It is no accident that literary studies devoted to the study of comedy should appear first in areas that are unquestionably perceived as belonging to 'high culture', as if their association with core concepts would protect them from accusations of low-mindedness. The trope of comedy as life-force is particularly evident in Shakespeare criticism, for example, much of it indebted to the distinguished work of the Canadian scholar Northrop Frye (1906–1991), who saw in Shakespearean comedy a spirit of regeneration in sympathy with the natural rhythm of the seasons. Based around a series of arche-typal structures in harmony with the four seasons of the year, Frye's *The Anatomy of Criticism* (1957) offers the idea that 'the fun-damental form of [mythical] process is cyclical movement, the alternation of success and decline, effort and relapse, life and death' (Frye, 1990: 158). Humanity, in other words, creates an imagina-tively inhabitable world of literary fiction carved from the patterns of life and death that assimilates the idea of seasonal rejuvenation into narrative. This is the case especially with narratives produced prior to the advent of modernity and the demythologisation of culture that accompanied it. Narrative patterns, writes Frye,

> are usually divided into four main phases, the four seasons of the year being the type for four periods of the day (morning, noon, evening, night), four aspects of the water-cycle (rain, fountains, rivers, sea or snow), four periods of life (youth, maturity, age, death) and the like.
>
> (Frye, 1990: 160)

From these archetypes are formed 'narrative categories of litera-ture broader than, or logically prior to, the ordinary literary genres', meta-generic forms from which more specific genres are derived: 'the romantic, the tragic, the comic, and the ironic and the satiric' (Frye, 1990: 162). These pre-generic 'moods' of nar-rative have in turn strong associative connections with the texture of the seasons: summer for romance, autumn for tragedy, winter for irony and satire, and spring for comedy.

Spring, the transitional season between hardship and repose, is placed perfectly to enact the theme of rebirth and the battle of winter and summer that is the dominant metaphor in Frye's theory of comedy. Shakespeare's comedy, he says, 'is the drama of the green-world, its plot being assimilated to the ritual themes of the triumph of life and love over the waste land' (Frye, 1990: 182). The 'green-world' is a phrase widely taken up by Shakespeare criticism because it offers a convincing template for the symbolism of the narrative structure of his comedy. 'Green-worlds' are wish-fulfilment locations, always rural, often enchanted, in which the normal business of the town is suspended and the pleasurable pastimes of holiday prevail. Shakespearean green-worlds include the wood outside Athens in *A Midsummer Night's Dream* (1605), the coast of Illyria in *Twelfth Night* (1601–2), Portia's Belmont in *The Merchant of Venice* (1596–7), and the forest of Arden in *As You Like It* (1599). Associated with love, leisure, levelled social hierarchies, and play, the green-world serves as a space in which solutions to urban problems can be worked through. As court or city rules no longer apply, gender distinctions can be disregarded, the mythical and the quotidian can intermingle, and drunks and braggarts may live freely away from the tyranny of work or the regime of the clock. The green-world is not only a place to escape from the problems of the town, most frequently represented by a 'blocking agent' – a father-figure or envoy of the older generation whose blind insistence on his authority forbids the success of relationships founded on love – but also a place where society can be divested of its most fundamental suppositions, such as the nature of law, or the relationship between the sexes. Through the relaxation of social conventions, the social fabric is allowed to heal. Immersion in the green-world, however, is always temporary; holiday is defined only as such because it must be distinguished from the everyday world of work. In the narrative of *As You Like It*, says Frye, Rosalind is the representative of spring, inspiring renewal in the dormant inhabitants of Arden and ultimately triumphing over the cruel and unforgiving winter of Duke Frederick. Through her intervention, made possible by her entry into the forest, the unlawfully usurped Duke Senior is reinstated, reconciliations are brought about, and, after a round of divinely sponsored weddings, society is rejuvenated with the promise of a new ruling generation and their heirs.

Frye's account is both convincing and symmetrically satisfying, but it brings with it two key objections. The first is the extent to which comedic structure is privileged over content, and the degree that his discussion of varied and distinct plays can become a list of titles whose similarity rests on their final reconciliations. This is a short-coming of all structuralist and narratological critical practices, and in mitigation it should be noted that Frye's project aims to study structural similarities and not to offer close readings of individual texts. However, through the reduction to narrative units, literary difference is absorbed into a homogenised structural model. A recurrent problem of comedy criticism is its focus on structure and plot over character and dialogue, a result of both the critical prejudice that tragic heroes are individuals, and the practice of writing comic ones as types. The second objection arises from the extent to which a large part of *The Anatomy of Criticism* depends on our acceptance of Frye's overall thesis that literary forms, at least in the originary phases of their development, mirror the procession of the seasons. Can all literature be read in this way? Are all writers informed by an unconscious force that imposes itself on their work through an enigmatic process of arboreal ventriloquism?

Another influential Shakespearean, C. L. Barber, believed that structural readings of literature failed to grasp the truth of art. In his *Shakespeare's Festive Comedy* (1959), he indirectly challenges Frye with the accusation that his ideas lacked nuance, writing that, 'No figure in the carpet is the carpet. There is in the pointing out of patterns something that is opposed to life and art, an ungraciousness which artists in particular feel and resent' (Barber, 1963: 4). For Barber, literature is full of moments of 'design beyond design' which possess a vitality that resonates much further than the generic and narrative structures in which they are placed. Barber's intention, and the nature of his contribution to the understanding of comedy, was to demonstrate the relevance of the Elizabethan social practice of holiday festivities that inform comedy and are reflected in it. This is a sixteenth-century remodelling of *The Origin of Attic Comedy*, privileging an historicist methodology that places an understanding of original context above other means of reading a literary text. The practices he invokes include festivals like 'the celebration of a marriage, the village wassail or wake ... Candlemas, Shrove Tuesday, Hocktide, May Day, Whitsuntide, Midsummer Eve, Harvest-home, Halloween and the twelve days of Christmas season ending with Twelfth Night' (Barber, 1963: 5). Such holidays provide the basis for the staged folly, disguise, and masquerade of a large number of Shakespeare's plays. For Barber, comedy is essentially 'saturnalian', an experience of pleasurable merrymaking and social inversion named after the revels devoted to the Roman god Saturn. Saturnalian comedy is neither satirical nor political, but devoted to a process Barber calls 'release and clarification'. 'Release' refers to the loosening of social controls during holidays, and leads Barber, like Freud, to ascribe comic pleasure to the redistribution of mental energy normally devoted to social conformity, so that 'the energy normally occupied in maintaining inhibitions is freed for celebration' (Barber, 1963: 7). 'Clarification' is comedy's ability to reaffirm the positive relationship of humanity to its environment, 'a heightened relationship between man and "nature"' (Barber, 1963: 8). Comedy thereby has the dual function of celebrating human relationships and merrymaking, while mocking what it identifies as 'unnatural', baiting kill-joys and miserly characters who fail to observe the feast or show some perverse aversion to happiness. From this perspective, Barber reads a character like Shylock from *The Merchant of Venice* as a representative of anti-festival, a usurer whose anxiety about money stands in joyless contrast to the Venetian Christians who use money 'graciously to live together in a humanly knit group' (Barber, 1963: 167). As the defeat of outsiders and the chastisement of scapegoats is a significant aspect of the comic celebration of communal identity and its life-experience, the vilification and forcible conversion of Shylock reveal him as a representative of egregious heterogeneity that must be made to conform to 'healthy' community values. However, Barber's insistence on holiday forms, while not absolute in his discussion of *The Merchant of Venice*, has the effect of naturalising folk practices and eliding the politics of race that can be made to speak through them.

CARNIVAL AND THE MARKETPLACE: BAKHTIN AND THE NEW HISTORICISM

With the re-emergence and dominance of forms of historicism in literary studies throughout the 1980s and 1990s, the work of

Mikhail Bakhtin (1895–1975) has exerted extraordinary influence on the study of comedy. Bakhtin, a Russian formalist who became interested in literary theory shortly after the 1917 Revolution, made his major contribution in the form of a monograph entitled *Rabelais and His World*, initially written as a doctoral dissertation in the 1930s and unpublished in English until 1968. Through a detailed analysis of the early-modern French comic novelist François Rabelais (c.1494–c.1553), Bakhtin argues that two synchronous but contradictory world views existed during the medieval period. 'Official' culture, which he characterises as ecclesiastical, sombre, excluding profanity and suppressing the body, driven by the bureaucracy of the Church and the administration of Grace; and 'the culture of the marketplace', the popular and boisterous voice of the people. The marketplace is a totemic location for Bakhtin, and one that has certain parallels with the rituals discussed by Cornford and the spontaneous expressions of vitality explored by Langer. 'This territory', writes Bakhtin,

> was a peculiar second world within the official medieval world order and was ruled by a special type of relationship. Officially the palaces, churches, institutions, and private homes were dominated by hierarchy and etiquette, but in the marketplace a special kind of language was heard, almost a language of its own, quite unlike the language of the Church, palace, courts, and institutions.
>
> (Bakhtin, 1968: 154)

The language of the marketplace is the idiom of the plebeian classes, the expression of 'natural' feeling, coarse, unlettered, and unmediated by the expectations of formality. This is a vision of culture at ease with, and making fun of, graphic descriptions of sexual activity and bodily functions, ridiculing officials and officialdom, and violating officially designated rules of etiquette and decorum. The world of the marketplace operates according to what is essentially a comic logic, one that runs parallel to official, serious, improving culture, laughing at it, and sometimes violently humiliating it.

Bakhtin's most important contribution to later analyses of comedy is his theory of Carnival, which he argues is the vehicle of an authentic proletarian voice answering the ascetic oppressions of the clerical classes. Carnival, literally 'a putting away of meat', is the period immediately before Lent, the Christian phase of abstinence that takes place over forty days in February and March and concludes on Easter Sunday. In British English this is known as 'Shrove Tuesday', while in French-speaking countries and much of the USA, it is known as '*Mardi Gras*', or 'fat Tuesday', helpfully signifying the sensual indulgence and misrule that comes before the Lenten fast. As a fixture of the medieval calendar, Carnival was a special holiday that permitted the temporary suspension of social rules and codes of conduct. The Flemish artist Peter Bruegel's painting of a popular medieval and early-modern theme, *The Battle of Carnival and Lent* (1559), presents Carnival as a gorged, corpulent, and self-indulgent figure, engaged in an endless contest with gaunt Lenten piety. In Bakhtin's work, this contest is more than an embodiment of the eternal struggle between the flesh and the spirit, comprising a political manifestation of popular opposition to the dominant order and the enactment of alternative regimes:

> As opposed to the official feast, one might say that carnival celebrated temporary liberation from the prevailing truth and from the established order; it marked the suspension of all hierarchical rank, privileges, norms and prohibitions. Carnival was the true feast of time, the feast of becoming, change and renewal. It was hostile to all that was immortalized and completed.
>
> (Bakhtin, 1968: 10)

The inversions and suspensions permitted and legitimised by Carnival represent substantive challenges to authority, therefore offering the possibility that comedy, invested with the spirit of festive and carnival traditions, may also be an expression of popular discontent. Some critics have seen in Bakhtin's work an almost utopian view of medieval culture that is more akin to wish-fulfilment than historical research. Aaron Gurevich, for example, questions whether Bakhtin had not 'transposed some aspects of contemporary life in Stalinist Russia into the epoch' he was dealing with (Gurevich, 1997: 58).

Whatever its weaknesses, many historicist and poststructuralist critics have found Bakhtin's theory of opposing cultures particularly productive. Such criticism is drawn to comedy via its thematisation of misrule and the visibility of characters from the lower social ranks. Perhaps the most influential critical position of this kind is New Historicism, a critical methodology that came to prominence in the 1980s, and whose practice is best summed up by Steven Mullaney, who writes that 'literary criticism is conceived not as an end in itself, but as a vehicle, a means of gaining access to tensions and contradictions less clearly articulated in other social forums but all the more powerful for their partial occlusion' (Mullaney, 1988: x). With this in mind, New Historicism reads comedy as a potential site of social disruption, using the comic as a possible medium for the message of dissent. However, according to New Historicist formulations of the configuration of state power, it is a medium that is simultaneously monitored and controlled by the authorities that it seeks to subvert. As the high priest of New Historicism, Stephen Greenblatt, writes of Shakespearean drama in his famous essay 'Invisible Bullets', during the process of transgression and inversion, 'authority is subjected to open, sustained and radical questioning before it is reaffirmed, with ironic reservations, at the close' (Greenblatt, 1985: 29). Discussing the representation of royalty in Shakespeare's *Henry IV* plays, Greenblatt argues that power absorbs the potential for change, permitting itself to be questioned for the tactical and pragmatic purposes of seeming to appear open, before finally re-asserting itself once more: 'Within this theatrical setting, there is a remarkable insistence upon the paradoxes, ambiguities, and tensions of authority, but this apparent production of subversion is ... the very condition of power' (Greenblatt, 1985: 44–45). Inversion and misrule, then, exist within a matrix of 'licensed transgression', and are expedient outlets for reckless behaviour that enable the continuance of the social order. As Olivia remarks of Feste, the representative of festival in *Twelfth Night*, 'There is no slander / in an allowed fool' (Shakespeare, 1989: 1.5.88–89). Greenblatt assesses the potential of comedy to cause social upset in the following terms:

> It is precisely because of the English form of absolutist theatricality that Shakespeare's drama, written for a theatre subject to state censorship, can be so relentlessly subversive: the form itself, as a primary

> expression of Renaissance power, helps to contain the radical doubts
> it continually evokes.
>
> (Greenblatt, 1985: 45)

In other words, an absolutist monarchical message is effectively
reinforced and validated through the dramatisation of objections
to it. Passages which are seemingly transgressive or dissenting are
permitted on account of their ultimate defeat and containment
within the form. Any potential for offence must have been coun-
tered by an affirmation of monarchical status quo, otherwise,
Greenblatt argues, the Master of the Revels, the official dramatic
censor, would have erased them and punished their author. How
convincing, however, is this concept of the 'Big Brother' state
that permits objection only that it might enforce itself at a much
more insidious level? Certainly, comedy was subject to censorship
in the early-modern period. We know that the *Henry IV* plays had
been modified by such an intervention, as the character of Sir John
Oldcastle, a Lollard martyr and member of the powerful Cobham
family, had to be renamed Sir John Falstaff to appease Oldcastle's
offended descendants. Ben Jonson, along with his collaborators,
was imprisoned in 1597 and the theatres made to submit to an
enforced closure due to the outrage caused by their satirical play
The Isle of Dogs, now lost. But the question is whether or not the
form invariably renders any potentially political content safe. As
Janet Clare states in her study of censorship on the early-modern
stage, the Master of the Revels could be both inconsistent and
arbitrary, which presumably allowed some satire to get through
unchanged (Clare, 1990: 122).

To be fair to Greenblatt, nowhere does his model suggest that
the exercise of power is co-ordinated and efficient at every level,
or utterly immune to inconsistency, mistake, and oversight. That
sometimes containment fails and comedy can become the site of
genuine opposition is the premise of Peter Stallybrass and Allon
White's *The Politics and Poetics of Transgression* (1986). Their text is
a radical materialist reading of Bakhtin that can be said to have
rescued some of his ideas from the romanticisation of the marketplace and reformulated them as a more credible political force
in which the marginal is understood to be genuinely creative and

disruptive. Stallybrass and White see Carnival and comic forms addressing 'the social classifications of values, distinction and judgements which underpin practical reason', where Carnival 'systematically inverts the relations of subject and object, agent and instrument, husband and wife, old and young, animal and human, master and slave' (Stallybrass and White, 1986: 56). These upheavals reformulate, for a temporary period at least, socially sanctioned power relationships, bringing the margin to the centre, making it visible and giving it voice. This is not to say that Carnival is suddenly a politically progressive force, however, since, 'although it re-orders the terms of the binary pair, it cannot alter the terms themselves', as inversion of the terms of normal social operation is not the same as re-defining them (Stallybrass and White, 1986: 56). The carnivalesque is not then equipped to topple the dominant order, but neither is the dominant order able to silence the carnivalesque. Stallybrass and White imagine both terms engaged in a mutually dependent but antagonistic relationship, in which each contains an element of its other that it uses to define itself. 'A recurrent pattern emerges', they write:

> the 'top' attempts to reject and eliminate the 'bottom' for reasons of prestige and status, only to discover, not only that it is in some way frequently dependent upon that low-Other ... but also that the top *includes* that low symbolically, as a primarily eroticised constituent of its own fantasy life.
>
> (Stallybrass and White, 1986: 7)

Comic inversion not only makes visible those excluded from the hierarchy, therefore, but also symbolically foregrounds the tensions and desires that are elided parts of the identity of power itself, revealing power not to be the coherent and all-pervasive monolith of New Historicism, but constituted of contradictions and unacknowledged dependencies.

A further challenge to the critical tendency to reduce dissent to collusion in support of the absolutist tactics of the state appears in Michael Bristol's *Carnival and Theater* (1985). Bristol takes issue with the New Historicism's conception of power as 'always singular, a unity and also a plenitude', since it means that it would be 'necessary for festivals to be completely unselfconscious occasions in which nothing was ever learned, and for the participants to cooperate, year after year, in an oppressive routine contrary to their interests' (Bristol, 1985: 15, 27). Finding the containment model of power unsubtle and unrealistic, he invokes the work of anthropologist Victor Turner to understand the relationship between carnival and authority. Turner makes a distinction between types of festive activity that are 'liminal' and those that are 'liminoid'. 'Liminal' phenomena are those carnival or festive activities that remain bound by their archaic forms to the extent that they are simply the residue of a previously significant ritual or the repetition of an inversion that remains entirely unanalysed by its participants. An example of this might be the erection of a Maypole or performance of Morris dance at an innocuous church fête. 'Liminoid' activities, however, are 'not merely reversive, they are often subversive, representing radical critiques of the central structure and proposing alternative models' (Bristol, 1985: 38). Liminoid activities, then, contain the elements of genuine social commentary and conflict, and can extend the definition of festivity to include theatrical performances, drag shows, political stand up, and riots. Rather than being contained by an authority that tacitly permits festive outbursts,

> Popular festive form reminds the ruling elite that they may actually rule relatively incompletely and ineffectively. Much of the conduct of everyday life, and many of the details of political and economic practice, proceed quite independently of the wishes of the power structure. Carnival is an heuristic instrument of considerable scope and flexibility. Though it is a festive and primarily symbolic activity, it has immediate pragmatic aims, most immediately that of objectifying a collective determination to conserve the authority of the community to set its own standards of behavior and social discipline, and to enforce those standards by appropriate means.
>
> (Bristol, 1985: 52)

Festival is not contained by authority, therefore, but rather overrides it in certain circumstances by asserting local plebeian codes of conduct over the representatives of officialdom. Social practices like the *charivari*, a cacophonous procession and serenade undertaken by the inhabitants of a village or district for the purposes of deriding and humiliating an unpopular couple or person, are clearly used as a means of regulating the life of the community outside official legislation. The humiliation of Malvolio in *Twelfth Night* also serves as a useful illustration. The gulling of Malvolio and the presentation of him as an extravagant lover 'cross-gartered' is a festive castigation of the sour puritan steward whose very name means 'ill-will'. Sir Toby, Sir Andrew, Feste, and Maria ridicule Malvolio's pretensions to marry the wealthy Olivia, and then continue to torment him until he is perceived to be mad. Festivity therefore pursues authority, portrayed as ridiculous because of its inflexibility, and forces it to adapt to the demands of the community.

Comedy's perceived association with a kind of folk politics has therefore given it legitimacy in modern academic discourse. Following Cornford's literary anthropology and reading it through Bakhtin's concept of Carnival, comedy becomes useful to academia as a literary counter-weight to strict regimes, an expression of a communal life-force that inverts the social order and offers short-term liberation from authoritarian pressure. By associating it so clearly with plebeian culture, however, modern critical interest may be guilty of retaining the elitist generic divisions that once denigrated comedy, keeping it as the working-class cousin of aristocratic tragedy and other 'serious' forms.

2

COMIC IDENTITY

Two babies were born on the same day at the same hospital. They lay there and looked at each other. Their families came and took them away. Eighty years later, by a bizarre coincidence, they lay in the same hospital, on their deathbeds, next to each other. One of them looked at the other and said, 'So. What did you think?'

Steven Wright

Woody Allen's film *Zelig* (1983) concerns a character whose desire to belong is so acute that he physically transforms himself into the likeness of whoever is around him. Coming to the attention of a baffled medical establishment and a frenzied press that dubs him 'the human chameleon', Zelig becomes the biggest celebrity in America. Troops of people are brought to meet him and each time he mimics their appearance, turning into a Rabbi, a 300-pound overeater, an African-American musician, or a French-man. While *Zelig* plays on core American themes, most obviously the immigrant experience and the struggle of assimilation, it also highlights a recurrent theme of comedy: the nature and limits of identity. Leonard Zelig is so shy and self-effacing that he is pathologically driven to assume the identities of others. This not only involves absurd physical transformations, but also presents an image of failed interiority, of a man who is a reflective surface. Many comic characters might be said to play on our fears of being incomplete human beings through their failures of self-awareness or inability to reflect on the nature of experience. Comic characters are traditionally one-dimensional in the sense that they are apparently unable to learn and change. Homer Simpson in the TV cartoon series *The Simpsons* (1989), for example, is reckless, hungry, transgressive, and dumb, and completely incapable of reflecting upon his actions in anything but the most superficial manner. Homer lives in a perpetual series of excitable nows, led by impulse and steered by whim. Seemingly unable to recall the mistakes of the past, he is inexorably anchored to an identity that is doomed to repeat its failings.

Homer Simpson borrows something from Roman New Comedy, where character types are so rigidly defined that their behaviours are entirely predictable within given situations. The miser will always be miserly, and the braggart will always boast. In this case, comic identity is derived from a sense of atrophied consciousness stripped of subtlety or the ability to learn, leaving behind only monstrously repetitive activity. Thus, while comic characters can be infinitely diverse, it is possible to identify certain common forms among them. This chapter will consider some of those forms.

STEREOTYPES

As we have seen, comic drama is largely plot-driven, moving towards ritualistic resolutions such as feasts, marriages, or revelations. Comic characterisation is usually subordinate to the demands of plot, and therefore more effectively realised with stereotypes and one-dimensional characters than anything approaching the realistic portrayal of human emotions. Like *The Simpsons*, many of our most popular comedies are little more than an opportunity for characters dominated by a single prevalent characteristic to find themselves in new situations upon which to assert those qualities. The comedian Mike Myers has said that the principle of single-mindedness is essential to successful comedy, suggesting that 'Comedy characters tend to be a machine; i.e., Clouseau was a *smug* machine, Pepe

Le Pew was a *love* machine, Felix Unger was a *clean* machine, and Austin Powers is a *sex* machine' (quoted in Friend, 2002: 82). Consciously or otherwise, Myers is adapting the Bergsonian view that 'what is essentially laughable is what is done automatically' (Bergson, 1980: 155). Automatism, or the channelling of diverse thoughts and feelings through one overriding principle, has been the impetus behind comic characterisation since the New Comedy of the third century BC, and provides us with the set of comic stereotypes that have provided the blueprint for comic characterisation from the Renaissance to the present.

New Comedy is derived from the work of the Greek dramatist Menander, whose plays, up until the discovery of papyrus fragments in 1905, were known only through the adaptations and embellishments of the Roman comic authors Plautus and Terence. Considering the enormous impact Menander has had on comedy, very little is known about him. He was an Athenian, who, according to one account, wrote 108 plays, but had only modest success during his lifetime due to his eclipse by other authors of New Comedy, of whom even less is known. His standing was completely revised in later antiquity, however, when he was prized for the quality of his plots and the excellence of his characters. Whereas Aristophanic Old Comedy dealt with political institutions, public figures, and fantastical situations, Menandrine New Comedy was concerned with the intimate themes of domestic and private life. New Comedy dramatised the lives of citizens rather than gods and politicians and was interested in romance, sexual desire, the circulation of money, and the imposition of patriarchal order. New Comedy was also the first to conclude with the promise of marriage. Concomitantly, its repertoire of stock characters emerged from the household and orbits around this central domestic space. Menander, Plautus, and Terence populate their plays with variations on the same basic character types: the profligate or impractical young man; the *senex*, or parent; the matronly wife; the *meretrix*, or accomplished courtesan; the clever slave; the nervous parasite; the vulnerable maiden; and the *miles gloriosus*, or swaggering soldier. These characters appear to reflect Menander's absorption of the philosophy of Theophrastus (c.370–c.288 BC), head of the Peripatetic School after Aristotle, and the author of *Characters*, thirty sketches of types embodying particular human faults and follies. Like stage comedy itself, these amount to possibly the most resilient character types in all Western fiction, with several remaining, in the words of Northrop Frye, 'practically unchanged for twenty-five centuries' (Frye, 1953: 271).

New Comedy is generally considered to be a more conservative form than its Aristophanic predecessor, reflecting a change in the context of Greek drama from the fourth to the third centuries BC. The shift in emphasis from the public arena to life indoors was probably a response to Athens's decreasing political indulgence, and the fact that its leadership was largely supported by foreign powers, resulting in a loss of the political immediacy that motivated Aristophanes. Audiences may also have changed as the subsidies which allowed people from all walks of life to attend the theatre disappeared, and a more resolutely middle-class audience came to dominate. Their taste, suggests Geoffrey Arnott, was escapist, interested less in the 'recurring disasters of life' and more in stories in which problems were 'always resolved in the inevitable happy ending which celebrated and cemented family unity' (quoted in Konstan, 1995: 167). Just as its characterisation was formulaic, so were plots, featuring variations on familiar themes. Roman comedy deals repeatedly with the forbidden love of a young man for a prostitute, slave, or otherwise ineligible woman, and the complications of their romance in the face of fierce parental disapproval before finally, through some contortion of the plot, a recognition scene reveals her true identity as a citizen.

> With this device, the conflicting claims of private passion and social responsibility are neatly reconciled, for the waywardness of desire proves to be illusory. The impulse that aspires to the forbidden is domesticated, gratified without danger to public convention, and thus the threat to the city-state ideal of a closed conjugal group is averted.
>
> (Konstan, 1983: 24–25)

Given that these narratives tend towards the reinforcement of family ties and the maintenance of dynastic status, supporting the privilege of a racially homogenous group in an ethnically diverse empire, stereotypical characterisation might be seen as a reassuring ploy that confirms a hegemonic view of the world, and appeals to the comprehensive systems of taxonomy and categorisation that existed in Roman intellectual life. As Maurice Charney writes: 'Comic convention postulates a society that is rigidly hierarchical. By the laws of decorum, carefully formulated by such Roman rhetoricians as Cicero and Quintilian, different social classes have their prescribed styles, both of manners and of speech' (Charney, 1978: 51). Representing a range of clearly delineated social types supports a concept of order that asserts its totality by claiming to predict, know, and catalogue the behaviour of all kinds and types of people. Watching a parade of stereotypes, therefore, affords the comfort of confirming an audience's prejudices.

As previously discussed, the reputations of Terence and Plautus were upheld during the medieval and Renaissance periods by scholars who valued them primarily as examples of good style. The basic structure of New Comedy was also preserved in the Italian Renaissance form known as the *commedia erudita*, or 'learned' comedy, of which Niccolò Machiavelli's *La Mandragola* (c.1520) is an example. Italian drama has some influence on the structure of English playwriting throughout the 1580s and 90s, combined with a group of plays known as 'prodigal son' dramas, another fashionable continental model that dramatised the errant ways and eventual reformation of a wayward son. Eventually, these influences came to form city, or 'citizen', comedy, a branch of comic writing devoted to intrigue plots of love and money and the struggle between the older and younger generation amongst the merchant classes of contemporary London. A number of circumstances, including rapid population growth and the emergence of a predominantly capitalist economy over an agrarian one, had raised the visibility of the urban middle-classes in England. As a result, these citizens were identified solely with their economic interests, and almost every area of existence is subsumed into their financial dealings, including their sex lives. In city comedy, the slave girl is displaced and the energetic pursuit of the commodity becomes the new object of desire. William Haughton's *Englishmen for My Money* (1598) is generally held to be the first play to fit this description exactly, but it was Ben Jonson, the dramatist who most aggressively asserted his erudition, whose work most clearly exemplified the revived and anglicised Roman form. Jonson believed that comedy was a weapon aimed at the faults, follies, and hypocrisies of the world. The prologue to *The Alchemist* (1610) establishes both his targets and the authorial tone:

> Our *Scene* is *London*, 'cause we would make knowne.
> No countries mirth is better then our owne,
> No clime breeds better matter, for your whore,
> Bawd, squire, impostor, many persons more,
> Whose manners, now call'd humours, feed the stage:
> And which have still beene subject, for the rage
> Or spleene of *comick*-writers.
>
> (Jonson, 1979: Prologue, ll.5–11)

The prologue lists a number of malefactors, and promises the audience a procession of types, 'now call'd humours'. The word 'humour' has its roots in medieval physiology, meaning 'moisture' or 'vapour'. Principally employed to describe animal or vegetal fluids, the word came to its present meaning of 'amusement' via the application of medical theory to fictional characterisation. Medieval medicine, following Galen (AD 129–199), held that health was regulated by four essential fluids, blood, phlegm, black bile, and choler, existing equally within the human body. When balanced, the humours were complementary and the body enjoyed good health. When disproportionate, with one fluid coming to prominence over the others, the body experienced discomfort or disease. From this it followed that a person's mental qualities, character, and temperament could also be subject to overbearing influences. A preponderance of blood produced sanguinity, or a brave, hopeful, and amorous disposition; too much phlegm resulted in apathy; black bile led to melancholia; and disproportionate choler caused irascibility and hot-headedness. At the beginning of *Every Man Out of His Humour* (1600), Jonson tells us how humoral theory may be taken as a principle of characterisation:

> It may, by Metaphore apply it selfe
> Unto the generall disposition,
> As when some one peculiar qualitie

> Doth so possess a man, that it doth draw
> All his affects, his spirits, and his powers,
> In their confluctions, all to run one way,
> This may be truly said to be a Humor.
> (Jonson, 1920: Induction, ll.112–118)

The concept of dominating 'confluctions' is extended even further in Jonson's *Volpone* (1605–6), where greed has caused the characters to become so distorted and dehumanised they take on animal traits that are reflected in their names. The old magnifico Volpone is named after a fox, his servant Mosca, a gadfly, and the legacy-chasing flatterers Voltore, Corbaccio, and Corvino after carrion-eating vultures, ravens, and crows respectively.

Several aspects of *Volpone*, such as its Venetian setting, reveal the influence of not only the *commedia erudita*, but also the *commedia dell'arte*, an improvised, non-scripted form of 'popular' theatre first recorded in 1545, that based its action around set scenarios involving love intrigues and bits of comic business called *lazzi*. The *commedia dell'arte* employed a stable of reusable characters, most of whom wore expressive stylised masks, each actor dedicating themselves to the study of only one role. The origins of *commedia dell'arte* are obscure, but various types of performance appear to have contributed to its development, including the stereotypes of New Comedy, but also the Roman *fabula* (various types of comic interlude), mime and buffoon shows, mountebanks, carnival processions, and medieval stage devils. The main characters of *commedia* appear to have emerged from four principal types: two infuriating *vecchi*, or old men, usually parents or guardians, and two *zanni*, or clowns, principally responsible for the comedy. These characters came to be fixed into the identifiable roles of Pantalone, the old Venetian merchant; the Doctor, a tiresome pedant; Harlequin, a quasi-independent servant, whose familiar patch-work costume originally signified poverty; and Brighella, a street bully and unrepentant liar who may have helped shape Beaumarchais's Figaro, adapted for opera by Mozart and Rossini. Additional characters developed, each with their own mask, who were to infiltrate and influence Western comic literature in various guises for centuries. These included Pedrolino who was remodelled in France as the sad and lonely Pierrot, and Pulcinella, who eventually became the jovial sea-side wife-beater, Mr Punch. In the *commedia*, as well as all the comic forms that utilise stereotypes, identity is destiny, and characters are doomed to repeat their actions and live forever at the mercy of their flaws.

FOOLS AND FOLLY

Another prevalent figure of comedy is the fool. An historically complex and paradoxical character, claiming a variety of overlapping roles including clown, buffoon, jester, scapegoat, and clairvoyant, the fool recurs as a symbol of contradictions and quandaries. Often the fool is simply a low commoner possessed of shrewd practical sense, as in the popular late-medieval tales of the 'obscene and hairy' hunchback Marcolf, who repeatedly proved himself wiser than King Solomon in bouts of wit. Foolishness is not the same as idiocy, but rather an expression of the ambiguous, doubled, and inverted ideas of wisdom and folly that existed in the medieval period. Folly, incorporated into several strong currents of theology, saw foolishness as the overriding characteristic of a post-lapsarian humanity, revealing itself in all human endeavour as in the verse of 1 Corinthians 'the wisdom of this world is foolishness before God.' Knowledge was an especially tainted and problematic concept, as the intolerable desire to know had led to the expulsion from Eden and the fall from grace. God therefore favoured the foolish and inviolable innocents who could not be corrupted by their own ingenuity. Christ had appeared as a manifestation of this humility, presenting himself 'as a mock-king, riding into Jerusalem on an ass, to be displayed in purple, beaten and laughed at ... Christ and the fool as one in simplicity' (Jacobson, 1997: 167). The ecclesiastical establishment of the middle ages incorporated some of these beliefs into their liturgical activities. Church festivals such as the *festum stultorum* (the 'feast of fools'), the *fatuorum papam* (the 'fool's pope'), and the *festum asinorum*, a French feast celebrating Mary's flight into Egypt, during which the priest and congregation were required to bray like donkeys, emphasised the ineffable folly of status in ritual form. As the theologian Peter L. Berger writes, folly enabled a magical transformation of the world, or 'more precisely', was 'an act of magic by which a counterworld [was] made to appear' (Berger, 1997: 193). Yet foolishness for its own sake was neither condoned nor encouraged. Medieval scholasticism made a distinction between the natural and the artificial fool: the first category referred to someone who was considered a 'holy innocent', a child or an adult with a learning disability, where the second referred to those 'who counterfeited this state in order to amuse others ... in short, all clowns' (Palmer, 1994: 43).

As folly was a conventionalised means of expressing human nature, it could also be adopted as an ironic and paradoxical identity assumed for the purposes of social commentary and satiric attack.

At the close of the medieval period, folly became a distinct literary voice, mocking pretension and belittling pride. One of the most significant texts of this kind is Flemish writer Sebastian Brant's *Narrenschiff* (1494), or *Ship of Fools*, a long and popular moral satire that castigated people from all walks of life for their vanity and hypocrisy. Brant's conceit of doomed passengers haplessly sailing to the Land of Fools allowed him to parade a catalogue of social types who had failed to meditate on their eternal fate. Brant's text lacks humour, although it was published with a series of lively comic illustrations, but its device of social panorama was employed by a masterpiece of ironic fool-literature, Erasmus's *Praise of Folly* (1511 and 1515). Desiderius Erasmus (1466–1536), the great Dutch Humanist and reformer, took the idea for his text from the name of his good friend Sir Thomas More, which, he says, 'is as near to the Greek word for folly, *moria*, as you are from it' (Erasmus, 1993: 4). The *Praise of Folly* is in turns an ironic, ambiguous, and viciously satirical lecture on the benefits of folly delivered by Folly herself. Addressing a happy and receptive crowd who applaud her arrival, Folly, the daughter of Money, nursed by Drunkenness and Ignorance and attended by Self-Love, Flattery, Forgetfulness, Idleness, Pleasure, Madness, and Sensuality, explains her centrality to human affairs. All things are made possible through her mediation, she claims. Peace is the product of flattery, she says, vainglory has resulted in science, wisdom is the fruit of folly as the wise man is modest, but the fool tries, just as Christ used ignorant apostles and told them to think like children. Everywhere, folly is a condition of human nature and without it, social interaction would be unbearable. Consider marriage, for example:

> Goodness me, what divorces or worse than divorces there would be everywhere if the domestic relations of man and wife were not propped up and sustained by the flattery, joking, complaisance, illusions and deceptions provided by my followers! ... In short, no association or alliance can be happy or stable without me. People can't tolerate a ruler, nor can a master his servant, a maid her mistress ... unless they sometimes have illusions about each other, make use of flattery, and have the sense to turn a blind eye and sweeten life for themselves with the honey of folly.
>
> (Erasmus, 1993: 35)

Folly, in this case wilful blindness or the willingness to believe convenient fictions, is an essential component of a happy life; humanity is utterly dependent on it. Erasmus intended the *Praise of Folly* as a satire, a comic version of his *On the Education of A Christian Prince* (1516). Through the technique of praising that which is to be condemned, he produced a powerful ironic identity devoted to comic defamiliarisation as a means of revealing the truth. Folly, for example, is the only person able to speak freely to monarchs:

> It might be said that the ears of princes shun the truth, and that they steer clear of wise men for the simple reason that they fear there may be someone outspoken enough to risk saying what is true rather than pleasant to hear. The fact is, kings do dislike the truth, but the outcome of this is extraordinary for my fools. They can speak truth and even open insults and be heard with positive pleasure; indeed, the words which would cost a wise man his life are surprisingly enjoyable when uttered by a clown. For truth has a genuine power to please if it manages not to give offence, but this is something the gods have granted only to fools.
>
> (Erasmus, 1993: 56–57)

The notion of truth emerging in the guise of folly is clearly visible in the work of Shakespeare, where a fool's licence serves a number of dramatic ends. In theatrical practice, the concepts of folly and

clowning overlapped considerably. A 'clown' meant literally a
person from the country, a yokel whose rusticated ways were cause
for mirth. 'Clowning', however, indicated a number of performing
skills, such as dancing, juggling, and musicianship. The marriage
of clowning skills with folly's penetration of vanity and hierarchy
meant that the clowns of the early-modern stage became dramatically powerful characters, both agile improvisational performers
and important narrative units, childishly amusing and insightful
by turns.

Shakespeare's use of the clown is established in what is one of
his first plays, *The Two Gentlemen of Verona* (1592), where Launce
is given a tenuous relationship to the plot that closely follows the
action while remaining separate from it. This allows Shakespeare to
develop a detached but parallel commentary that unifies themes
raised throughout the play's symmetrical pairings of high and low
social groups. In the second half of his career, as Shakespeare moved
away from writing comedies to concentrate on tragedies and
romances, his use of the clown changes in a manner that reflects this
new generic context. Around this time (1599), William Kemp, a
bumpkin fool who had played most of the early clowns up to and
including the figure of Dogberry in *Much Ado About Nothing*, was
replaced in Shakespeare's company by Robert Armin, who possessed a much drier and more restrained style. Concomitantly,
Shakespeare's later clowns are darker figures, imbued with a sense
of mortality and melancholy, as in the figure of Feste in *Twelfth
Night* (1600–1). The porter in *Macbeth* (1606), for example, imagines himself as the gatekeeper of Hades, while the grave-diggers
in *Hamlet* (c.1600) make weary jokes about ageing and physical
decomposition, and literally preside over the death of clowning as
they dig up the skull of Yorick, Hamlet's favourite jester, now
only the memory of laughter. Both *Othello* (1604) and *Antony and
Cleopatra* (1606–7) contain only a single clown scene. In the first,
the clown jests with Desdemona over the whereabouts of Michael
Cassio, a conversation that immediately follows Othello's decision
to have Cassio killed. In the second, it is the clown who delivers
Cleopatra the venomous asp and wishes her 'joy o'the worm'
(Shakespeare, 1989: 5.2.270). Both clowns prefigure deaths, the
contrast of the lowly with the elevated lending the *memento mori* a

particular piquancy. The most powerful example of this is the fool in *King Lear* (1604–5), who is the only character in the wake of Cordelia's banishment who is able to speak the truth to the king. Lear's fool is rarely funny, but he is frequently barbed and morbidly apposite, openly abusing the old king: 'FOOL. If thou were't my fool, nuncle, I'd have thee beaten for being old before thy time. / LEAR. How's that? / FOOL. Thou shouldst not have been old till thou hadst been / wise' (Shakespeare, 1989: 1.5.36–39). As Lear's rage becomes increasingly futile, the fool's nonsense is the only appropriate retort. There is no use for him after the third act of the play, but he delivers a prophecy before he goes. Typically paradoxical and impossible, the fool's prophecy imagines the disarray England will fall into when vice is no longer a part of everyday life:

> When slanders do not live in tongues,
> Nor cutpurses come not to throngs,
> When usurers tell their gold i'th'field,
> And bawds and whores do churches build,
> Then shall the realm of Albion
> Come to great confusion.
> (Shakespeare, 1989: 3.2.87–92)

This parting speech is indebted to Erasmus's Folly in its belief that self-delusion and hypocrisy are integral to the health of the nation. This central contradiction, the inversion of the good and the bad, the wise and the foolish, the mad and the sane, lies at the heart of the 'eccentric' vision of comedy, where thoughts and experiences can coexist alongside ironic reflection on those same thoughts.

TRICKSTERS

Paradoxical folly has a close relative in a character known as the 'trickster' who appears in the folk-tales and religious myths of many cultures. Mythical tricksters include the Greek god Hermes, a liar, a thief, and a master of disguise; St Peter, who appears in Italian folk-tales as a shiftless opportunist whose quasi-criminal activities have to be continually remedied by a patient and forgiving Jesus; the Norse god Loki, the companion of the thunder-god Thor and personification of lightning; the Native American Coyote, a sacred progenitor, manic omnivore, and externalised taboo; and the Nigerian Yoruba Esu-Elegabara, a figure who carries the desires of man to the gods, and who limps 'precisely because of his mediating function: his legs are of different lengths because he keeps one anchored in the realm of the gods while the other rests in this, our human world' (Gates, 1988: 6). The trickster is a practical joker, a witty and irreverent being who violates the most sacred of prohibitions. The trickster is not confined by boundaries, conceptual, social, or physical, and can cross lines that are impermeable to normal individuals, between the living and the dead, for example, and can travel between heavenly and human worlds instantaneously. This is why, like Hermes, the trickster often doubles as the messenger of the gods.

The trickster has a religious significance in some cultures that takes a specifically didactic form. Here is an example of a tale featuring 'Coyote', a trickster often found in the Native American cultures of the southwestern United States:

> Hearing a strange sound coming from an old elk skull, Coyote looks inside and finds a village of Ants having a Sun Dance. He makes himself small in order to get inside the skull and see better, but presently his body returns to normal size and his head is stuck inside the skull.
>
> He wanders into a village and announces, 'I am holy; I have supernatural power; you must give me something!' The awe-stricken people pass him in a procession, marking him with pollen as is customary in that region. But the last person in line is a smart aleck boy who is carrying a stick behind his back. When he reaches Coyote he brings the stick down with all of his might across the old elk skull, and it cracks and falls off. 'That's what you should have done long ago', Coyote tells them, 'but instead you wanted too much supernatural power.'
>
> (Hynes and Doty, 1993: 3)

Only after Coyote has been confronted by an equally irreverent adversary does his greed become an admonition of the villagers' gullibility and a warning to treat supernatural events with caution. In this resides Coyote's moral ambiguity: he rightly berates the people, but only after his attempt to cheat them has failed. William Hynes and Thomas Steele see the trickster as a necessary by-product of social order:

> Systems normally busy generating firm adherence to their beliefs also maintain within these belief systems, somewhat contradictorily, a raft of tricksters who perpetually invert and profane these same beliefs. In myth and ritual tricksters seem to be officially sanctioned exception clauses by which belief systems regularly satirize themselves.
>
> (Hynes and Steele, 1993: 160)

The trickster, then, provides an integral failsafe that prevents believers from becoming too secure in their beliefs.

Trickster figures are everywhere in comedy from disguised lovers to legacy-hunting rakes. Obvious examples would include the cartoon anarchists Bugs Bunny and Daffy Duck, the bogus civil servant Khlestakov in Nikolai Gogol's *The Government Inspector* (1836), or the mute and infuriating Harpo Marx. In Roman New Comedy, trickster figures inhabit the skin of the ingenious slave character. In Plautus's *Pseudolus* (c.191 BC), the slave Pseudolus, his name itself meaning 'false one', addresses the audience with a proclamation:

> Now let all take notice – and let none say he has not received notice – all adults here present, all citizens of this city, all friends and acquaintances of mine, are hereby warned and advised, this day ... to be on their guard ... against me ... and not to trust a word I say.
>
> (Plautus, 1984: 221)

Pseudolus's low social status gives him the freedom to move across social boundaries, which includes awareness of the fictive nature of his existence, operating both within the frame of the fiction and without it, addressing the audience and acknowledging the fact of the performance, and at one stage even admitting to being an actor. Within the play, his trickster mobility makes him an intermediary between the lover, the patrician parent, the pimp, and prostitute, between illicit and legitimate love and respectable and shameful liaisons. In the end, Pseudolus forges domestic harmony from sexual and financial scandal and consolidates the system by flouting it.

Shakespeare's Puck is similarly the counter-intuitive provider of solutions in *A Midsummer Night's Dream*. Puck, also known as Robin Goodfellow, is a genius of minor mischief and domestic upsets, a 'merry wanderer of the night' devoted to practical jokes and turning sentiment into laughter:

> The wisest aunt, telling the saddest tale,
> Sometime for three-foot stool mistaketh me;
> Then I slip from her bum, down topples she,
> And 'tailor' cries, and falls into a cough,
> And then the whole quire hold their hips and loffe,
> And waxen in their mirth, and neeze, and swear
> A merrier hour was never wasted there.
>
> (Shakespeare, 1989: 2.1.50–57)

Puck is in fact a conflation of a number of spirits, including hobgoblins, changelings, and incubi. In the generations immediately prior to Shakespeare, fairies like Puck were styled as sinister demons who 'stole children, dispensed sudden illnesses, destroyed crops and flocks and were believed to live in hell' (Laroque, 1993: 22). The transformation of Puck from demonic spirit to playful trickster is partly due to the falling away of superstitious belief, as well as the transposition of character types from classical literature onto domestic writing. As Jonathan Gil Harris writes, the supernatural characters of *A Midsummer Night's Dream* are a:

> syncretic blend of powerful yet for the most part benevolent spirits taken from the seemingly disparate domains of Greek mythology, courtly romance and village folklore; ... Puck is a composite of 'high' and 'low', owing as much to Neoplatonic conceptions of Cupid as to the Robin Goodfellow of popular tradition.
>
> (Harris, 1998: 353–354)

In the psychoanalytic system of Carl Jung (1875–1961), the trickster is a remnant of an earlier state of consciousness before humanity had become fully civilised. In Jung's view 'all mythical figures correspond to inner psychic experiences and originally sprang from them' (Jung, 1959, vol. 9: 256). Jung sees the cycles of tales that feature the trickster as a means of narrating how 'a higher level of consciousness has covered up a lower one' (Jung, 1959, vol. 9: 266). Trickster narratives usually conclude with the meddlesome actions of the protagonist coming to serve some useful or illustrative purpose, as in the case of Coyote. As such, argues Jung, they mirror the development of human consciousness from a wilder and more savage state to a state of relative sophistication. 'The civilizing process begins with the framework of the trickster cycle itself', he writes. 'The marks of deepest unconsciousness fall away from him; instead of acting in a brutal, savage, stupid, and senseless fashion, the trickster's behaviour towards the end of the cycle becomes quite useful and sensible' (Jung, 1959, vol. 9: 266). Such is the trajectory of Puck, who initially serves as an agent of chaos, but is ultimately responsible for inducing Demetrius to love Helena and arranging the young couples in perfect symmetry, so that 'Jack shall have Jill / Nought shall go ill; / The man shall have his mare again, and all shall be well' (Shakespeare, 1989: A *Midsummer Night's Dream*, 3.2.461–3).

While Jung thought of the trickster as the 'shadow' of a former being, whose high visibility in narrative speaks of its refusal to be completely dissolved into modern consciousness, structural anthropologist Claude Lévi-Strauss (1908–2009) saw him as a symbolic agent who unified two otherwise contradictory concepts in the structure of understanding. In 'The Structural Study of Myth' (1958), Lévi-Strauss argues that in traditional cultures, two opposite and irreconcilable terms, such as life and death, are replaced by equivalent terms, such as agriculture and hunting, in order that a third term might be permitted as an intermediary. This is why carrion-eating animals like the coyote and the raven are given the role of tricksters in Native American myths. These animals possess some of the elements of both terms: they are like hunters because they eat meat, but also like farmers because they do not kill what they eat. 'The trickster', he says, 'is a mediator. Since his mediating function occupies a position halfway between two polar terms, he must retain something of that duality – namely an ambiguous and equivocal character' (Lévi-Strauss, 1963: 226). The comic mobility of the trickster, therefore, is a means of bringing about reconciliation through the interpenetration of apparently irreconcilable realms of existence. By having a foot in both the sub- and super-lunary worlds and embodying a moral ambiguity, he acts as a signifier in which opposites can come together: through the mediation of the trickster, life and death are reconciled.

WIT AND BATHOS

The versions of subjectivity we have seen so far have all been grounded in some sense of the essence of identity: whether it be the sanctified ambiguity of fool or trickster, or the supposed universality of types, each is supposed to be built around an essential grain of truth. In this final section, we shall look at comic techniques that arose in the late seventeenth century that demonstrate an attitude towards identity that might be characterised as especially ironic, or somehow standing at a remove from a genuinely anchored sense of self. These techniques would be 'wit', celebrated in Restoration and eighteenth-century literary culture, and 'bathos', the puncturing intrusion of reality that deflates rhetoric and lofty aspirations. Both techniques are generally associated with urban and sophisticated comedies from the seventeenth century onwards, comedies permeated with a non-committal individualism and defiance of seriousness, orthodoxy, and the grandiloquent claims of authority.

In Restoration comedy, the quality of wit – a quick inventiveness in language that takes advantage of the play of associations generated by any utterance – is a fashionable way of asserting social superiority and individuality above the ordinary dullness of society. This idea is derived in part from earlier conduct books, such as Baldesar Castiglione's *The Book of the Courtier* (1528) that declares witticisms 'diverting and sophisticated', and considers spontaneous displays of wit perfect examples of the courtly ideal of *sprezzatura*, or effortless grace and accomplishment (Castiglione, 1986: 172). The plots of Restoration comedy differ from their Renaissance predecessors inasmuch as the desires of the individual take priority over the needs of the community. According to Edward

Burns, "'Wit" – the ability to use social and linguistic artifice for personal ends – overrides "decorum" – the affirmation of an intrinsically self-righting social order – and thus plays reach their endings on kinds of contracts, not an order re-discovered, presumed to have been somehow always "there" and hence presented as natural' (Burns, 1987: 17). This change reveals a new disillusionment with ideologies of absolute order following the social upheavals of the English Civil War. Authority had disgraced itself, it seemed, and sincerity and conviction were exposed as currencies debased by ideology. For Joseph Addison, writing in 1711, people were no longer marked by 'a noble Simplicity of Behaviour', but had become expert 'in Doggerel, Humour, Burlesque, and all the trivial Arts of Ridicule' (Addison and Steele, 1979, vol. 2: 238). With this post-lapsarian cynicism came the enormous popularity of parody and irony as literary modes, along with an appreciation for artifice and 'playing' as comic themes, confirmed by an extravagant use of masks, disguises, impersonations, and subterfuges. Richard Brinsley Sheridan's *The Critic* (1779), for example, represents the culmination of knowing meta-theatricality of this kind, as the entire play, set at a rehearsal, is an extended parody of literary and dramatic conventions continually interrupted by inept discussions of style and merit. William Congreve's *The Way of the World* (1700) opens just after its hero Mirabell has lost a card game, and continues to dramatise the theme of playing for high stakes until it ends. In this play, performance, the appearance of action, and the concealment of intention, is unproblematically offered as the route to gratification and reward. The Restoration comic hero is a male fantasy of libertinage, where wit is the verbal manifestation of agile virility that triumphs over the neutered fops and the Witwouds, gaining wealth, respect, and women as returns.

If wit is the ability to out-run conformity and out-manoeuvre the leaden world of norms, then bathos is the experience of having the leaden world impose itself on one's most vaulted plans. Bathos, a rhetorical term whose usage derives from Alexander Pope's Scriblerian tract *Peri Bathous, or the Art of Sinking in Poetry* (1727), involves a sudden transition in tone from the elevated to the quotidian to produce a moment of incongruous anti-climax, such as when romantic, utopian, or glamorous concepts encounter a dull reality. Mock epics make particularly good use of the bathetic effect. Henry Fielding's *Joseph Andrews*, for example, mimics Homer's *Odyssey* in its descriptions of the muddy brawls of Andrews and Parson Adams to produce a kind of low-rent, vernacular heroism. Pope's poem, *The Rape of the Lock*, similarly seeks to juxtapose the high formality of epic with the quotidian reality of the banal, making use of a rhetorical device known as 'zeugma' in which the author makes a single word apply to two or more others to produce a bathetic effect:

> Whether the nymph shall break Diana's law,
> Or some frail china jar receive a flaw;
> Or stain her honour, or her new brocade,
> Forget her pray'rs, or miss a masquerade;
> Or lose her heart, or necklace, at a ball;
> Or whether Heav'n has doom'd that Shock must fall.
>
> (Pope, 2012: I.2693)

To make an equivalence of 'honour' and a 'new brocade' or give equal weight to prayers and parties, as Pope does in these lines, reduces the former to a frivolous accessory and shows us the real priorities at work.

Just as the eighteenth-century version of bathos plumbed the space between the mythical and modern worlds, more recent manifestations have explored the gulf between the promises of modernity and their reality. The bathetic heroes that appeared after the Second World War, for example, might be considered the comic equivalent of the 'angry young men', romantic individuals in Britain whose consternation at the pressures of conformity and poverty of ambition among the working classes of the 1950s was drawn from their sense that there was another world beyond the one they inhabited, a larger, more dangerous, world but one that enabled them to think freely and live an authentic life. Dark examples of comic bathos appear in the dramatic writing of Joe Orton and Harold Pinter, both of whom use laughter as a means of attacking middle-class sensibility and hypocritical establishment values. The model for the bathetic hero in British comedy, however, is Tony Hancock (1924–1968), whose popular radio show

Hancock's Half Hour transferred to television in 1956 and ran for five years. Stephen Wagg has described Hancock's persona as 'the model of a dyspeptic, status-anxious, petit-bourgeois suburbanite stomping grumpily about the lower reaches of Middle England' (Wagg, 1998: 7). Everything was disappointing in Hancock's world. He was an unemployed actor, living in rented accommodation in Railway Cuttings in East Cheam (his address itself emblematic of failed gentility), sharing his house with a resolutely working-class lodger played by Sid James. An episode called *The Big Night* (1959), that sees Hancock and Sid preparing for a blind date, encapsulates his bathetic world view perfectly. Mimicking the sophistication of the monied classes, Hancock imagines himself an international playboy, despite the fact that the demands of the working week confine his leisure to a Saturday evening. Such is the constant theme of the *Hancock* series: the distance that emerges between the concept of the self generated by the individual desiring ego, especially one who 'was not only forever seeking to better himself but believed at the same time that he was already superior', and that produced by the reality of economic status (Neal and Krutnik, 1990: 248). Not only is Hancock economically confined, but we find there are erotic limits imposed on him as well. Sid's hyperbolised physical description of Hancock's blind date, built up by swelling romantic music, abruptly ends when we learn that her name is the emphatically working-class and old-fashioned 'Gladys'. Similarly, Hancock's home, the place where he should be master, revolts against him in the form of his elderly maid, Mrs Cravat, who refuses to conform to any of the conventions of polite domestic service, just as Hancock fails to be an aristocrat: she is surly and dismissive of Hancock's pretensions to social nicety, even amplifying his own pomposity by bringing in the breakfast and announcing it as '*oeuf scrambléd*', transformed by bad French into a parody of an expensive restaurant. The expanse between Hancock's bathetic mediocrity and the glamour to which he continually aspired was also the subject of a film-length treatment, *The Rebel* (1960), in which he travels to Paris to become an artist, enjoying immense success despite an acute lack of ability. By the end of this film we are thoroughly convinced that high art is fraudulent nonsense, and the best thing that Hancock can do is return to the suburbs and remain an unfulfilled eccentric. In this sense, bathos is not only a voicing of one's imprisonment within class structures, but also a statement of reconciliation that acknowledges suburban 'normality' as the only identity that is truly honest.

In the twenty-first century, the underwhelming reality of the world has risen to become perhaps the single most influential mode of television comedy thanks to the success of shows such as *Curb Your Enthusiasm* (2000–), *The Office*, *Arrested Development* (2003–2006, 2013), *Extras* (2005–2007), *The Thick of It* (2005–2012), and *Parks and Recreation* (2009–). What these programmes share is a loose narrative form and improvisatory feel, often shot in a single-camera, hyper-realistic 'mockumentary' style that leaves behind the slick format of the studio sitcom and seeks to belie their scripted nature. Key to their comedy is a sense of discomfort, heightened by the presence of awkward silences and uncomfortable moments that are amplified by the absence of canned laughter. Both the British and American versions of *The Office* (UK 2001–2003; US 2005–2013), for example, contain deliberately jarring notes, including dead time, non-sequiturs, and the sadness of an office environment made up of dull colours, mass-produced furniture, and the enforced jollity of inspirational posters and coffee mug slogans, all of which underline the space between the reality of the office world and the delusions of its inhabitants. In the words of *Office* co-originator, Stephen Marchant, it was 'a fascinating stew of discomfort and ignorance that becomes a great recipe for laughter' (quoted in Sacks, 2009: 30).

In terms of comic identity, what these shows dwell on is the essential awkwardness of many human interactions. Much of this awkwardness appears to be derived from what we might call an urge to inhabit an ironised and inauthentic self, as the documentary style allows us to observe the actions of characters both at candid moments and in instances of direct address. Thus, when attempting to represent themselves in a favourable light, the characters of *The Office* continually fall into traps of hypocrisy and contradiction that they have set for themselves, or get lost in the thrall of irrelevant or incoherent thoughts. That so many comedies of discomfort are set in the workplace is particularly telling, especially as so many of these shows have flourished during times of economic crisis. They reveal the alienation, mundanity, and pettiness of so much work life, and comment on the extent to which the promises of late capitalism and its life of leisured satisfaction have failed to live up to the banality of the corporate existence. There is no struggle in these narratives, and nothing larger at stake. Instead, bathos has expanded, imposing itself on everything in the form of an affectless neutrality that says 'we have everything we wanted, and it amounts to what?'

3

THE BODY

Man consists of two parts, his mind and his body, only the body has more fun.

Woody Allen

'The comic hero, by his very nature', writes Maurice Charney, 'needs to declare himself the patron of everything real, physical, material, enjoyable, and the enemy of all abstractions, moral principles, seriousness and joylessness. This is a matter of basic allegiance to the life force' (Charney, 1978: 160–161). If the comic hero is a sensualist, then his or her main ally in hedonism must surely be the body, that medium in comedy through which humanity's fascination with its instinctual and animal nature is best explored. The comic body is exaggeratedly physical, a distorted, profane, ill-disciplined, insatiate, and perverse organism. Any Tom and Jerry cartoon exemplifies this extenuated corporeality in its parade of bodies that mutate, disassemble, reconfigure, and suffer endless punishment while refusing to die. Comic heroes are often disproportionate caricatures themselves, excessively fat or ludicrously thin like Laurel and Hardy, small and hapless like Buster Keaton, or elastic like Mr Bean. We might also say that the comic body privileges the facts of physicality over the ideal of the physique, its functions over poise, however those ideas might be structured at any particular historical moment. Jerry Seinfeld once said that conventionally attractive people do not make good stand-up comedians as the audience distrusts beauty in comedy and prefers their clowns imperfect. An ideal of physicality must exist against which the comedian can be found lacking, thereby reassuring an audience that comic substance will be found in departure from those ideals.

BEAUTY AND ABJECTION

In Western culture, the human body is subject to discourses and regulatory regimes that form and instruct it according to an ideologically driven idea of how it should appear and how it may be properly used. A key theme is its divided nature, capable at once of stunning beauty and grace, but also disease and foul excretions, a temple built over a sewer. The idealisation of beauty in the West has one root in the Platonic system that understood the contemplation of physical perfection as a necessary step on the course to absolute knowledge. In *The Symposium* (c.371 BC), Socrates encourages his friend to use beauty as a ladder to the truth, urging him

> to begin with examples of beauty in this world, and using them as steps to ascend continually with the absolute beauty as one's aim, from one instance of physical beauty to two and from two to all, then from physical beauty to moral beauty, and from moral beauty to the beauty of knowledge, until from knowledge of various kinds one arrives at the supreme knowledge whose sole object is that absolute beauty, and knows at last what absolute beauty is.
>
> (Plato, 1951: 94)

Beauty in human beings is therefore a partial reflection of an absolute beauty that is good, virtuous, and metaphysically inseparable from truth. For Aristotle, the kernel of beauty lay in perfect orderliness, writing that 'the chief forms of beauty are order and symmetry and definiteness' (quoted in Synott, 1993: 80). A parallel idea can be found in the Old Testament's book of Isaiah: 'The carpenter stretcheth out his rule; he marketh it out with a line; he fitteth it with planes, and he marketh it out with the compass, and maketh it after the figure of a man, according to the beauty of a man' (44:13). Classical architecture used perfect bodily proportion as a divinely ordered template for the organisation of buildings, especially temples, a principle developed by the Roman architect and military engineer Vitruvius (fl. first century AD). In Book III of his *De Architectura* Vitruvius writes, 'No temple can have any compositional system without symmetry and proportion, unless, as it were, it has an exact system of correspondence to the likeness of a well-formed human being' (Vitruvius, 1999: 47). A beautiful human form is therefore the perfect compositional template, its symmetry and proportion constituting an embodiment of the divine plan.

Concomitant with the idealisation of beauty is a cultural insistence on mastering the body, and making it conform to ideas of deportment and appropriate behaviour, regulating its functions and odours according to what is considered acceptable while suppressing all that is crude and bestial. Norbert Elias, whose groundbreaking work *The Civilizing Process* (1939) demonstrated how a concept of the body and its management lay at the heart of ideas like refinement and civilisation, argues that one of the principal means of governing bodily manners has been through the invocation of shame. Feeling ashamed, or developing a heightened sense of delicacy about nakedness, table-manners, flatulence, and other 'unpleasant' biological facts, requires disciplining the bodily functions in order to conform to the standards of etiquette and avoid being shunned. As the rules of bodily discipline become increasingly refined, a parallel sense of the primitive and brutish is created in its wake:

> The greater or lesser discomfort we feel toward people who discuss or mention their bodily functions more openly, who conceal and restrain these functions less than we do, is one of the dominant feelings expressed in the judgement 'barbaric' or 'uncivilized'. Such, then, is the nature of 'barbarism and its discontents', or, in more precise and less evaluative terms, the discontent with the different structure of affects, the different standard of repugnance which preceded our own and is its precondition.
>
> (Elias, 1978: 58–59)

By demonstrating our disapproval of standards lower than our own we construct a category of barbarism against which we guarantee our elevated level of civility.

It is against these ideals of beauty and manners that physical comedy is produced. Put simply, comedy strategically by-passes civility to return us to our bodies, emphasising our proximity to the animals, reminding us of our corporeality and momentarily shattering the apparently global imperatives of manners and beauty. Obscene, sexual, or taboo humour is predicated on an understanding of the socially tolerable body that it perverts in order to provoke laughter. Yet this does not amount to an authentic moment in which we are granted a genuine and unmediated experience of our material selves, but rather a discovery of the body through the contravention of civility. Out of the concept of bodily order, then, emerges the comic body.

One idea that may help us understand the place of the body in comedy is the notion of 'abjection'. This concept, developed in its most familiar form in the psychoanalytic criticism of Julia Kristeva, contemplates those things which repulse or nauseate the subject but which do not utterly belong outside him or her. In his study of abjection in stand-up comedy, John Limon describes it as 'a psychic worrying of those aspects of oneself that one cannot be rid of, that seem, but are not quite, alienable – for example, blood, urine, feces, nails, and the corpse' (Limon, 2000: 4). The abject is an ever-present site of horror and fascination that pollutes the self, because the self partly consists of it. This is most clearly characterised by the actual body, which will eventually die. As Kristeva writes:

> The corpse, seen without God and outside of science, is the utmost of abjection. It is death infecting life. Abject. It is something rejected from which one does not part, from which one does not protect oneself as from an object. Imaginary uncanniness and real threat, it beckons to us and ends up engulfing us.
>
> (Kristeva, 1982: 4)

We see here that the abject is a physical reality that cannot be defeated through the simple application of additional layers of cultural refinement. In Limon's terms, the abject 'worries' at us, refusing to be sublimated, never entirely forgotten and implicated in one's very existence. Abjection may explain why 'sick', morbid, or scatological humour, or comedy that involves violence and pain, is so popular. Such examples go straight to the worry, addressing the inescapably bodily facts of existence that are suppressed by the varnish of manners and acknowledging the omnipotence of filth. Medieval Biblical drama often incorporated elements of farce and burlesque, styles that use violence, physical predicaments, and scatology in their comedy, as if indicating a desire to raise the troubling issues of bodily existence in the presence of God. By foregrounding the functions of what Bakhtin calls the 'lower bodily stratum', the genitals, the anus, urine, excrement, and excrescences, and invoking the abject body as a risible concept to be laughed at rather than feared, its power of horror may be lifted and our fear of decay and degeneration alleviated. A modern analogue of this might be found in the 'gross out' comedies that were popular in the 1990s and early 2000s. Movies such as the Farelly brothers' *There's Something About Mary* (1998) and Paul Weitz's *American Pie* (1999) derive much of their humour from the physical anxieties of adolescence, such as failed, imperfect, or humiliating sexual escapades and explosive acts of flatulence, vomit, and ejaculation. By enacting these moments of traumatic mortification, we laugh at them as if to ward them off, and in so doing, are reconciled, just a little bit, to our bodily selves.

THE GROTESQUE

The grotesque could be described as an embodiment of the abject. A form of humorous monstrosity devised for satiric purposes, the grotesque marries the comic to the repulsive, as in the paintings of Hieronymus Bosch (c.1450–1516) or George Grosz (1893–1959), or even in the spirit of pantomime dames. Retrospectively applied to the decorative arts of Ancient Rome, the term originally referred to an imaginative combination of the real and the fantastic, and especially to an unnatural or stylised distortion of organic nature in stark contrast to the regularity of classical order that Vitruvius himself complained of bitterly. 'Grotesque' was a term initially reserved for the visual arts, but it was later extended to include anything that contained elements of the incongruous, the ridiculous, the monstrous, or the bizarre. The grotesque is a form of exaggerated and ambivalent social commentary produced by the violent clash of opposites, especially those that are comic and terrifying, that exist in a state of unresolved tension. The site of the grotesque clash is the human body, resulting in deeply ambiguous and divided reactions to the horror of corporeality and oneself as an organism. Mr Creosote, the diner from Monty Python's 1983 film *The Meaning of Life*, might serve as an example. Here is a man so gluttonous that his eating causes him to vomit torrentially until ultimately exploding after consuming a 'wafer thin' mint. Creosote survives but finds himself ripped apart and staring down at his open ribcage and enlarged heart. As viewers, we are amused by the absurdity of the spectacle and are appreciative of its poetic justice, but the image is also brutal and disgusting, a visceral rendition of a body destroyed by its own appetite and forced to witness the consequences of its actions. It is this unresolved tension that gives the grotesque its particular force as a humorous mode that aims to produce an ambiguous feeling pitched somewhere between pleasure and disgust.

By far the most notable author of grotesque comic fiction is François Rabelais (c.1494–1553). Rabelais's stories of the giants Gargantua and Pantagruel follow them through a series of absurd adventures and grotesque scenarios that celebrate physicality by means of unremitting obsession. The giants and their companions engage in a continual round of eating, drinking, defecating, urination, sweating, copulating, and passing wind. They are insatiately anal, oral, and phallic monstrosities whose sexual and scatological openness hopes to release the world from pathological inhibitions and the stress of maintaining manners. What they champion is unruly, desiring, animal existence in the face of a censorious and ascetic intellectualism. The proximity of humanity to the body is continually stressed from the moment Gargantua's mother goes into labour in Book I. His birth is prefaced by a characteristic case of mistaken identity:

> A while later she began to groan and wail and shout. Then suddenly swarms of midwives came up from every side, and feeling her

> underneath found some rather ill-smelling excrescences, which they
> thought were the child; but it was her fundament slipping out,
> because of the softening of the right intestine – which you call the
> bum-gut – owing to her having eaten too much tripe.
>
> (Rabelais, 1955: 52)

The confusion of the baby and bodily waste is symptomatic of the text's substitution of subjectivity with materiality, and its paralleling of cognitive categories with bodily functions. However, Gargantua and Pantagruel are not only representatives of an infantile or hedonistic id, but rather the medium through which Rabelais launches satirical attacks on a range of subjects including education, medicine, the ecclesiastical establishment, monastic life, and the nature of justice. Rabelais deployed his satire in the Erasmian style, ridiculing pretension and ignorance by enlarging them through exaggeration. For Mikhail Bakhtin, of course, Rabelaisian grotesque was the purest possible manifestation of the popular-festive folk identity. Arguing that Rabelais's novels reject any kind of boundaries between the mannered and disciplined body and the procreative, alimentary, corpulent, or offensively abject body, Bakhtin claims that Rabelais's 'grotesque realism' demonstrates 'the body in the act of becoming' (Bakhtin, 1984: 317). 'We find at the basis of grotesque imagery', he writes, 'a special concept of the body as a whole and of the limits of the whole. The confines between the body and the world and between separate bodies are drawn in the grotesque genre quite differently than in the classic and naturalistic images' (Bakhtin, 1984: 315). The grotesque body is not a closed system defined by clear limits, but a body that reaches out beyond its boundaries and interacts with the world on a sensual level:

> The stress is laid on those parts of the body that are open to the
> outside world, that is, the parts through which the world enters the
> body or emerges from it, or through which the body itself goes out to
> meet the world. This means that the emphasis is on the apertures or
> the convexities, or on various ramifications and offshoots: the open
> mouth, the genital organs, the breasts, the phallus, the potbelly, the

nose. The body discloses its essence as a principle of growth which exceeds its own limits only in copulation, pregnancy, child-birth, the throes of death, eating, drinking or defecation.

(Bakhtin, 1984: 26)

The grotesque is therefore a vivid celebration of inter-connectedness, growth beyond death and the continuity of existence, where the body is triply significant as a representation of ideal community, the embodiment of festivity, and inter-penetration and connection of the human body with the universe. Once expressed in these terms, it is clear why some critics have accused Bakhtin of a 'romanticization and heroization of the body' (Critchley, 2002: 51).

A modified example of Rabelaisian grotesque would be Shakespeare's Sir John Falstaff, a figure for whom the celebration of corporeality always takes place within the context of a direct challenge to the disciplines of order and self-control. Falstaff is often thought of as a representative of Carnival, his Eastcheap antics standing in contrast to the statesmen and soldiers of the rest of the play. Falstaff, a liar, a glutton, a coward, and the consort of prostitutes and thieves, is a symbol of degeneracy and perpetual leisure. In a passage where Prince Hal mimics his father's displeasure, we can see how Falstaff is imagined as a parade of meats:

There is a devil haunts thee in the likeness of an old fat man; a tun of man is thy companion. Why dost thou converse with that trunk of humours, that bolting-hutch of beastliness, that swollen parcel of dropsies, that huge bombard of sack, that stuffed cloak-bag of guts, that roasted Manningtree ox with the pudding in his belly?

(Shakespeare, 1989: *1 Henry IV*, 2.5.407–413)

Falstaff's body is a distempered creation stitched together from organs, fluids, and edibles: 'In each image', writes Neil Rhodes, 'Falstaff is ... a barrel of diseases or a horn of plenty which can be exchanged and replenished at any moment' (Rhodes, 1980: 109). For Anne Barton this constantly changing grotesque makes Falstaff a hero, the descendant of a long line of characters who 'detest war and the ideals of military glory':

> They are healthily sceptical of the pretensions and promises of politi-cians, and their own unabashed physicality makes them insist on recognizing and celebrating man's links with nonhuman creation. Monstrous egoists and opportunists, they are enemies of society, but also its raffish saviors.
>
> (Barton, 1985: 133)

In the final battle at Shrewsbury, Falstaff carries a bottle of wine where his pistol should be, falsely boasts of killing Percy, feigns death to avoid injury, and ultimately lives, enacting the image of a carnival resurrection and a life-affirming, if dishonourable, alter-native to politics and warfare. As C. L. Barber writes: 'Whereas, in the tragedy, the reduction is to the body which can only die, here reduction is to a body which typifies our power to eat and drink our way through a shambles of intellectual and moral contradictions' (Barber, 1963: 213).

Just as the end of *2 Henry IV* sees Falstaff banished from Hal's presence on pain of death, thereby setting kings and carnival strictly apart, at the close of the Renaissance the grotesque appears to have been relegated to the margins of comedy. Neo-classical come-dies of manners privileged wit over physical humour, and revised concepts of authorship meant that the onus fell increasingly on performers to respect the integrity of the text to the detriment of clownish improvisation. At this stage, comedy draws away from the body to privilege persiflage and plot, as evinced by the plays of Molière, Marivaux, Etherege, Wycherley and others, whose dramas accelerate action verbally while simultaneously decreasing the space it occupies. But while the grotesque may withdraw in comic literature, it enjoys a coincidental rise in the graphic arts, especially as caricature, a term taken from the Italian, *caricare*, meaning 'to overdetermine' or 'to overload', which isolates parti-cular features in its subjects (such as the nose) and enlarges, alters, or otherwise manipulates them in order to emphasise particular qualities of appearance. Charles Baudelaire (1821–1867), who wrote a series of articles on caricature, considered it an example of the '*comique absolu*', or absolute comic, because its grotesque distortions had the power to shock the viewer into an awareness of the ironic duality of life, 'at once embodying and exposing the division and fragmentation of the modern subject, representing and revealing the terrifying and exhilarating otherness of modern experience' (Hanoosh, 1992: 4). Caricature operates according to the principle that we are all potentially monstrous, as the prominently exaggerated or altered features communicate the identity of the subject depicted, and so caricature makes us identifiable by deforming us. Caricature is most readily associated with satire, with physical distortion commensurate to the vices of its targets. William Hogarth (1697–1764), the painter and engraver best known for his series of 'modern moral subjects' *The Harlot's Progess* (1732), *The Rake's Progress* (1733–5), and *Marriage à la Mode* (1743–5), used caricature in a distinctly literary fashion, adopting a tone of Horatian satire to belittle greed and condemn hypocrisy.

Caricature's place in national political debate was also established in the eighteenth century, where cartoonists used it as a means of transforming its targets into the personifications of their vices. For Freud, the pleasure in caricature is derived from its ridiculing of political figures, even when the image itself is unsuccessful, 'simply because we count rebellion against authority as a merit' (Freud, 2001: 105). Martha Banta, who has studied nineteenth- and twentieth-century caricature in both Britain and the USA, sees it as a subtle but powerful forum for establishing the nature of normality. The questions that were being asked in these cartoons, she writes, dealt with 'essential (essentialist) concerns', which 'broke through as a series of pictorial enquiries: "What is 'English'?" "What is 'American'?" "What is 'civilized'?" "What is 'barbaric'?" and the most basic anxiety of all, "Where can we feel safe?"' (Banta, 2003: 23). Caricature helped to mediate these questions by pictorially imagining the 'other' and making it monstrous or ludicrous in order to service the anxieties of the white, urban middle-class readership of magazines like *Punch* and *Life*. Pictorial caricature is therefore a shorthand that uses elements of the human figure as a means of conveying a complete set of ideologically correlated ideas.

SLAPSTICK

'Slapstick' is generally understood as physical humour of a robust and hyperbolised nature where stunts, acrobatics, pain, and violence are standard features. While broad comedy of this type has been around since Aristophanes, the golden age of slapstick came with early American cinema, where, in the hands of skilled performers such as Charlie Chaplin, Buster Keaton, and Harold Lloyd, and through the enterprise of legendary producers like Mack Sennett, it became practically the sole form of comedy. Slapstick is a perfect example of the way in which genres are shaped by the media that present them, as moving pictures remained soundless until 1926, forcing humour to be silent and visual. For Stanley Cavell, the technological considerations of early film were absolutely central to the comedy it produced for two reasons:

> First, movie performers cannot project, but are projected. Second, photographs are of the world, in which human beings are not onto-logically favoured over the rest of nature, in which objects are not props but natural allies (or enemies) of human character. The first necessity – projected visibility – permits the sublime comprehensibility of Chaplin's natural choreography; the second – ontological equality – permits his Proustian and Jamesian relationships with Murphy beds and flights of stairs and with vases on runners on tables on rollers.
>
> (Cavell, 1979: 36–37)

Thus we are presented with the projected body that draws attention to its surface and movements, negotiating a world of things over which it cannot claim superiority. Ironically for silent film, the term 'slapstick' is onomatopoeically derived from the sound made by the hinged wooden paddle, primed with a pinch of gunpowder, that Harlequin used to beat his enemies in the eighteenth-century pantomime. This was in turn a version of the inflated sheep bladders filled with dried peas that accompanied clowns on the early-modern stage, themselves an echo of the tools used to beat the 'scapegoat' in ancient ritual. The scapegoat, a person onto whom the accumulated evils of the community were transferred prior to his or her expulsion, might also be a useful way of understanding the hero of slapstick comedy. Slapstick comedians generally play the role of outsider, such as Keaton's unsmiling, diminutive loner, or Chaplin's Tramp character: marginal men who find themselves swimming against the tide of modern living. Thrust as innocents into a world they have never apparently mastered, their hapless bodies endure every indignity and hardship so that we do not have to. The suffering of slapstick performers liberates us in other ways too, as by watching them court death, or be repeatedly assaulted and still get back up for more, we are freed from the need to sympathise, and our laughter can be pleasurably sadistic.

The slapstick protagonist is continually prone to attack through either a bodily revolt or the loss of self-control, or from an external source that aims to dismantle his or her dignity. In both slapstick movies and the cartoons they inspired, the body is malleable, resilient, and infinitely resourceful. At the heart of slapstick is the conceit that the laws of physics are locally mutable, that the world can rebel against you, or that a person can be suddenly stripped of their ability to influence their environment or anticipate how it will behave. The body in slapstick is often at odds with the mind that inhabits it, suggesting a dysfunction of the mind/body dualism that emphasises the divided nature of human experience. Slapstick historian Alan Dale reads the beleaguered hero as a reconfiguration of the relationship between the mind and the body that has been a feature of conceptions of humanity since classical antiquity. 'One of the central elements of ... theology', he writes –

> the debasing effect of the body on the soul – enables Christians to overcome this discord only by denying and finally getting rid of the body, whereas slapstick achieves accord here on earth by a comic concession to the body at its most traitorous. Both of these stand in contrast to the pagan approach of the Olympic Games, in which athletes attempt to achieve a perfect union of body and will. These three ritualistic approaches form a gamut: Christianity seeks eternal triumph over physicality after life; Olympians seek by means of the body a temporal triumph that will be remembered long after the athlete's prowess has faded; slapstick seeks a temporal acceptance of physicality by a cathartic exaggeration of its very limitations.
>
> (Dale, 2000: 14)

As well as being a vicarious outlet for cruelty, then, the humour in slapstick may also help to reconcile us to a body that obstructs the will and insubordinately thwarts desire.

Slapstick is also where the body meets the world of things, and hence it is suitably fascinated with objects. By examining the identity and utility of things and playing with the spaces they occupy, their dimensions, properties, and cultural significance, the body's relationship to the external world is made strange. Typical gags might involve disproportionate sizes, the animation of the inanimate, the slowing down or speeding up of temporality, the personification of objects, and the reversal or rejection of linear cause-and-effect that allows things to be re-contextualised or entirely re-used, all of which belongs to a rich tradition of clowning. Some of the most popular routines performed by the famous Regency clown, Joseph Grimaldi (1778–1837), were known as 'tricks of construction', visual gags where Grimaldi would take seemingly innocent and unconnected items and build them into something new, taking a child's bassinet and four cheeses and making them into a coach, for example, or fashioning a hussar's uniform from two coal-scuttles and a ladies' muff. The Swiss-born clown Charles Wettach, better known as Grock (1880–1959), speaks tellingly of his relationship to objects in his autobiography: 'Ever since I can remember', he wrote, 'all kinds of inanimate objects have had a way of looking at me reproachfully and whispering to me in unguarded moments: "We have been waiting for you ... at last you've come ... take us now, and turn us into something different"' (quoted in Welsford, 1935: 309). Laleen Jayamanne sees the clown's ingenuity as 'an unsevered link between perception and action' that amounts to the ability to think with the body rather than the more familiar coordinates of subject–object relations, resulting in 'the capacity to make correspondences, the perception of non-sensuous similarities across incommensurables', such as eating an old shoe as if it were a gourmet meal as in Chaplin's *The Gold Rush* (1925) (Jayamanne, 2001: 189). The idea that the slapstick gag represents an interruption of conventional knowledge is put forward by Donald Crafton, who argues that the utility-turned-unpredictability of slapstick gags amounts to a rupture in the linear process of understanding. 'One way to look at narrative', he argues,

> is to see it as a system for providing the spectator with sufficient knowledge to make causal links between represented events. According to this view, the gag's status as an irreconcilable difference becomes clear. Rather than provide knowledge, slapstick misdirects the viewer's attention, and obfuscates the linearity of cause-effect relations. Gags provide the opposite of epistemological comprehension by the spectator. They are atemporal bursts of violence and/or hedonism that are as ephemeral and as gratifying as the sight of someone's pie-smitten face.
>
> (quoted in Jayamanne, 2001: 185)

Rather than taking events and shaping them into coherent order, slapstick events treat the world as if it were capricious, unpredictable, and suddenly explosive. To think of a gag as an 'irreconcilable difference' is to emphasise its incompatibility with our understanding of how the world normally works. Slapstick, then, opens up the possibility of the world becoming inhospitable and strange to us.

Another useful way to consider slapstick is through the work of Henri Bergson. Bergson, as discussed in Chapter 1, believed that human beings exist in a state of continual awareness of the animated 'vital spirit' of themselves and others, and that when a situation causes that vitality to be obscured and the 'humanness' of humans to be lost or denuded, comedy is born from the sudden eclipse of life. 'The comic', he says, 'is that side of a person which most reveals his likeness to a thing, that aspect of human events which, through its peculiar inelasticity, conveys the impression of pure mechanism, of automatism, of movement without life' (Bergson, 1980: 117). This especially includes moments where judgement is overridden by the actions of the body, such as any situation 'that calls our attention to the physical in a person, where it is the moral side that is concerned' (Bergson, 1980: 93).

Many great moments in slapstick have drawn our attention to the fraught interactions between the human and the machine. At the beginning of the nineteenth century, for example, Joseph Grimaldi expressed scepticism about the benefits of industrial progress, particularly the desire to harness power in order to move faster. Routines in the pantomimes *Harlequin and the Sylph of the Oak* (1816) and *Harlequin and Mother Bunch* (1821) both featured steam engines and steamboats that would explode or run wild the moment he came upon them. As David Mayer has noted, so insistently did Grimaldi invoke the dangers of steam that the *Morning Post* complained that he should desist from jokes of this kind in case they poisoned the public's mind to inventions of 'great importance to the world of science, and to mankind in general' (quoted in Mayer, 1969: 204).

Charlie Chaplin was similarly interested in the encroachment of mechanisation, and the extent to which the body is able to resist integration into the machine constitutes the theme of one of his greatest movies, *Modern Times* (1936). Set against a backdrop of mass labour and industrialisation, the unique and individuated body is contrasted with the faceless and automated machines of production-line capitalism. Essentially, the film asks whether it is possible for individuals to retain their sympathetic emotional qualities when their lives are controlled by the working week and subservience to heartless institutions. The film opens in a steel mill with Chaplin performing repetitive tasks at a conveyor belt, an action that penetrates him so deeply he adopts its automated twitch. While, from one perspective, this is a dark comment on the reification of labour, from a Bergsonian view it represents comedy in its purest form, insofar as 'The attitudes, gestures and movements of the human body are laughable in exact proportion as the body reminds us of a mere machine' (Bergson, 1980: 79). The mechanised body is one of the key symbols of the film, with two set-pieces built around the uncomfortable meeting of body and technology. The first features an automatic feeding device to which the worker is strapped and fed by robot arms, with the result that the meal is smeared all over Chaplin's face and clothes, as if he were an infant in a high chair. The second involves Chaplin's co-worker becoming stuck in the enormous cogs of a machine while Chaplin tries to feed him his lunch. In both predicaments, something particularly human, meal-times, with their array of cultural meanings, rituals, and strong associations of need and sensual enjoyment, are marred through the intervention of something senseless, inorganic, and utterly unsympathetic. In fact, missed or frustrated meals recur throughout the film, underlining the extent to which the Tramp is always at some distance from bodily satisfaction and economic success. The alternative to faceless frustration is the 'gamin', Paulette Goddard, Chaplin's real-life wife at the time, who plays a female representative of authentic vitality. After her father is killed in a labour riot, the gamin comes under the protection of Chaplin who instantly assumes the over-lapping roles of protector and uncertain mate. An absence of obvious sexual interest was typical of Chaplin's character, and his thin cane and voluminous trousers have been taken as symbols of waning male sexuality (Segal, 2001: 432). For the new couple, respite from privation takes priority over sex. In a scene in which Chaplin takes the job of night watchman in a department store, the new couple enact a fantasy of leisure and plenty, characterised by their unfettered access to the luxury goods on the shelves. A similar bourgeois 'green-world' idyll is conjured up as the couple sit on the lawn of a suburban bungalow and imagine life as middle-class pastoral, where the trees are heavy with fruit and the cows deliver fresh milk. Ultimately, Chaplin's slapstick in *Modern Times* is the dumb-show of bodily cravings and social denial.

Chaplin's incredulity at the innovations of modern life is a comedic thread that continues in the work of the French comedian, Jacques Tati (1907–1982). Tati, who was greatly influenced by the silent era of Chaplin, Keaton, Lloyd, and Sennett, introduced his best-known character, a lanky, guileless, pipe-smoking gentleman in a raincoat, in a 1953 movie titled *Les Vacances de Monsieur Hulot*, although it was in three later films – *Mon Oncle* (1958), which won an Academy Award for Best Foreign Language Film, *Play Time* (1967), and *Traffic* (1971) – that Tati best used him as a medium through which to explore the alienating effects of modern living. Monsieur Hulot is very much a slapstick being, although his interactions with the world are much subtler and less violent than those of the American performers that preceded him. The difference can perhaps be explained by the fact that whereas Chaplin and Keaton interacted with a modern world characterised by steam trains, cannons, factories, and heavy industry, Hulot's world is largely defined by design. For Hulot, the industrial world has been succeeded by a post-industrial one, in which the cogs of toil and heavy infrastructure have been replaced by an alienating world of sleek finishes and glass atriums. In *Play Time*, Hulot visits a floor of an office building that has been sub-divided into work cubicles to form an impenetrable labyrinth from which he cannot escape, a situation that is reflected in the outside world, where the traffic moves bumper to bumper in circles from which their drivers are unable to escape. That the sterility of modern environments and the loneliness they induce are Tati's constant themes is underlined by the fact that his movies rarely feature standard dialogue, but are rather made up of muted snippets of overheard speech, layered on to the ambient sounds of the everyday, amplified and foregrounded, so that exaggerated sounds of doors opening and heels clicking on the floors of marble foyers occupy more aural space than language. The contrast between the old world and the new is best represented in *Mon Oncle*, where Hulot moves between his dilapidated apartment in the old part of town set on a market square near a congenial café, and an ultra-modern suburb where his sister lives in a house made of glass and steel, filled with uncomfortable chairs and modern appliances activated by the push of a button, and where the local school and plastic extrusion plant are indistinguishable from one another. To move between these two worlds – one clearly intended as 'organic', the other artificial – Hulot cycles past a bombed-out wasteland and through a ruined gate onto slick black roads painted with idiot-proof lines that even instruct you in the correct way to exit a doorway. The transition is intended as a comment on the decline of traditional French culture following the Second World War and the increasing adoption of American-style consumerism as a way of life. As Tati himself said:

> I noticed people following the white lines on the road more and more and having less and less fun. I thought it would be good to point out 'This is all nicely laid out. It's tidy, clear, and wonderful. But you don't seem to be having much fun.' I have the right to say 'There's more to life than that.'
>
> (Tatischeff, 1989)

THE FEMALE BODY

As Morwenna Banks and Amanda Swift's history of female performers in music-hall has shown, there have been many accomplished women who were physical performers, but still their legacy has failed to endure (Banks and Swift, 1987). The golden age of Hollywood slapstick was not a golden age for female comedians. Women rarely performed the kind of stunts their male counterparts were famous for, and were used instead as figures of romantic interest or ridicule. Mack Sennett, the prolific producer of silent-era slapstick, even went as far as imposing rules for the use of women in his films according to a descending scale of hilarity that held that old maids were the funniest targets, mother-in-laws were second, but that it was absolutely forbidden to make a mother the butt of jokes for fear of alienating the audience (Dale, 2000: 92). Women who occupy the roles traditionally considered sacrosanct by men, such as the girlfriend or the mother, could not be represented as either physical or humorous in slapstick cinema, whereas the old or the unattractive were fair game.

This clear case of inequity, combined with a pervasive prurience, has been commonplace when it comes to comic representations of the female body. From extremes such as the American sitcom *I Love Lucy* (1951–1957 and 1957–1960) – which in 1952 was unable to mention pregnancy, even though its star Lucille Ball was heavily pregnant and the show featured an episode in which Lucy was delivered of a son – to the role of women in the long-running *Benny Hill Show* (1969–1989), where female actors wore 'revealing frocks … an expression of perpetual surprise (men are so clever/naughty) and a special way of moving that jiggles as many separate parts of the body as possible while covering the minimum ground', the female body has been either objectified, reduced to sexless motherhood, or derided as belonging to spinsters, harridans, and crones. 'What unites the narrow spectrum of female types', writes Lorraine Porter, 'is their a priori definition by physicality and sexuality: the tart or dumb blonde by her over-determined sexuality, or her excess of sexual difference, and the tyrant or spinster by her absolute asexuality, or her lack of sexual difference' (Porter, 1998: 70).

For female bodies to be prominently featured in comedy, they have generally been required to stand outside normative notions of female beauty. Kathleen Rowe has called these 'unruly women', and enumerates the ways in which they have been depicted:

1. The unruly woman creates disorder by dominating, or trying to dominate, men. She is unable or unwilling to confine herself to her proper place.
2. Her body is excessive or fat, suggesting her unwillingness or inability to control her physical appetites.
3. Her speech is excessive, in quantity, content, or tone.
4. She makes jokes, or laughs at herself.
5. She may be androgynous or hermaphroditic, drawing attention to the social construction of gender.
6. She may be old or a masculinized crone, for old women who refuse to become invisible in our culture are often considered grotesque.
7. Her behavior is associated with looseness and occasionally whorishness, but her sexuality is less narrowly and negatively defined than is that of the femme fatale. She may be pregnant.
8. She is associated with dirt, liminality (thresholds, borders, or margins), and taboo, rendering above all a figure of ambivalence.
                                                                (Rowe, 1995: 31)

Rowe includes figures such as Roseanne Barr and *The Muppets'* Miss Piggy as examples of unruly women, as well as their most famous literary antecedent, Ursula the Pig Woman in Ben Jonson's play, *Bartholomew Fair* (1614). An obese, greasy, uninhibited pig breeder, who eats, curses, brawls, steals, and urinates her way through the play, this 'sow of enormity' (5.6.51) is a female Falstaff, grotesque in the extreme, what Stallybrass and White call a 'celebrant of the open orifice ... belly, womb, gaping mouth, udder, the source and object of praise and abuse ... Above all, like the giant hog displayed at the fair, she is excessive' (Stallybrass and White, 1986: 64).

Unruly women serially challenge patriarchal definitions of femininity through the performance of excess. Consider, for example, the double-act of Patsy and Edina in Jennifer Saunders's *Absolutely*

Fabulous (1992–1996), a pair of women whose grotesque physicality has become so penetrated by the contradictory and dictatorial demands of diet and fashion that they have become utterly misshapen. *Absolutely Fabulous* ridicules the consumer culture and worship of youth and beauty to which its characters are slavishly devoted, and which in its purest form demands that women subjugate their bodies entirely to become demure and non-corporeal. The satire of the industry and its vacuous beliefs is literally performed on the bodies of the women, through the garish and ill-chosen clothes they wear, to Patsy's promiscuity, Edina's immaturity, and the drunkenness of both.

While Patsy and Edina certainly appear on the spectrum of female grotesques, the movie *Bridesmaids* (2011) has offered a more nuanced interpretation of the roles women may play outside comedy's 'sex object/grotesque' binary. Here, women *are* permitted to be conventionally feminine and conventionally attractive, while also swearing, puking, defecating, acting as sexual aggressors, and occasionally smashing things up. Indeed, Helen Harris, the only character who appears to embody the demure feminine ideal, is shown to be duplicitous, calculating, and profoundly unhappy. Of these women, the most obviously 'slapstick' is played by Melissa McCarthy, who, upon first introduction, tells us how she recently fell off a cruise ship:

> Yeah 'oh shit.' YEAH 'oh shit.' Took a hard, hard violent fall. Kind of pinballed down, hit a lot of railings, broke a lot of shit. I didn't … I'm not going to say I survived, I'm going to say I thrived. I met a dolphin down there and I swear to God that dolphin looked, not at me, but into my soul. Into my goddamn soul, Annie, and said 'I'm saving you, Megan.' Not with his mouth, but he said it. I'm assuming, telepathically.
>
> (Feig, 2011)

Megan's report of her painful, cartoonish bounce represents the emergence of a previously rare manifestation of female corporeality in comedy, one where her full bodiliness is neither exploited nor denied, nor made the object of spectacle, but is rather a joke, equivalent to those made by men.

While female comedians have steadily addressed the elision and appropriation of the female body in comedy, new grounds of contestation have also opened up, in particular, the controversy concerning jokes about rape. As comedy has challenged taboo after taboo, claiming always its right to say the unsayable, there has been a certain inevitability to the fact that eventually someone will find these jokes defensible in a mainstream context. Most recently protest was sparked by the American comedian, Daniel Tosh, who in a live show in 2012 responded to a female heckler by saying 'Wouldn't it be funny if that girl got raped by, like, five guys right now? Like, right now?' (Holpuch, 2012). Tosh subsequently apologised, although the fallout remained angry and contentious, with one side defending comedy as privileged space beyond censorship (thereby pushing responsibility for offence onto the offended), while the other argued that it trivialised rape and mocked the victims of sexual violence (as the comic Sarah Silverman remarked, 'Whose gonna complain about a rape joke? Rape victims? They don't even report rape' [Pozner, 2012]). For the media critic, Jennifer Pozner, this was not a moment to call for censorship or the removal of all references to rape in comedy, but rather an opportunity to make a distinction between '"rape jokes" that target victims and mock their pain, and "rape culture jokes" that dismantle the systems that protect rapists and blame women for sexual assault' (Pozner, 2012). Perhaps the most creative response, however, came from the comedian and performance artist, Adrienne Truscott, whose 2013 show at the Edinburgh Fringe Festival, *Asking For It: A One Lady Rape about Comedy Starring Her Pussy and Little Else!* addressed the extent to which the discussion around rape and comedy has at its heart the ownership of the female body. Seemingly drunk, naked from the waist down, and wearing a variety of wigs, bras, and dresses which she puts on and removes throughout the show, Truscott examines the extent to which the discourse of sexual violence seeks to indict women as provocateurs incapable of appropriately managing their own bodies. As a means of underscoring the extent to which female sexuality is policed by men, she turns herself into a screen, projecting a series of male talking heads onto her naked torso, each one expressing some kind of doubt that women are capable of properly controlling themselves. Meanwhile her pubic hair acts as a beard.

Truscott's work is just one example of the way in which comedy has drawn attention to the issues of gender throughout history, an issue which the following chapter will explore in further detail.

4

WOMEN IN COMEDY

Men find funny women threatening. They ask me, 'Are you going to be funny in bed?'

Joan Rivers

While women have been prominent protagonists in tragedy (as evidenced in the figures of Medea, Hedda Gabler, and Lady Macbeth), when it comes to comedy, they have been far less visible. Suffering ennobles women and even sanctifies them as part of what Kathleen Rowe has called 'the cultural preference for women's tears over their laughter', but imagining them as the generators of comedy has seemingly set them at odds with traditional notions of femininity (quoted in Bociurkiw, 2005: 179). The prejudice is longstanding. William Congreve, for example, believed that women were both emotionally and biologically incapable of being funny: 'I must confess I have never made any Observation of what I Apprehend to be the true Humour in Women', he wrote in 1695. 'Perhaps Passions are too powerful in that Sex to let Humour have its Course; or maybe by reason of their Natural Coldness, Humour cannot Exert itself to that extravagant Degree, which it does in the Male Sex' (Congreve,

1997c: 479). Three hundred years later, when Joan Rivers, one of the world's most famous and recognisable comedians, began her career in the 1960s, very few women were performing stand-up comedy: 'If you saw a pretty girl walk into a nightclub', she told *The Hollywood Reporter*, 'she was automatically a singer. Comedy was all white, older men' (Rivers, 2012). At that time, the notion of a female performer who was witty, outspoken, and claimed all the privileges of free and profane speech was seen as a direct challenge to the prevailing views of how a woman should comport herself. Rivers came to prominence through regular appearances on *The Tonight Show*, whose host, Johnny Carson, was responsible for introducing hundreds of comedians to mainstream audiences between 1962 and 1992. But even Carson found many female comedians to be coarse and masculine. As he told *Rolling Stone* magazine in 1979:

> A woman is feminine, a woman is not abrasive, a woman is not a hustler. So when you see a gal who does 'stand-up' one liners, she has to overcome that built-in identification as a retiring, meek woman. I mean, if a woman comes out and starts firing one-liners, those little abrasive things, you can take that from a man. The ones that try sometimes are a little aggressive for my taste. I'll take it from a guy, but from women, sometimes, it just doesn't fit too well.
>
> (quoted in Knoedelseder, 2011: 78)

Carson's objection appears to stem from the oft-repeated opinion that comedy is a combative form requiring a level of aggression unattainable by women. Ironically, it is a view shared by Rivers herself, although for her, it is an issue of acculturation. 'Comedy is masculine', she says. 'To stand up and take control of an audience verbally is very difficult. Women are oppressed in childhood and not allowed to do this' (quoted in Horowitz, 1997: 107).

While we might like to disregard these attitudes as relics of a less-enlightened era, even today it is estimated that only 20 per cent of US, and 12 per cent of British, touring comedians are women (Lockyer, 2011: 114–115). Meanwhile, as recently as 2007, the late polemicist Christopher Hitchens published an essay entitled 'Why Women Aren't Funny' that echoed Congreve by arguing that humour is a trait valued and honed by men as a means of assisting them in their reproductive goals. Just as women have learned to enhance their physical appearance to attract a mate, claims Hitchens, so men have learned to make women laugh. The only funny women, he suggests, are those he perceives as somehow standing outside the mainstream of heterosexual desireability, women he characterises as 'hefty or dykey or Jewish' (Hitchens, 2007). Just as with Johnny Carson, the argument partakes of a longstanding anxiety that funny women are a direct affront to the authority of men: 'Precisely because humor is a sign of intelligence', Hitchens writes '(and many women believe, or were taught by their mothers, that they become threatening to men if they appear too bright), it could be that in some way men do not *want* women to be funny. They want them as an audience, not as rivals' (Hitchens, 2007).

In expressing a preference for women as passive auditors rather than active participants in the production of comedy, Hitchens replicates the prejudice that has seen women demoted to what Frances Gray has called the role of 'handmaid of laughter, not its creator' (Gray, 1994: 21). Where female characters have enjoyed prominence, they have often been represented by surrogates: boys dressed as women on the Shakespearean stage, for example, or dragged-up dames in British pantomime. Even the sketch show *Monty Python* had most of its female roles played by men in drag with the notable exception of the actress Carol Cleveland, who appeared whenever the script called for a glamorous blonde. Needless to say, while a notion of femininity lies at the heart of cross-dressing and drag, as Lucy Fischer has argued, transvestite comedy ultimately 'privileges the male and claims his dominance even when woman is apparently there'. This is 'particularly bizarre', she continues, 'given the origins of the mode in female fertility rites' (Fischer, 1991: 62, 63).

This chapter will consider the historical role of women in comedy, before looking at the ways in which traditional gender expectations have been challenged by comedians in more recent years.

MARRIAGE

One of the stock narratives featuring women in comedy has been the marriage plot. As we have seen in Chapter 1, comedies from classical antiquity through to the romantic comedies of the present day have conventionally ended in marriage, as an affirmation of the social contract and a commitment to the future peopling of the world. However, while marriage may be seen as affirming the status quo, when looked at from the perspective of female characters, it may be seen as a rigid cultural structure against which women can test the limits of their freedom, agency, and identity.

Consider, for example, Aristophanes's *Lysistrata* (412 BC), one of the earliest stage comedies and also the earliest to give significant speaking roles to women, possibly in the whole of Western literature. The plot of *Lysistrata* involves a group of Athenian women who stage a sit in at the Acropolis in order to force their warring husbands into peace negotiations with Sparta. The group, led by the eponymous Lysistrata, are out-spoken women driven by the desire to force the state into seeing sense. The bargaining tool they use is sex, which they withhold from their husbands until their demands are met. However, Lauren K. Taaffee has argued, this is not necessarily the first step in a struggle for broader emancipation. Rather, the central conceit of *Lysistrata* is the world turned upside down, a role-reversal that places women in masculine positions and vice versa, which ultimately only serves to draw out the subordination of women. 'The integrity of male identity is kept whole,' writes Taaffee,

> while the absurdity of women in public life is played up. The play confirms and celebrates an ordered sense of gender identity in which male is stable and female is unstable, in need of control through marriage. Finally, the convention of male actors in female roles ensures that masculinity is always present on stage, even when all the characters are female.
>
> (Taaffee, 1993: 51)

The representation of women in *Lysistrata*, then, is largely symptomatic of the representation of woman in Western comedy as a whole. As Susan Carlson writes:

> In the comic plays populated by women, two features proscribe what comedy's women can be: a basic inversion and a generally happy

ending. To understand these two aspects of comic structure is to understand the limitations of comic women. Women are allowed their brilliance, freedom, and power in comedy only because the genre has built-in safe-guards against such behavior.

(Carlson, 1991: 17)

To see this in action, we need only turn to the transformation of Katherine in Shakespeare's *The Taming of the Shrew* (1593–4), a play that sees her go from a 'shrewd ill-favoured wife', to a compliant woman who argues that a husband should be 'thy lord, thy life, thy keeper / ... thy sovereign' (Shakespeare, 1989: 1.2.59; 5.2.146–147). Like Lysistrata's band of rebellious wives, Kate's volatile behaviour is permissible because it is both temporary and necessary if it is to be finally overcome, and patriarchy reasserted. Rather than providing a nuanced or realistic insight into the conditions of espousal, therefore, the play works because its view of women is so formulaic. It is entirely appropriate that the first wife we meet in the play who conforms to Petrucchio's ideal ('My husband and my lord, my lord and my husband / I am your wife in all obedience' [Shakespeare, 1989: Induction, ii, 104–5]), is a male, the page Bartholomew in disguise, underlining the extent to which play-acting and male fantasy override anything like the realistic portrayal of women (Leggatt, 1998: 121).

During the early-modern period in which *The Taming of the Shrew* was first performed, the official discourse of marriage held that the domestic arena was a microcosm of the state, with the husband the head of the household just as a monarch rules over his people. While this trope of domestic government epitomises a harmonious ideal, numerous treatises concerning the proper conduct of husbands and wives suggested that, just as the state was imperilled by enemies and espionage, marriage was continually threatened by 'adultery and whoredom' (Newman, 1991: 20). The question of female constancy, then, provides another means of framing women's participation in marriage narratives, as they are forced to negotiate the opposing poles of subordination and infamy. The courtesans of Roman New Comedy connect the threat of whoredom with that of foreign invasion particularly well, as they tended to belong to the *hetaerae*, a class of foreigners who enjoyed some freedoms as citizens but who were denied citizenship and were generally considered aliens. As an outsider, the courtesan was granted a certain amount of sexual licence that would have been unacceptable in a Roman citizen. Yet the desire to become a Roman remains strong, and so New Comedy features a number of plots in which the courtesan attempts to transform herself by reforming her sexual behaviour and changing her ethnic identity. Terence's *Eunuch* (161 BC) is one such example, in which the recovery of the slave Pamphila's true identity as a Roman citizen clears the way for her marriage to the young Athenian aristocrat, Chaerea. However, before hearing the news, Chaerea, thinking his beloved is still beyond his reach, switches places with a eunuch servant, enters her house, and rapes her. Chaerea's pride in his fortune and pleasure in his escapade are not censured by his family or peers, aside from the mildest chastisement he receives for his rascally behaviour. Rather, as the title suggests, the play diverts attention from the issue of rape to consider the comic improbabilities of a eunuch's sexual performance. That Chaerea and Pamphila are eventually married supposedly negates the crime against her, and confirms for us the view that alien women outside the institution of marriage are legitimate sexual targets.

Similar formulations are found in early-modern comedy, where a woman's social acceptance is linked to her sexual standing in the eyes of men. The sexual defamation of Hero in Shakespeare's *Much Ado About Nothing*, for example, results in a supposed death which can only be reversed after her name has been cleared. Similarly, the tragi-comic *The Winter's Tale* sees the accused Hermione reborn once her innocence is assured, but only after an intervening period of sixteen years. Thomas Middleton's *A Chaste Maid in Cheapside* (1613) features Moll Yellowhammer's sudden resuscitation as she lies in her coffin. In all these cases, women are wrongly accused of improper sexual conduct, an accusation that demands the highest punishments that strict social codes permit. To all intents and purposes, Hero, Hermione, and Moll die, and remain dead until the slander against them has been disproved. Only when the meanings that men attach to women have been redefined, may the women be reborn and their roles as the faithful wives and chaste servants of their husbands be re-affirmed.

In opposition to chaste wives stands the constant threat of the fallen women. Jacobean city comedies are particularly well stocked with prostitutes who serve to chastise prodigal behaviour, or are married off to moral bankrupts, as evidenced at the end of both Middleton's *A Trick to Catch the Old One* (c.1605) and David Lord Barry's *Ram Alley* (1608), where the villain of the piece is delivered a deliciously ironic punishment by being tricked into marrying a prostitute he had thought to be a desirable heiress. Sexual incontinence is viewed here as the moral equivalent of veniality, an example of comic *contrapasso* where the punishment is tailored to fit the nature of the crime. There are occasional variations on this theme where the prostitute turns out to have a heart of gold, but, as Alexander Leggatt writes, 'None of the attempts to complicate the conventional opposition of chaste maid and vicious whore really amounts to much: they are all minor effects, frequently uncertain and apologetic' (Leggatt, 1973: 109).

As always, there are exceptions. Middleton and Dekker's city comedy *The Roaring Girl* (c.1611), for example, provides us with a radical alternative to prescribed female roles in the unusual character of Moll Cutpurse, also known as Mary Frith. Moll is unusual because not only does she defy all the conventions of acceptable female behaviour, but she manages to retain her unimpeachable chastity. The play is based on the life of the real Mary Markham née Frith (c.1584–1659) who began to dress as a man and inhabit the London underworld in the early seventeenth century. Her unique character occupies a singular position in the play, which otherwise conforms to standard city comedy conventions, and which seems continually to struggle to know what to do with her. The first discussion of her by Sir Alexander Wengrave makes this clear:

> It is a thing
> One knows not how to name: her birth began
> Ere she was all made. 'Tis woman more than a man,
> Man more than a woman, and – which to none can hap –
> The sun gives her two shadows to one shape.
> (Middleton and Dekker, 1994: 1.2.128–132)

It is easier for the men having this conversation to believe that Moll is the victim of a bizarre birth-defect, than to accept her as a woman wearing men's clothing. While more than forty plays used the convention of women cross-dressed for the purposes of disguise between 1603 and 1619, including the *Roaring Girl* in the character of Mary Fitzallard, it is important to remember that Moll is resolutely *not* in disguise (Stuart, 1993: 41). Rather her attire flaunts indeterminacy and taunts male opinion. This liminal relationship to categories of definition is further underlined by her mobile relationship to the city, living in several homes at once, and slipping 'from one company to another like a fat eel / between a Dutchman's fingers' (Middleton and Dekker, 1994: 2.2.206–207). That Moll does not really belong in her own play is accentuated by the fact that instead of following comedic convention and donning female attire to marry at the end of act 5, she vows to stay single and to remain always dressed as a man. Moll's exclusion from the resolution grants her leave to comment on patriarchy's orthodox views of women. Challenging the female role in marriage, she declares that

> I have no humour to marry. I love to lie o' both sides o'th' bed myself; and again, o' th'other side, a wife, you know, ought to be obedient, but I fear me I am too headstrong to obey, therefore I'll ne'er go about it ... I have the head now of myself, and am man enough for a woman; marriage is but a chopping and hanging, where a maiden loses one head, and has a worse i'th' place.
>
> (Middleton and Dekker, 1994: 2.2.36–45)

Moll sees marriage as a resignation of her liberty, losing her 'head', her virginity, or at least, sexual integrity, to a man, who then becomes the 'head' of the household.

The comedy of the Restoration period provides a different perspective on the relationship of the heroine to the twin polarities of chastity and whoredom. It may be worth reminding ourselves that the Restoration saw the first female actors perform in theatres, which must have changed the dynamic of the representation of the sexes considerably in contrast to the exclusively male actors of the Elizabethan and Jacobean stage, while simultaneously foregrounding the tension inherent in featuring authentic female voices that was a consequence of putting women on public display. As such, Restoration heroines must at once prove their virtue while also running dangerously close to compromising it through demonstrations of wit that constitute the basis of their desirability. This fear is best articulated by Pinchwife in William Wycherley's *The Country Wife* (1675), who declares, 'he's a fool that marries, but he's a greater that does not marry a fool. What is wit in a wife good for, but to make a man a cuckold' (Wycherley, 1996: 1.1.388–390). Near the end of William Congreve's *Way of the World* (1700), the heroine Millamant, who has been pursued shrewdly and ardently by Mirabell, makes a series of demands, in the form of conditions that must be satisfied if she is to be his wife. These include:

> liberty to pay and receive visits to and from whom I please; to write and receive letters, without interrogatories or wry faces on your part; to wear what I please; and choose conversation with regard only to my own taste; to have no obligation upon me to converse with wits that I don't like, because they are your acquaintance; or to be intimate with fools, because they may be your relations. Come to dinner when I please; dine in my dressing room when I'm out of humour, without giving a reason. To have my closet inviolate; to be sole empress of my tea table, which you must never presume to approach without first asking leave. And lastly, wherever I am, you shall always knock at the door before you come in. These articles subscribed ... I may by degrees dwindle into a wife.
>
> (Congreve, 1997b: 297)

At first sight, these privileges look like an attempt to retain independence within marriage, remaining the mistress of her own affairs and gate-keeper of her private space. Yet they also suggest an attempt to avoid the necessary familiarities of married life and to retain the formality of courtship. 'What seem like provisions by Millamant for freedom and power', writes Pat Gill, 'are endeavours not to extend her prerogatives but to freeze time, to remain eternally the same' (Gill, 1994: 121). Thus, Millamant finds herself attempting to negotiate an impossible thing.

In the twentieth century, the convention of marriage continued to impose limits on the ability of women to determine their own affairs in comedy, while also becoming a place to consider the impact of the consumer society that had developed in the wake of the Second World War. One of the clearest iterations of this was in the hugely successful sitcom *I Love Lucy*, a show in which the comedian Lucille Ball played a character called Lucy Ricardo alongside her real-life husband Desi Arnaz. Finding herself continually hemmed in by expectations of domesticity, Ball's character Lucy was forced to adopt the tactics of a female trickster in order to get what she wanted. As Lori Landay explains:

> Lucy's ambitions are thwarted in part because of her status as a woman, particularly as a married woman without financial or creative autonomy, so the object of her trickery is often to subvert her husband's authority through the covert tactics of 'feminine wiles' available to her.
> (Landay, 1998: 67)

The lack of autonomy in Lucy's affairs meant that she adopted a persona that was essentially childlike and in constant need of affectionate correction. Frequently, her most errant behaviour concerned her status as a voracious consumer, as her desires and schemes often focused on the culture of acquisition that was also at the heart of the *I Love Lucy* phenomenon. The show was financed by a number of sponsors, including the tobacco giant, Philip Morris, and several of its episodes revolved around Lucy's desire to attain home comestibles such as household appliances, furniture, and clothing. This in turn was reflected in the range of *I Love Lucy* merchandise and tie-ins that earned millions for Ball and Arnaz. Despite this being a family affair, as far as the show was concerned, it was predominantly women who craved possessions. As Lucy's neighbour Fred joked in one episode, 'when it comes to money, there are two kinds of people: the earners and the spenders. Or as they are more popularly known, husbands and wives' (quoted in Landay, 1998: 76).

While Lucy was portrayed as a child who needed to be managed, other twentieth-century sitcoms have treated wives as jailers to their long-suffering husbands. This is a particularly noticeable trend in many of the British television comedies of the latter twentieth century such as *Whatever Happened to the Likely Lads?* (1971), *Bless This House* (1973–1976), *The Good Life* (1975–1978), *George and Mildred* (1976–1979), and *Keeping Up Appearances* (1990–1995), all of which view marriage as the site of struggle between easy-going men and their despotic wives. In these shows, a woman's role is to thwart her husband's attempts to act 'naturally' – a concept usually defined by drinking beer, watching television, gambling on racehorses, or attending football matches – whilst simultaneously pursuing some pretentious project of middle-class social mobility. The sitcom wife in this incarnation is both overly socialised and rigorously abstemious in proportion to her husband's desire to be left alone to engage in sensual pleasures or be 'free to be what they so enjoyably were, precisely because there were no women around to "spoil things" with common sense' (Gray, 1994: 84). Status-obsessed and riven with the inauthenticities of etiquette, the wives in these sitcoms fulfill the role of joyless authority figures, both wife and mother to her infantilised husband. 'Women are forced … to *be* the establishment', writes Frances Gray of this period of comedy. 'This is clear from innumerable sitcoms in which female absence is the condition that permits male individuality by liberating them from the confines of the family "norm"' (Gray, 1994: 84). Such a dynamic is clearly built into the marriage of Bob and Thelma in *Whatever Happened to the Likely Lads?*, which, argues Maggie Andrews, continually makes an issue of 'the boundary between adulthood and lad that Bob is constantly crossing and re-crossing' while living at all times in fear of provoking his wife's ire (Andrews, 1998: 57). Bob's bourgeois lifestyle, nurtured and encouraged by his wife Thelma, is continually troubled by contact with his friend Terry, whose stint in the army, bachelor life, and unapologetically working-class values amount to the freedom Bob has renounced for his steady job and annual holidays in Spain. For Bob, marriage is not only the embodiment of lost liberty, but also a denuded proletarian authenticity, resulting in 'a comedy of entrapment within the rigid and class-based social structure' (Gray, 1994: 83).

Perhaps the predominance of these stereotypes is not surprising given that for much of its history, television production, just like any other workplace, was predominantly the province of men. Very few women were in a position to write, commission, or produce shows, but just as the demographics of the workforce have changed, so the entertainment industry has begun to portray different conceptions of marriage (Hallam, 2005: 39). A generation of sitcoms emerging from the USA in the 1990s, for example, represented marriage as something that was either unattainable, or at best deferred. Shows such as *Seinfeld* (1989–1999), *Friends* (1994–2003), and *Frasier* (1993–2004 reveal little faith in the ability of relationships to last while holding up the the prison-like marriages of the older generation, such as *Seinfeld*'s unspeakable Frank and Estelle Costanza, as a cautionary warning. The figure of the female 'singleton' has also attained prominence with books, shows, and movies such as *Sex and the City* (1998–2004) and *Bridget Jones's Diary* (1996) taking as their cue the romantic failures and dating misadventures of single women. However, as Deborah Chambers has written, whereas Seinfeld and Frasier were free to enjoy the privileges of bachelorhood, 'a striking feature of [female] narratives is the characterisation of women's single status as a problem':

> The pleasure of the female singleton sitcom text involves a nervousness about the predicaments of the single woman in her attempt to carve out an identity that transcends the conventional married, domestic role.
>
> (Chambers, 2005: 162)

While many female protagonists refuse traditional stereotypes and claim for themselves a fully autonomous agency, ultimately they remain locked into a narrative structure whose gravitational pull revolves around an idealistic portrayal of the happy marriage. The female singleton poses a kind of existential threat, and is the source of quirky but ultimately troubling adventures that will remain unresolved until she finds her mate. 'As women glide from their twenties to thirties', writes Helen Fielding's Bridget Jones, 'the balance of power subtly shifts. Even the most outrageous minxes lose their nerve, wrestling with the first twinges of existential angst: fears of dying alone and being found three weeks later half-eaten by an Alsatian' (Fielding, 1996: 20). Are these representations of women so different from those of Aristophanes's *Lysistrata*? As Stacey D'Erasmo has argued, the answer is 'not really':

> The new single girl, tottering on her Manolo Blahniks from misadventure to misadventure, embodies in her very slender form the argument that not only is feminism over, it also failed: look how unhappy the 'liberated' woman is! Men don't want to marry her!
>
> (quoted in Chambers, 2005: 177)

SILENT WOMEN

As so much comedy concerns the voicing of the unsayable, it is interesting to consider how much revolves around the question of when, where, and how women are allowed to speak. Whereas men have enjoyed outspokenness as a marker of their authority and freedom, the notion of uncontested female speech has resulted in a long tradition of anti-feminist stereotypes. From the ferocious termagant popularly associated with Socrates's wife, Xanthippe, the Roman satirist Juvenal's portrayal of the droning female bore, and outspoken women such as Chaucer's Wife of Bath and the garrulous Nurse in *Romeo and Juliet*, voluble women have been portrayed as scolds, gossips, and fools. This has itself been at the heart of many comic plots. The central conceit of Ben Jonson's play *Epicene, or the Silent Woman* (1609), for example, is that the merchant Morose's blissfully quiet wife turns out not to be a woman at all, but a boy. Even into the twentieth century, Jimmy Durante's crack, 'my wife has a slight impediment in her speech. Every now and then she stops to breathe', or Groucho Marx's 'women should be obscene and not heard', stand as expressions of the patriarchal view that talkative women stand in violation of their presumed role as sexually attractive objects who are subservient to men.

Thomas Middleton's play, *A Chaste Maid in Cheapside*, takes this idea one step further to show how women's speech may be indicative of more fundamental failings. Middleton's play features a notable scene in which three puritan 'gossips' attend a christening, get drunk, talk, and then pee themselves. Gail Kern Paster has shown how this scene, and the play's attention to urinary tropes in general, draws together a number of patriarchal assumptions about female vocal, sexual, and physical 'incontinence' that locate cultural views of femininity in medical discourse. Early-modern theories of sexual difference believed that men were essentially 'hotter' than women, accounting for their supposedly active dispositions and external genitals. By contrast, women's relative coolness and supposedly idle lives made them considerably more 'watery'. This medical 'fact' produced a series of associations that connected women with water, especially the sense of a woman as a vessel whose impermeability was an allegory for her chastity and moral worth. In contradistinction to the Roman story of Tuccia, the Vestal virgin who proved her virtue by being able to carry water in a sieve, the puritan gossips are shown to be 'leaky' women, their unrestrained talking revealing a lack of discipline that is reinforced by their weak bladders (presumably caused by repeated childbearing). 'The female characters of *A Chaste Maid in Cheapside*', writes Paster, 'reproduce a virtual symptomatology of woman which insists on the female body's moisture, secretions, and productions as shameful tokens of uncontrol' (Paster, 1993: 52). That much of the play's action takes place during Lent draws out the iniquities of character by emphasising their total lack of abstinence.

With such visceral illustrations of female incontinence in mind, it is no surprise that an equally long tradition of conduct and etiquette literature evolved charged with instructing women on how to control their public speech. As John Gregory's *A Father's Legacy to His Daughters* (1774) warns, wit in women was especially to be discouraged:

> Wit is the most dangerous talent you can possess. It must be guarded with great discretion and good nature, otherwise it will create you many enemies. Wit is perfectly consistent with softness and delicacy; yet they are seldom found united. Wit is so flattering to vanity, that they who possess it become intoxicated, and lose all self-command.
>
> (quoted in Burney, 1998: 341–342)

This is reminiscent of Jane Austen's Emma, sharply reprimanded by Mr Knightley for making a joke at the expense of the meek

Miss Bates (Austen, 1987: 368). Gregory's equation of wit with vanity repeats a misogynist commonplace that women are prone to an unsettling narcissism, and will succumb to it as easily as Eve did to temptation in the Garden of Eden. Indeed, the connection between laughter and sinning has often been made: Joseph Addison mentions that he once heard a sermon on the belief that 'laughter was an effect of original Sin, and that Adam could not laugh before the Fall' (Addison and Steele, 1979, vol. 2: 237), while Baudelaire held that 'Laughter is Satanic; it is therefore profoundly human' (Baudelaire, 1992: 148).

Regina Barreca, one of the preeminent writers on women and comedy, has described how the association between comedy and sin operates within the realm of gendered language. 'In communities throughout the world', she writes,

> women who tell jokes are regarded as sexually promiscuous. The connection between humor and sexual invitation is made up of many links, among them the thought that it takes a certain 'fallen' knowledge to make a joke. Women in some Greek and Italian villages, for example, are considered less than virtuous if they so much as laugh aloud in mixed company. Only old women – or women who are somehow outside the sexual marketplace – are permitted to make lewd remarks.
>
> (Barreca, 1991: 50)

But not only does laughter gesture in the direction of some forbidden, 'unladylike' knowledge, it also has physical effects on the body concomitant to a loss of self-control as it dissolves good posture, contorts the face, causes physical abandon (such as incontinence), and generates loud, extra-linguistic sounds. Laughter shatters the illusion of women as quiet and poised and reveals them as fearfully bodily and biological creatures, and as such, the horror of the discomposed female body threatens to undo the ideals of beauty and romance projected onto them by men, as in Jonathan Swift's poem, 'The Lady's Dressing Room' (1730), where the voyeur Strephon cannot believe 'Such order from confusion sprung / Such gaudy tulips raised from dung' (Swift, 2012: ll.143–144). It is no surprise, then, that women might avoid public displays of wit in order to preserve themselves. 'There is a reason for our apparent lack of humor', wrote the American writer and professor, Kate Sanborn, in 1885,

> which it may seem ungracious to mention. Women do not find it politic to cultivate or express their wit. No man likes to have his story capped by a better and fresher from a lady's lips. What woman does not risk being called sarcastic and hateful if she throws back the merry dart, or indulges in a little sharp-shooting? No, no, it's dangerous – if not fatal.
>
> (Sanborn, 1885: 205–206)

Even as late as 1922, the etiquette writer Muriel White Dennis counselled young ladies to suppress their laughter. A sense of humour is a wonderful thing, she said, but 'it frequently happens that those who possess it do not laugh aloud at all. They laugh with their eyes' (Dennis, 1922: 115).

FAST TALKING DAMES

The biggest challenge to the figure of the demure lady of the Victorian and Edwardian drawing room may have been the introduction of sound technology to the cinema, an innovation that brought a new dimension to the representation of women, especially in comedy. Prior to sound, the women of silent movies had either followed the blueprint established in Mack Sennett's slapstick films, or were portrayed as predatory harpies or submissive victims. The popularity of 'screwball' comedies, however, a term applied to a number of classic Hollywood movies from the 1930s and 40s created by writers and producers such as Preston Sturges and Billy Wilder, provided strong roles for their central female characters while also putting a plethora of words into their mouths. Screwball comedies were battle-of-the-sexes narratives in which duelling opposites would eventually fall in love and marry. Movies such as *It Happened One Night* (1934), *Bringing Up Baby* (1938), and *His Girl Friday* (1940) were notable for the speed of their dialogue, containing speech at speeds of up to 240 words per minute (compared to an average of 100 to 150 for normal speech), suggestive of a clamorous and teeming world that could only be calmed by successfully finding one's true mate (DiBattista, 2001: 18). But instead of seeing the 'fast-talking dame' (as the film historian, Maria DiBattista, has dubbed them), as yet another manifestation of the loquacious shrew, 'screwball' speech mirrored that of the women in Shakespearean comedies (while also featuring *actual* women). For Shakespeare (as we shall see in Chapter 6), witty badinage is used as a kind of foreplay, a means of assessing the sexual compatibility of potential partners, and of establishing the erotic bond between them. The fast talking women of screwball comedy were not only unrepentant wise-crackers, they were also given the chance to enact their own sexual agency. As DiBattista writes, 'When film found its human voice, it simultaneously gave to the American woman, as performer and heroine, a chance to speak her mind, to have a real, not just a presumptive, say in her own destiny' (DiBattista, 2001: 11–12).

The visibility and, of course, audibility, of women in comedy is most clearly evident in stand-up, where, in the absence of sets and props, the comedian is required to produce a performance merely from the elements of voice and persona. The US comedian, Phyllis Diller, one of the first modern female stand-ups who made her debut in the mid 1950s, negotiated the audience's scepticism regarding her gender by appearing on stage as a cackling harridan in flamboyantly ugly make-up and chaotic wig, thereby limiting her novelty through the mobilisation of familiar tropes. Diller blazed an important trail in stand-up comedy that enabled comedians such as Joan Rivers to present a more authentic female voice. Rivers's half-century of material has dealt with consistent themes: the hubris of celebrities, the indignities of ageing, managing beauty, and the economics of marital sex. For Rivers, women occupy an inferior position by default. Their bodies are constantly rebelling in spite of uncomfortable and time-consuming beauty routines, and they are forced to barter for material possessions in return for having sex with lustful but unlovely husbands. An example of this is when Rivers holds up Jacqueline Kennedy Onassis as 'the smartest woman of our generation':

Ah! And not that gorgeous. Did you ever meet her? Funny eyes that worked independently. They were like lizard eyes looking for rich guys ... But she married that little pig Onassis. Would any woman here sleep with Onassis? He was this big [holding hand a foot above the floor] used to walk around, boogies coming out of the nose, bad breath, hair all over, knuckles hitting the ground ... But wasn't she smart? 'Cos when he dropped dead she got 158 million dollars. Do you hear me? 158 million dollars! I'd hit the sheets for that so damned fast. I'd even move!

(Rivers, 2004)

While Rivers's comedy is firmly rooted in the context of gendered presuppositions, her work consistently presents women as independent thinkers required to negotiate and succeed in a system in which they are automatically disadvantaged, including, in the latter part of her career, giving a voice and visibility to older women within a culture that does not value them highly. Indeed, 'what Joan represents', writes Camille Paglia, 'is the power of voice' – the candour, audacity, aggression, and sarcasm that gives expression to the female experience of living in a sexist, materialistic culture (Paglia, 2013: 104).

Where Phyllis Diller and Joan Rivers have blazed a trail, they have done so by expressly speaking from their position as women. One of the key indicators that female comedians have achieved parity with their male peers, however, would be an environment in which they were able to move on from the confinement of specifically gendered material to one in which they could feel authorised to address the same range of topics as men. An example of this would be Sarah Silverman, a comic whose diverse material touches on a variety of themes, many of them offensive or taboo. Key to Silverman's act is her knowing projection of a persona that is at once entitled, privileged, and horribly ignorant, furnishing a context that allows her to initiate discussions that mobilise offensive discourse as a means of focusing satiric attention on the way in which prejudice is filtered in contemporary culture. Illustrative jokes include a narrative detailing how she was raped by a doctor, 'which is so bittersweet for a Jewish girl', and how Nazis are cute when they're little (Silverman, 2005). As Aaron Tillman has argued, Silverman's meta-language comprises a satirical examination of the formation of self within the context of an American popular culture that is characterised by its confusing cacophony of materialism, narcissism, and ethnic anxiety. Silverman, he writes,

> uses stereotypes of her Jewish American identity to indulge a conversation about extreme materialism ... she uses religious mythology to claim a 'chosen' privilege; she uses a connection to historical atrocity to perform self-righteous indignation; she uses her fair complexion to deny any ethnic association. The absurdity of her observations and conclusions shed light on the environments that can produce such a character.
>
> (Tillman, 2009: 66)

For Silverman, then, gender is not the sole referent, but rather one of the many that contribute to the formulation of a polyvocal identity in the modern world.

THE FEMALE BODY AGAIN

While Sarah Silverman is an example of a comedian who has successfully challenged the male dominance of the form, it has still proven difficult for female comedians to escape being judged on their appearance. Seinfeld's rule, outlined in Chapter 3, that conventionally attractive people do not make good comedians, applies, it would seem, only to men, whereas women have been held to a different standard. When the British comedian, Jo Brand, first entered the comedy circuit in the 1980s, for example, she billed herself as the 'Sea Monster', an acknowledgement that this large, short-haired, Doc Marten-wearing person did not conform to a conventional standard of grace or femininity. While Brand soon dropped the nickname, the comic motif of her own monstrosity remained central to her on-stage persona to the extent that it acted as a necessary prologue through which she had to pass before she could move on to material of any other kind. 'It gets it out of the way', she has said, 'because as a woman you know when you come on stage, the first thing you're judged on is your appearance' (Wagg, 1998: 134). Brand's comedy frequently attacks conservative perceptions of appropriate female behaviour and the media that colludes in perpetuating a male ideal of femininity. 'If a Martian came down to earth and just had to watch telly and read magazines to find out what women were like', she says, 'he'd think that they were all blonde and 25 with big tits'.

> Also he would think they were never rude and always looked nice, they always deferred to men, a lot of the time. Obviously there are exceptions ... but I'm saying that's the general essence of it. So I like not to be like that ...
>
> (Brand, in Wagg, 1998: 122)

That it is even necessary for Brand to have to 'explain' her appearance on stage or television speaks to the fact that it is considered exceptional to have a non-conventionally attractive woman (whatever that means) in the spotlight. This bias within the entertainment industry is an issue addressed by the comedian Rachel Dratch, a member of the *Saturday Night Live* cast from 1999 to 2006, who has discussed the extent to which her physical appearance has shaped the roles she has been asked to play. 'These are pretty much the only parts I'm offered since I've been off *SNL*', she writes. 'Lesbians. Secretaries. Sometimes secretaries who are lesbians. Usually much older than I am in real life. I am offered solely the parts I like to refer to as The Unfuckables' (Dratch, 2012: 5).

Dratch's sometime collaborator, Tina Fey, the writer and producer of the sitcom *30 Rock* (2006–2013), and recipient of numerous awards including the Mark Twain Prize for American Humor, has also written about the degree to which assessments of a woman's appearance can inform business decisions within the entertainment industry. 'This is the infuriating thing that dawns on you one day', writes Fey. 'Even if you would never sleep with or even flirt with anyone to get ahead, you are being sexually adjudicated by these LA creeps. Network executives really do say things like "I don't know. I don't want to fuck anybody on this show"' (Fey, 2011: 271). 'Maybe the way it works for a new show', writes Dratch, 'is a bunch of TV execs sit around a room with some wires and EKGs attached to their wangs, and when I was on screen, the needle dipped dangerously into the Code Red Anti-Boner Zone' (Dratch, 2012: 14).

Of course, there is also the risk of being considered *too* attractive, as has happened with the comedian Whitney Cummings, who, in a 2011 interview with *The New York Times Magazine*, was asked if she had succeeded in getting two sitcoms on television by sleeping with influential producers (Goldman, 2011). The vitriol aimed at Cummings for her success resulted in her becoming what the TV critic Emily Nussbaum has called a 'sexy-girl hate magnet' (Nussbaum, 2011). Clearly, while women have succeeded in comedy to a hitherto unprecedented extent, they are still required to negotiate professional obstacles that do not apply to men, many of which are related to the patriarchal assumptions regarding a woman's appearance and her licence to speak. Tina Fey has noted how often women are dismissed as 'crazy' in the entertainment business if they have the confidence to speak over men. 'I have a suspicion', she writes, 'that the definition of "crazy" in show business is a woman who keeps talking even after no one wants to fuck her anymore' (Fey, 2011: 271).

5

RACE AND ETHNICITY

Heard about the Irish lamp post? Pissed on a dog.
Trevor Griffiths, Comedians

'Although the phrase "ethnic humor" may be of recent origin', writes the anthropologist Mahadev Apte, 'humor disparaging other groups is probably as old as contact between cultures' (Apte, 1985: 108). Not only has racial or ethnic humour been around for millennia, it has also been used by some of our greatest writers. *The Merchant of Venice*, for example, is a comedy that not only revolves around the ethnic caricature of the Jewish Shylock, but also involves the humiliation of all but one of Portia's various suitors, as through the Prince of Morocco, the Prince of Aragon, the Duke of Saxony's nephew, and so on, Shakespeare leads us in a pageant of early-modern racial stereotypes.

Like most racial and ethnic joking, the racialised comedy of *The Merchant of Venice* helps to establish group identity by demarcating the line between 'us' and 'them', while also acknowledging the anxiety induced by racial difference, which it seeks to mitigate through laughter. This need is felt especially keenly in Venice, where the free circulation of money and proximity to the sea exposes Christian culture to myriad racial differences against which there are only limited defences. Joking is one of the means by which the Christians tackle the ambiguities of living with heterogeneity and thereby establish the cultural, geographic, and moral boundaries of their own group in contradistinction to those of outsiders (Davies, 1982: 400).

While the scapegoating and ultimate conversion of Shylock might serve to reinforce order in sixteenth-century Venice, to contemplate the same strategy in the modern societies will seem contemptible, yet it happens all the time, as racial and ethnic jokes seek to limit, dehumanise, and belittle the scope of agency accessible to members of a target group. As Dennis Howitt and Kwame Owusu-Bempah write, 'Not only do racist jokes provide ready opportunities to give expression to ideas of "racial" superiority of one group to another, but they continually reinforce the use of race categories in our thinking', thereby supporting the kind of ideation that justifies racist perceptions and perpetuates racist behaviours (Howitt and Owusu-Bempah, 2005: 62).

However, while racist joking is offensive, there are times when joking around racial differences might provide a welcome relief from the pressures of feeling that our speech is being constantly policed regarding its likelihood to offend. As the African American critic Joy Viveros has written, racial comedy permits people 'to extricate themselves from a suffocating sincerity that most discourses anatomizing the operations of race seem unable to map a way out of' (Viveros, 2011: 149). This would certainly seem to inform much of the comedy of Sarah Silverman, for example, who seeks to shed light on the torturous gridlock surrounding the discourse around race by attempting to satirise racist thinking from within as part of an ignorant and self-regarding persona. Silverman's 'meta-racist shit', as she has called it, can be extremely effective, but it also reveals how fraught such joking can be. In 2001, Silverman found herself in trouble with the Media Action Network for Asian Americans for using the word 'Chink' while on *Late Night With Conan O'Brien* (Silverman, 2010: 163). The word was used within the context of a joke about trying to avoid jury duty by writing 'I hate niggers' on the form, and then, not wishing to be thought of as racist, changing it to 'I love niggers'. Producers from NBC naturally objected to the use of the N-word on television, and after considering changing it to 'Jew' (Silverman is herself Jewish), and then 'Spic', Silverman settled on 'Chink' as her final choice.

In the wake of the indignation, Silverman appeared on television to debate with Guy Aoki, president of the Media Action Network for Asian Americans, and by her own admission found herself unable to defend the joke satisfactorily without invoking a convoluted theory of context and irony against an interlocutor determined to take the insult at face value (Silverman, 2010: 145–154). Silverman has acknowledged that she finds it 'horrifying' when offence is taken at her routines, or 'when a person in the audience is laughing at the wrong thing – the ugly part of the joke – the part intended for irony or insidiousness' (Silverman, 2010: 94). Indeed, a section of her movie *Sarah Silverman: Jesus is Magic* reflects at length on the experience, and on the moment at which a joke ceases to exert an ironic force on the language of racism and is thereby reduced to being just plain racist. Discussing 'midgets', Silverman says:

> I'll tell you why we make fun of midgets. We're not afraid of them. That's what it always boils down to, across the board, you know. I mean, I had a joke with the word 'nigger' in it that I thought was so edgy, you know, so hip, and I was doing it all over town at comedy clubs, and I was at this one club doing my show, and I look in the front row and the whole front table is black people ... But the point is, I didn't do the joke, you know. And you gotta ask yourself, is that an edgy joke or is that a racist joke, you know, and I didn't do it because I was afraid of them, you know. I didn't. And I ended up changing that joke to 'chinks'.
>
> (Silverman, 2005)

The point here is that Silverman's persona is straightforwardly insensitive and not 'edgy' at all. Indeed, describing something as 'edgy' is a lazy way to excuse and glorify racism. Neither does she abandon her joke because of any sudden epiphany or ethical worry that it will cause offence, but only because she feels intimidated by the fact that the audience contains a large group of black people. This is itself a racist reaction. It is a highly conceptual joke that cleverly foregrounds the problems of context and intention, with the payoff that even when making a conscious effort not to be offensive, there is always another group somewhere that can be safely victimised.

From Shakespeare's Venice, to our globalised and integrated world, racial and ethnic joking is complex. This chapter will consider some of that complexity, from the first challenges to racist humour in British comedy, to the ways in which African American comedians have tackled the invidious racism of minstrelsy, before looking in greater detail at the nature and value of comedy that, like Silverman's, aims to satirise negative attitudes to race from within the discourse of racism.

COMEDIANS AND COMEDIANS

In 1971, Granada Television first broadcast *The Comedians*, a simple and popular show that ran for more than fifty episodes and countless repeats. The show is notable because its stars, many of whom had never appeared on television before, came to epitomise a style of stand-up comedy that was vilified during an unprecedented re-evaluation of comedy that took place in Britain throughout the 1970s and 1980s, which became known as 'alternative comedy'. *The Comedians* featured a high turnover of routines, edited into a fast-paced package that involved each comedian telling only one or two jokes. Many of its performers were seasoned professionals drawn from the privately owned night-clubs and working-men's clubs run by the Club and Institute Union (CIU). The comedians of the CIU circuit had an enormous repertoire of formulaic jokes, many of which had been purchased in bulk rather than individually written to order, and over which comedians themselves had no proprietary rights. Much of this material had an aggressive sub-text, expressing, in particular, racist, sexist, and homophobic sentiments, such as Bernard Manning's: 'There was a plane crashed in Madrid about six month ago, two hundred Japanese on that plane, broke my fucking heart. Six empty seats there was' (Manning, 1993). To a certain degree, the material reflected the context of the performance, inasmuch as the style suited a rapid non-narrative delivery, that comprised a practical means of coping with large and sometimes difficult crowds for whom the comedian was simply one more act on a variety bill.

From this comedy came a new sensitivity to the practice of joking and its implicit politics. 'Alternative' comedians rejected the easy racism and fast delivery of the gag comedian, replacing it with revised form and content. One of the first, and probably the most articulate, formulations of these issues is found in Trevor Griffiths's play *Comedians* (1976). Griffiths, a playwright whose work tackles questions of class consciousness and left-wing politics, examines the power of comedy to support prejudices and instruct people in bigotry. The setting of the play is an evening class where a group of men who aspire to become comedians learn their craft and perform at a debut show in front of a judge. Griffiths alludes to the construction of jokes in his choice of characters, a proportion of whom belong to the groups stereotyped by the CIU-style comedians: two Irish labourers, a Jewish club-owner called Sammy Samuels, Gethin Price, a British Rail van driver, and a walk-on part by a lost Indian named Patel. Their tutor is Eddie Waters, the retired 'Lancashire Lad', a principled Shavian socialist who believes strongly in the transformative power of comedy. After warming his students up with a tongue-twister, 'the traitor distrusts truth', Waters matter-of-factly launches into an abusive tirade against the Irish: 'flapping hands, stinking of soil and Guinness. The niggers of Europe', before moving on to Jews: 'Say Jew, say gold' (Griffiths, 1979: 18–19). The class laugh in embarrassment and shuffle their feet but Waters continues:

Negroes. Cripples. Defectives. The mad. Women ... Workers. Dirty. Unschooled. Shifty. Grabbing all they can get. Putting coal in the bath. Chips with everything. Chips and beer. Trade Unions dedicated to maximizing wages and minimizing work. Strikes for the idle. Their greed. And their bottomless stupidity. Like children, unfit to look after themselves. Breeding like rabbits, sex-mad. And their mean vicious womenfolk, driving them on. Animals, to be fed slops and fastened up at night. (*Long pause.*) The traitor destroys the truth.

(Griffiths, 1979: 19)

This shopping list of prejudices is intended to shock, a deliberate ploy used by Waters to warn his students away from the easy targets and lazy jibes of the club comedian. In essence it invokes the spirit of club comedy without the punch-lines, exposing it for the lightly sugared tirade of bigotry that it is. For Waters, the repetition of prejudice in comedy reinforces ignorance in the minds of the audience by consolidating it through intolerant laughter. Turning that laughter back on bigotry, however, is the most positive thing that comedy can do; it should tell the truth, reveal things for what they are, delivering people from the constraints of prejudicial ideologies, to become 'a radical mode of social communication' (Garner, 1999: 133). In this credo, entertainment is not diversionary but secondary to the redemptive and revelatory function of the 'true' joke. 'We work *through* laughter, not *for* it', Waters explains:

> It's not the jokes. It's not the jokes. It's what lies behind 'em. It's the attitude. A real comedian – that's a daring man. He *dares* to see what his listeners shy away from, fear to express. And what he sees is a sort of truth, about people, about their situation, about what hurts or terrifies them, about what's hard, above all, about what they *want*. A joke releases the tension, says the unsayable, any joke pretty well. But a true joke, a comedian's joke, has to do more than release tension, it has to *liberate* the will and the desire, it has to *change the situation*.
>
> (Griffiths, 1979: 20)

Comedy retrieves a suppressed truth, but not in purely Freudian terms as a means of keeping larger repressions in their place, but as a revolutionary force that liberates people from their fear, interrogates repression and converts it into positive political energy to effect change. 'Most comics *feed* prejudice and fear and blinkered vision', he says, 'but the best ones, the best ones ... illuminate them, make them clearer to see, easier to deal with' (Griffiths, 1979: 23).

Waters's philosophy contrasts strongly with that of Bert Challoner, a talent spotter for the clubs and the man who represents the path to the professional comedy circuit. His advice advocates conformity to a particular style: 'Don't try to be deep.

Keep it simple. I'm not looking for philosophers, I'm looking for comics' (Griffiths, 1979: 33). The abdication of responsibility implied by Challoner's vulgar consumerist view that 'we're not missionaries, we're suppliers of laughter', or the logic of the argument that jokes are 'only' jokes, is precisely the consumerist fallacy that Griffiths condemns in this play (Griffiths, 1979: 33). Waters sees a direct relationship between an exclusionary form of popular racist humour and the logic of fascism. Recalling a visit to a German concentration camp while in the army entertainment corps ENSA, he sees a horrific correspondence between jokes and the brutality of anti-Semitism. 'In this hell-place', he says, he saw

> a special block, 'Der Straf-bloc', 'Punishment Block'. It took a minute to register, I almost laughed, it seemed so ludicrous. Then I saw it. It was a world like any other. It was the logic of our world ... extended ... And I discovered ... there were no jokes left. Every joke was a little pellet, a final solution.
>
> (Griffiths, 1979: 64)

In this obscene absurdity, that those incarcerated in a concentration camp should have a special place reserved for further punishment, as if such a thing were possible, he sees that the cruelty of the joke and the perversity of the camp are cut from the same cloth, different in degree, but not in kind (Garner, 1999: 141). And yet, in the midst of that horror Eddie Waters experiences the subversive stirrings of 'life' that this regime has failed to suppress:

> I got an erection in that ... place! An erection! Gethin. Something ... (*He touches his stomach.*) ... loved it too. (*Silence.* PRICE *turns away from* WATERS, *takes two precise paces towards the back of the room, turns back again.*) We've got to get deeper than hate. Hate's no help.
>
> (p.67)

Having established the insidiousness of club-comedy, the play presents its audience with the problem of what a responsible, inclusive, and liberating comedy might look like. Act 2 of *Comedians* tries to demonstrate this through the performances of the students. Here, what would normally be a middle-class theatre audience is transformed into the fictional audience of a working-men's club, a device that dares the 'real' theatre audience to laugh at the acts it is about to see. The first student, Mick Connor, appears to follow Waters's advice. His routine is drawn from his own background, with material on the Catholic confession, the prurience of priests, and the inconsistencies of sex and faith. Connor seems at least to be confronting his fears, even including a rather standard joke about the IRA, which in his mouth comes across as an anxious gag about stereotypes and the violence pla-guing his country. Sammy Samuels, who has already signalled his ambition to play the 'tops', begins his routine in similar fashion with comments on his Jewish upbringing. When he sees that Challoner is unimpressed he loses his nerve and launches into a routine that targets the Irish, West Indians, feminists, homo-sexuals, and sexual assault. The Ulsterman George McBrain fol-lows the same path, although his routine is marked by a deep misogyny that appears in the refrain 'my wife, God she's a slut'. Samuels and McBrain, predictably, are the only students signed up by Challoner to play the clubs. The centre-piece of act 2, and indeed the entire play, is Gethin Price's routine, a bizarre and aggressive act that owes more to Grock and Antonin Artaud's theatre of cruelty than to Frank Randle, the northern comic he purports to idolise. Price is clearly the most artistically gifted and ideologically motivated of the comedians, yet he produces work that is dramatically out of place in the club setting and stretches the definition of comedy to a virtual breaking-point. He enters white-face in denim jacket and boots, *'half clown, half this year's version of bovver boy'* (Griffiths, 1979: 48). The act begins with a piece of mime, setting fire to a violin bow and crushing the violin underfoot. His first words sum up the violence and frustration that characterise him and his routine: 'Wish I had a train. I feel like smashing a train up. On me own. I feel really strong. I wish I had a train' (Griffiths, 1979: 49). After a complicated series of Kung-Fu exercises, a couple of mannequins are brought on, male and female, dressed for a night out at the theatre. We imagine them waiting for a taxi as Price enthusiastically greets them, before it becomes apparent that the couple have nothing to say to him: 'Been to the match, have we? Were you at t'top end wi'lads?

Good, wannit? D'you see Macari? Eh? Eh? (*Silence.*) P'raps I'm not
here. Don't you like me? You hardly know me. Let's go and have
a pint, get to know each other' (Griffiths, 1979: 49). Through a
coarse and disjointed dialogue, Price conveys the inarticulacy and
anger he perceives in the working-class male, marginalised by
middle-class society and reduced to expressing himself through
violence and sexual aggression; becoming, in fact, a stereotype of
the prejudices that define his class. His routine does include two
standard jokes, one sexual, one racial, but both are delivered
maniacally and to the dummies rather than the audience. In this
context, they seem like desperate and pathological symptoms of
rage rather than pleasurable social exchanges. Towards the end of
the routine, Price offers the lady a flower:

> Here. (*He takes a flower out of his pocket, offers it to them.*) For the lady.
> No, no, I have a pin. (*Pause. He pins the flower – a marigold – with the
> greatest delicacy between the girl's breasts. Steps back to look at his
> work.*) No need for thanks. My pleasure entirely. Believe me. (*Silence.
> Nothing. Then a dark red stain, gradually widening, begins to form
> behind the flower.*) Aargh, aagh, aagh, aagh ... (*The spot shrinks slowly
> on the dummies, centring finally on the red stain. PRICE's 'aaghs'
> become short barks of laughter. Innocence.*) I wonder what happened.
> P'raps it pierced a vein.
>
> (Griffiths, 1979: 51)

This disturbing image, followed by a simple rendition of the socialist anthem the 'Red Flag', is an explicit expression of the mili-
tant sub-text of Price's act, where revolutionary politics are
confusingly mixed with aggression and sexual threat. While
Challoner can only describe it as 'repulsive', Eddie Waters calls it
'*brilliant*', but the final discussion between Price and Waters
reveals considerable tensions between the two men. Price is full of
revolutionary anger and the desire for violent change, whereas
Waters retains faith in political truth, an evolutionary politics,
and social redemption through education. Yet something has
been satisfied by Price's iconoclastic performance. Politics, commitment, and the articulation of experience have all been drawn
upon to produce a genuine and truthful event. No conventional

description would call it comedy, however. There is not one single laugh in the fictional club, and one doubts there are many in the theatre either. Is it possible, then, to have entertaining comedy on these terms? The play does not reach a conclusion on this issue, but in its final moments, it does seem to suggest that comedy is capable of distinguishing between dogma and genuine humanity that Price's routine so oddly pleads for. Throughout the evening, the character of Mr Patel, an Indian immigrant to Britain, has been wandering in and out of the classroom, seemingly lost. Just as Price and Waters are leaving, he appears again, hoping to retrieve a package he has left behind. He works in an abattoir, and the package contains beef, food he is forbidden as a Hindu. As if to reconcile this irregularity, Patel tells Waters a joke:

> A man has many children, wife, in the South. His crop fail, he have nothing, the skin shrivel on his children's ribs, his wife's milk dries. They lie outside the house starving. All around them, the sacred cows, ten, twenty, more, eating grass. One day he take sharp knife, mm? He creep up on a big white cow, just as he lift knife the cow see him and the cow say, Hey, aren't you knowing you not permitted to kill me? And the man say, What do you know, a talking horse.
>
> (Griffiths, 1979: 67)

Comedy may not be enough to spark a revolution, but it can help to reveal the distinction between ideology and shared humanity.

In the same year that *Comedians* appeared, amateur club promoter Peter Rosengard opened the doors of the Comedy Store in a strip club in London's Soho district. This venue, based on the famed stage of the same name in Los Angeles, proved to be of immeasurable importance for the development of a British comedy scene that worked through many of the experiments proposed by Griffiths's play. In Oliver Double's terms, it brought 'a handful of comic revolutionaries together, [and] gave them a stage on which they could learn to be funny' (Double, 1997: 165–166). Alternative comedy was overtly political from the start, informed by a punk ethos that dominated British counter-culture in the mid to late 1970s. It defined itself against the expectations of mainstream performance and encouraged people to write their own material, set up their own gigs, and perform without the need for agents or the approval of the concert secretaries of the CIU. Looking back across alternative comedy, *Guardian* comedy critic William Cook described its ideals in terms reminiscent of the ethics of Eddie Waters, as a form that celebrated 'similarity, rather than condemning difference. The best of it hits hard and it hurts, but it's philanthropic not misanthropic, a bridge and not a wall. Above all Alternative Comedy reveals, via laughter, something of the real life of the comedian' (Cook, 1994: 16).

One of the first casualties of the new comedy was the joke-form itself, which had become guilty by association. Alternative comedy deliberately parodied and derided the idea of 'jokes' as reactionary and dull, as in Peter Richardson and Nigel Planer's anti-joke 'what's yellow and goes into the toilet? Piss' (Sayle, 1988). While many routines now seem hopelessly naive, the movement had the momentum and the talent to bring an entire generation of performers to the attention of the public. Most important was the work it did in raising awareness of the prejudice that lurked near the surface of much mainstream comedy, and in making audiences increasingly intolerant of it. In time, however, alternative comedy became mainstream, and as such was able to retain only the merest hint of its original political consciousness as it became big business and was incorporated into the commercial world of radio and television. The market dominance of a diluted alternative comedy also had the peculiar effect of allowing comics like Bernard Manning to portray himself as the victim of censorship and a martyr to political correctness. Before his death in 2007, Manning's publicity machine presented him as the man they could not gag, a modern comic outlaw who dared to challenge the thought police. This was presented as an authentically working-class position, dispossessed by the anxious 'nanny' state: 'Can't stop us laughing can they?', he says in an aside. 'It's the only thing we've got left' (Manning, 1993).

AFRICAN AMERICAN COMEDY

The extent to which racism was normalised in the British entertainment culture of the late 1970s is perhaps best illustrated by the popularity of *The Black and White Minstrel Show*, a variety programme that featured white performers wearing blackface make-up with white lips and circles around their eyes while performing songs in the style of Al Jolson. The show, which demonstrated a deep nostalgia for slavery and the plantations of the American south, ran for twenty years on Britain's national broadcaster, the BBC, even winning a prestigious Golden Rose of Montreux television award despite protests from the Campaign Against Racial Discrimination. It was finally cancelled in 1978 (Howells, 2006: 163).

While minstrelsy has been popular in Europe, its legacy is felt most strongly in the USA, where it is regarded as an unwelcome force of considerable significance that has shaped the representations of African Americans on stage and in the media. Minstrelsy has its roots in the American theatre of the 1820s, when the theatrical impresarios Edwin Forrest and Charles James Matthews brought their representations of southern plantation negroes to audiences in the north-eastern regions of the United States. It was the performances of Thomas D. Rice (1808–1860), however, and his song 'Jump Jim Crow' that truly established the popularity of minstrel shows. Within the space of twenty years, minstrelsy had established itself as one of the most popular forms of stage entertainment in America, with groups like the Virginia Minstrels, the African Melodists, the Congo Minstrels, and the Ethiopian Mountain Singers combining songs, dances, and antic routines into a formulaic three-act pattern. Like Rice himself, the performers in these minstrel shows were almost always white, and their representations of African American speech, dress, and mannerisms were highly caricatured and largely concocted, as was much of the culture they purported to represent. For example, while some of the music in minstrel shows was inspired by black culture, many of the songs that sparked the original craze for blackface have been shown to be European in origin (Watkins, 1999: 86).

Minstrel performances offered an idyllic portrait of plantation life that was slow, sociable, and full of jokes and music, a view that suited the pro-slavery states while also pandering to the anxieties of the northern audiences who objected to slavery on principle, yet worried about the demographic impact of mass migration to the north (Watkins, 1999: 93). Blackface provided a kind of cover for white performers to offer a more frenetic, ludicrous, and sexually suggestive performance than they might otherwise have been able to do when performing as themselves. Characters were frantic and malaprop, and dominated by three recurrent types – the slow-witted rural 'coon', the northern 'dandy', and the 'artful trickster', thereby further reducing the identities of individuals who had already been lumped together and stripped of their history by force (Taylor and Austen, 2012: 7). As Yuval Taylor and Jake Austen write, minstrelsy was 'a fundamentally racist undertaking, neutering a race's identity by limiting it to demeaning stereotypes' (Taylor and Austen, 2012: 3). Yet its popularity permeated much of American culture, from beloved songs such as 'I'm Going Home to Dixie', to the joke 'why did the chicken cross the road?', both of which had their inception in minstrel shows (Watkins, 1999: 92). Of minstrelsy, comedian Deon Cole offers this useful summary: 'That shit was horrible' (quoted in Lyttleton, 2006: 17).

Minstrel shows lost ground after the Civil War and the introduction of female entertainers and vaudeville, but endured in provincial troupes, and, most notably, in the unprecedented celebrity of performers such as Al Jolson, who continued to perform in blackface well into the twentieth century. But while it eventually fell from favour, the racial stereotypes it drew from, and the view of black culture it offered, served to pigeonhole black comedians for considerably longer, providing, in the words of Mel Watkins, 'the barometer of whites' assessment of black Americans in general' (Watkins, 1999: 100). As Watkins continues,

> Minstrelsy had established a fraudulent image of Negro behavior (in both the serious and comic vein) to which all African-Americans were forced to respond. And early black entertainers – perhaps even more than blacks in less visible occupations – bore the burden of working within the strict confines of that distorted standard. Indeed, they were expected not only to corroborate white minstrels' illusionary specter but, because they were authentic examples of the type, to heighten it.
>
> (Watkins, 1999: 103)

Given the reality of slavery and inequality and the legacy of minstrel performances, African American comic performers in the twentieth and twenty-first centuries have had to face the burden of not only dealing with negative perceptions, but with negotiating stereotyped expectations of what their humour will be like. An example of this is the career of Lincoln Perry (1902–1985), who used the stage name Stepin Fechit. Perry enjoyed a lucrative stage and film career in the 1920s and 30s, and was the first black actor to become a millionaire, yet his persona repeatedly validated the racist view of African Americans as lazy and dim-witted. As with many African American performers throughout the nineteenth and twentieth centuries Perry found that only by conforming to stereotypes could his portrayal be perceived as believable.

Such is the power of stereotypes that even those performances that depart from them are drawn back into addressing them, albeit obliquely. Take, for example, the *Cosby Show*, a sitcom starring Bill Cosby and Phylicia Rashād that ran for six years between 1984 and 1992, winning numerous awards and reaching audiences of up to 30 million. The show, which centred on the family life of middle-class African Americans, was groundbreaking inasmuch as its lead characters, Heathcliff and Clair Huxtable, were a doctor and lawyer respectively. As Wendy Alexia Rountree has noted, however, for critics of the *Cosby Show*, the sitcom created

> the false impression that most African Americans had achieved 'the dream' and had entered mainstream middle-class America. The show supposedly promoted the idea that African-Americans had 'over-come' racism and discrimination (as exhibited by the ethnically diverse friendships and working relationships on the show) while in actuality, the African-American community, especially the urban underclass, continued to suffer from poverty, high unemployment, increased teen pregnancy, gang violence, and the rise of AIDS and crack cocaine addiction.
>
> (Rountree, 2011: 101–102)

The oppressive legacy of minstrelsy, then, has complicated what it means to be 'authentic' within African American comedy. For the literary critic Glenda Carpio, however, the idea of an authentic black comedy is inseparable from an analysis of the forms of comic appropriation that have developed from within a tradition of paralysing stereotypes. Surveying African American humour from the nineteenth century to the present, Carpio argues that African American comedians have been most successful not when searching for something 'real', but when appropriating and occupying stereotypes for their own ends. 'African Amercian humor', she writes, 'has frequently made art out of carrying out white fantasies about race to their most absurd levels' (Carpio, 2008: 111). To describe the appropriation of racist fantasies by the oppressed, Carpio uses the term 'conjuration', a concept she adapts from voodoo, 'a practice that was transported by enslaved Africans across the Middle Passage, which is a form of ancestor worship in which the souls of the dead ... are evoked and made manifest through ritual' (Carpio, 2008: 15). Attaching this concept to humour, Carpio argues that African American comedians have adapted 'conjure' as a means not only of invoking and inhabiting the stereotypes that pre-determine the representation of African Americans in popular culture, but also as a way of 'caricaturing the caricatures that minstrelsy produced, [and] of animating them in a hyperbolic mode' (Carpio, 2008: 16).

An example of 'conjuration' appears in the stand-up comedy of Richard Pryor (1940–2005), a comedian who has been praised for both 'the literal emancipation of African American humor', and 'breaking with the blacks' long standing tradition of subterfuge and concealment of inner-city customs' (quoted in Simpson, 2008: 120). In the 1960s, Pryor had been a comedian in the style of Bill Cosby – well-dressed, paternalistic, and unthreatening – until one night in 1970 while onstage in Las Vegas he stopped his act, said 'what am I doing here?' and walked out of both the theatre and mainstream comedy for several years (Knoedelseder, 2009: 20). In the interim, Pryor spent some time in the California town of Berkeley absorbing the political and counter-cultural influences of the hippies, anti-war protestors, the Black Power movement, and the Black Panthers, the result of which was the development of a much freer, autobiographical, and politically aware style that directly addressed the issues that seemed most immediate to him. As such, Pryor's routine moved away from the fast-paced delivery of punchlines to reflect the kind of black street life he had witnessed around the impoverished Peoria, Illinois, neighbourhood where he had grown up in a brothel.

Though fuelled by rage at the injustices of the system, Pyror's stand-up routine was neither angry nor polemical. Rather, he allowed his point of view to speak through a cast of characters he created that lived with the realities of crime, poverty, and police brutality, characters who included preachers, pool hustlers, drug addicts, petty criminals, drunks, prostitutes, uptight white men, and one of Pryor's most famous creations, an ancient wino philosopher named 'Mudbone'. All these performances might be considered 'conjuration', in Carpio's terms, since through the personification of different voices, racist stereotypes are dislocated from the structures of oppression that engendered them and thrown back on themselves as a means of examining both their own formation and what it is about them that has made them so appealing. Pryor's specific facility with language was an aid to this sense of unmaking, as he liberally assailed his audiences with words that were vulgar, caustic, and profane. It is Pryor who is credited with bringing the N-word into mainstream usage of performers and hip hop artists, revealing to white audiences that this hate-filled epithet was not only the preserve of racists, but was also a 'mainstay in non-elite black linguistic expression', that many in his community used regularly among themselves (McCluskey, 2008: 13). His uncensored use of the term divided audiences, some of whom applauded what they saw as his brave embracing of the truth, while others condemned it on the grounds that the word remained the word no matter what, and that 'white people had found a black man who could call other black people "niggers" for them' (Williams and Williams, 2008: 158).

The work of comedian Dave Chapelle similarly explores racial politics, yet whereas Pryor's comedy focused on giving voice to individuals who lived marginalised lives, Chapelle takes an interest in the larger structures of the conversation governing race in America. *Chapelle's Show* (2003–2006) was an enormously popular sketch comedy in which he repeatedly poked fun at the discourse that produces cultural identifications and concomitant prejudice. Sketches such as the one featuring 'Clayton Bigsby', a blind white supremacist who has never been told that he is black, a game show that parodies African American popular culture called 'I Know Black People', or a sketch in which members of different races engage in a 'racial draft', claiming individuals for their own race while rejecting those they don't want, all sought to highlight the absurd reductionism of the discussion of race that results in the construction of artificial boundaries.

Chapelle's comedy, in sympathy with Carpio's theory of conjuration, works through the subtly graded application of excess, climbing into well-worn stereotypes and inhabiting them until they burst at the seams. The effect is to interrogate the language of racism until it seems not so much racist, but rather a bizarre obsession with phantasmal concepts of race. Joy Viveros has called this 'racial drag', a form of performance she describes as

> the display of an embodied racial identity, the purpose of which is not to ridicule 'the other race', but rather to parody race itself. The mismatch between performer and performance in Chapelle's comedy, and the fluid movement between racial sensibilities, constructs race as a wished for rather than actual certainty.
>
> (Viveros, 2011: 144)

As such, the multiplying incongruities that Chapelle develops are intended to reveal the concept of 'race' as a mobile fiction (just as drag will be seen to operate in relation to gender in Chapter 6), inviting scrutiny of what Viveros calls 'the peculiar conventions of identity-in-race' (Viveros, 2011: 151).

Chapelle's deep satire has caused some controversy, not least for its portrayal of African Americans. A study of the representation of African Americans on *Chapelle's Show*, for example, found that they 'are commonly portrayed as violent, drug using, and irresponsible' (Perks, 2008: 93), resulting in what Carpio has described as laughter that is 'in and out of symmetry depending on race, gender and ideological leanings, with the volatile history of race relations, specifically as produced by slavery, as common ground' (Carpio, 2008: 111). As with Sarah Silverman's inability to satisfactorily explain the intention behind her 'Chink' remark, Chapelle voiced concern that sections of his audience were focusing on literal interpretations of his work that failed to allow for the social and political commentary that inspired it. Specific problems arose around a series of sketches in which Chapelle played a 'racial pixie', an imp appearing on the shoulders of its host and which goaded him or her into behaving according to racial stereotypes. Having performed the white and Hispanic versions of this sketch, Chapelle prepared the African American version, donning black-face, a bellhop uniform, and a hat and cane, all chosen, in his words, because 'it was going to be the visual personification of the N-word' (Chapelle, 2006). However, while filming the segment, Chapelle observed a white crew member laughing in a way that he considered to be against the spirit of the show, and subsequently abandoned the series and a television contract worth many millions. While the true psychological intent of the crew member's laugh is impossible to determine, Chapelle's reaction points to the dangers ever-present in racial joking, as for all its fluidity and postmodernity, comedy remains subject to the gravitational pull of the sociological facts of race relations and racial sensitivity in the modern age. Just as Pryor stopped using the N-word following a trip to Africa in 1979 where he had seen it deployed with the full force of the racism that had inspired it, Chapelle also came to revise some elements of his thinking, telling chat-show host Oprah Winfrey in 2006 that 'I was doing sketches that were funny, but socially irresponsible' (Chapelle, 2006). At the root of Chapelle's discomfort lay the legacy of minstrelsy. 'I feel like they got me in touch with my inner coon', he said. 'They stirred me up. When we was doing that sketch and that guy laughed, I felt like, man, I felt like they got me. They got me' (Chapelle, 2006).

'IS IT 'CAUSE I IS BLACK?': THE MANY ETHNICITIES OF SACHA BARON COHEN

The comic portrayal of ethnicity has proven highly lucrative for Sacha Baron Cohen, whose movie roles include Frenchmen (*Talladega Nights*, *Hugo*, *Les Misérables*), Austrians (*Bruno*), Kazakhs (*Borat*), middle eastern despots (*The Dictator*), and even an African ring-tailed lemur (*Madagascar*). Cohen initially rose to prominence in the role of Ali G, a 'wannabe' gangster rapper from the London suburb of Staines who made his debut on a satirical British news programme called *The 11 O'Clock Show* (1998–2000), and in subsequent spin-offs including the eponymous *Da Ali G Show* (UK 2000; US 2003–2006). At first, Ali G focused on conducting interviews with people unaware that they were in the presence of an actor, including politicians, clergymen, celebrities, sportsmen, and prominent shapers of public policy, all of whom had been chosen because the producers felt they would serve their 'unrepentant satirical purpose' and 'because we found something pompous or objectionable about them, or we thought we could make a point about society through them' (quoted in Sacks, 2009: 61). The hope was that by placing the interviewee in uncomfortable territory and priming them with questions laced with Ali G's misogynist patois and ignorant logic, the interviewee would either reveal his or her own unvarnished opinions, or at least show the contradictions inherent in attempting to maintain a palatable public persona. The effect was magnified by the ambiguity regarding Ali G's racial identity as Cohen, a Cambridge graduate of Jewish origin who was clearly white, dressed and spoke in a style associated with black youth culture. The result was a series of entertaining moments of referential dissonance, such as the time he asked an on-duty policeman 'Why are you treating me like this? Is it 'cause I is black?', which immediately placed the policeman on the defensive, anxious not to appear to transgress cultural taboos about race, or confirm the racism that many have seen as institutionally endemic within the British police force, while also appearing visibly perplexed at the self-identification of the white man standing before him.

In time, Ali G became too well known to successfully exploit his interviews and so the focus of the comedy shifted to the character himself. Ali G was an appealing cartoon, popular because he was so absurd, and like many good comedy characters, so lacking in self-awareness that much of the ridicule fell back on himself. This did not prevent criticism being levelled at Cohen by some black comedians for his negative portrayal of black culture and representations of youth fashions and slang, which, it was noted, would not have received anywhere near as much attention had the performer actually been black himself. Yet accusations of straightforward stereotyping or even outright minstrelsy have been confounded by the ambiguity surrounding Ali G's race. Several theories regarding Ali G's racial identity have been floated, the most prominent of which is the notion that he is a satire of white, middle-class youth from a nondescript British suburb desirous of emulating American gangster rappers, an idea that was reinforced in the 2002 feature film, *Ali G Indahouse* (2002), which provided more of the character's backstory and showed his Caucasian family and all-white circle of friends (Howells, 2006: 167). A second theory, however, brings an additional layer of ethnicity to bear on the character in its supposition that Ali G is an Asian man pretending to be black, an idea supported in part by the fact that the name 'Ali' was deliberately chosen in order to provide an additional oriental ethnic dimension. As the producer Harry Thompson remarked of the initial conception of the character: 'If he had a whiff of Islam about him, we thought people would be afraid to challenge him … If Muslims took offence, there was a plan to explain that the name was short for "Alistair Graham"' (quoted in Howells, 2006: 166). Ali G co-writer Dan Mazar has also said that Ali G represents 'kind of a weird mishmash of cultures' (quoted in Sacks, 2009: 63). As such, Ali G might employ the same kind of characterisation that Viveros has called 'racial drag', or that Richard Howells, in specific relation to Ali G, has labelled 'poly-semic', that is 'both multi-layered and open to differing and even opposing interpretations' (Howells, 2006: 169). In constructing this notion, Howells invokes the postcolonial theorist Homi Bhabha's notion of 'hybridity', inasmuch as, like Bhabha's work, Cohen's comedy draws on the tension between national and global cultures, and the continual friction, exchange, and integration that takes place between them.

For Howells, Ali G's polysemy ultimately outsmarts and resists retreat into any of the prescribed responses that are entrenched in inflexible definitions of race, encouraging instead a discussion of the issues that he labels 'intelligent, sophisticated and constructive' (Howells, 2006: 171). Simon Weaver, however, has offered an alternative reading of this polysemy to which he attaches the label 'liquid racism', which he defines as the combined confusion caused by multiple readings of Ali G's ethnicity and the 'erasure they inflict on one another' (Weaver, 2011: 150). By leaving the question of Ali G's ethnicity indeterminate, Weaver argues that it partakes of a humour in which authorial intention and the grounds for critique remain deliberately inchoate. This idea is familiar from satire, inasmuch as it opens up the space for parallel and incompatible readings that are at once legitimate and irreconcilable. The question raised here is: is this defensible when some of these readings may be overtly racist and/or class-based?

Cohen's pursuit of the themes of multiculturalism was furthered in his movie *Borat: Cultural Learnings of America for Make Benefit Glorious Nation of Kazakhstan* (2006), in which he played the Kazakh journalist, Borat Sagdiyev, who journeys to America to make a documentary. As with Ali G, Borat's principal tactic is to adopt a position of *faux naiveté*, playing a character whose ignorance of cultural standards allows him to elicit revealing reactions from his interlocutors that thereby illuminate their prejudices. The ostensible target appears to be American ignorance of the outside world, as well as normal people's willingness to believe that a foreigner can be so idiotic, as when Cohen cheerfully leads a rodeo crowd in a rendition of the 'star spangled banner' that glorifies the war on terror, encourages a group of men in a bar to sing 'throw the Jew down the well', or persuades a group of fraternity brothers into volunteering racist and sexist remarks.

Borat's constant theme, therefore, is the continual and repeated production of alterity. Not only does Borat elicit responses as an exotic 'Other', he generates them by means of constant references to an imagined homeland that is backward, destitute, misogynist, incestuous, and relentlessly anti-Semitic. That this should take place in a post-9/11 America, already hyper-vigilant in relation to the issue of Muslim radicalisation and troubling cultural differences, manages to produce an atmosphere that is virtually Wagnerian in the pitch of its near-universal intolerance. However, while emphasising the degree to which Americans collude to construct the 'Other', the movie also demonstrates (perhaps unwillingly) the extent to which North America believes in its own ability to assimilate. At an etiquette dinner in Alabama, for example, Borat reveals that he doesn't know how to operate a toilet or what to do with his shit, at which point one of the elderly guests tries to reassure her friends by saying 'He'll be Americanized in no time.'

All are amenable and welcoming, until, that is, the appearance of an African American woman playing a prostitute disturbs them. External difference is embraced. Domestic difference in not.

But what does *Borat* ultimately tell us about race? Perhaps initiating a debate about race is not the ambition of a movie that simply aspires to becoming a vehicle for testing one of the last taboos, becoming what the film critic Owen Gleiberman calls 'an equal opportunity offender' (Lehrer, 2006). On the other hand, in its attempts to fashion a form of absolute Otherness, it may be highlighting the practical complexities of multiculturalism and the limits of inclusion.

6

COMEDY, QUEERED

If you remove all the homosexuals and homosexual influences from what is generally regarded as American culture, you are pretty much left with *Let's Make a Deal*.

Fran Lebowitz

It would be fair to say that comedy treats matters of sex more often and more openly than any other form. Its festive structure and Dionysial associations afford sexual themes greater liberty, while also providing a fictional arena within which cultural taboos may be openly discussed in a way that inoculates them from the fear of social contamination. As Freud writes, 'the spheres of sexuality and obscenity offer the amplest occasions for obtaining comic pleasure ... for they can show human beings in their dependence on bodily needs ... or they can reveal the physical demands lying behind the claim of mental love' (Freud, 2001: 222). As such, comedy affords a means of circumnavigating the limitations placed upon expressions of sexual desire by cultural expectations, affording pleasure as it permits some elided aspect of the animal subject to peep through the civilised exterior and reveal itself. Similarly, detailed studies of sexual humour, such as G. Legman's epic two-volume *Rationale of the Dirty Joke* (1975), or Christopher Wilson's scientific study of joke-function, stress that sexual jokes 'offer the furtive joy of ignoring taboos' (Wilson, 1979: 131).

However, while sexual content in comedy may be pleasurable because it outruns censorship, it is also important to acknowledge the extent to which many sexual themes play a part in establishing or consolidating conservative norms of sexual behaviour by focusing their attention on deviance. Wilson, for example, discusses the use and effect of incest jokes, and concludes that 'Humour that dismisses incest and other socially disapproved relationships as "laughable" may be seen to illustrate and reinforce sexual convention' (Wilson, 1979: 177). Indeed, the impulse to police sexuality through humour is not dissimilar to the way in which issues of cultural identity are policed through racist and ethnic joking. But unlike jokes about race, the history of comedy is filled with examples of sexualised joking that indicate a greater permissiveness and tolerance of ambiguity and excess that may in turn lead to a bursting of the boundaries that seek to contain 'self' and 'other'. Consider the popularity of a number of openly gay comedians – Julian Clary, Ellen Degeneres, Margaret Cho, Graham Norton – all of whom have, at one time or another, directly addressed issues of sexual identity in their acts while still managing to prosper in a society that has yet to fully escape its homophobia. All of these comedians highlight a strange but fascinating dichotomy that allows us both to police and resist heteronormativity. Joking around sexualities, therefore, reveals first and foremost the anxieties we have around these subjects. As Andy Medhurst has written, 'humour thrives at flashpoints of cultural nervousness, offering soothing balm for such ideological ailments whilst rubbing salt into the very same wounds' (Medhurst, 2007: 112).

Consider, for example, the way comedy seeks to test and bend the limits of heteronormative relationships and gender roles, such as the bed-sharing and co-dependency of Laurel and Hardy. While we might attempt to rationalise their shared bed by appealing to the austere necessities of Great Depression economics, the intimacy and gender-play evident in Laurel and Hardy movies is suggestive of something altogether more complex. In *Their First Mistake* (1932), for example, Oliver Hardy's wife, Arabella, is angered by the amount of time her husband spends with Stan Laurel, and so threatens to leave him if he doesn't stop seeing him. 'Well what's the matter with her anyway?', asks Stan:

OLLIE: Oh, I don't know. She says that I think more of you than I do of her.
STAN: Well you do, don't ya?
OLLIE: But we won't go into that.

Hoping to help his friend, Stan convinces Ollie that his wife needs a baby to occupy her time, and in the very next scene the two men have adopted one, only to find that Arabella has not only filed for divorce, but she is also sueing Stan for 'the alienation of Mr. Hardy's affections'. As the difficulty of the situation becomes apparent, Stan hands Ollie the adoption papers and turns to leave:

STAN: Well, I'll be seeing you.
OLLIE: [Holding the baby] Where are you going?
STAN: I'm just going down ...
OLLIE: Well you can't leave me here with this child.
STAN: Why?
OLLIE: Why? Why, you're just as much responsible for it as I am.
STAN: What have I got to do with it?
OLLIE: What have you got to do with it? What have you got to do with it? [Shifts posture, and adopts a tragic tone] Well, you were the one that wanted me to have a baby, and now that you've got me into this trouble, you want to walk out and leave me flat.
STAN: But I don't know anything about babies.
OLLIE: Well you should have thought about that before we got it.
STAN: I don't want to get mixed up in this thing. I have my future. My career to think of.
OLLIE: Your career. What about me? What will my friends say? Why, I'll be ostracized.
STAN: Well, I'm going to lose my hook, line and sinker.
OLLIE: So, you're going to desert me, just when I need you most. [Turns as if to weep over the infant. Stan makes quick exit. Ollie chases him and bars the door.]

(Marshall, 1932)

Notice how effortlessly the two men slip into the role of lovers and play out a melodramatic narrative in which a 'girl in trouble' pleads with the heartless bounder who is about to abandon her. Yet the roles are not stable, for in the scene that follows, it is Stan who occupies the maternal position by taking the screaming baby and attempting to suckle it at his breast to the accompaniment of Ollie's irritated, sleep-deprived commentary. That the entire scene takes place in a bedroom dominated by one large, messy bed, with both men dressed in long, asexual night shirts, creates the impression of a shared domestic space that is at once intimate and informal, and conducive to occupying interchangeable gender roles.

To read Laurel and Hardy as pioneers of 'queer' comedy might seem a particularly modern affectation, but it is actually one that the term itself permits. While 'queer' is often taken as a shorthand for the gay and lesbian communities, its evolution as a critical concept was intended to be much more disruptive, a way of not only challenging the cultural default of heteronormativity, but also the extent to which terms such as 'lesbian' and 'gay' delimit the conversation by the inference that they represent fixed identities, albeit ones that are socially marginalised. Take, for example, the bed sharing of the British comedy duo Morecambe and Wise, who regularly demonstrated the same inseparable closeness, and who, during a running series of sketches in the 1980s, could often been seen conversing in bed. Unlike their predecessors, Morecambe and Wise had to field the question of whether or not their bed sharing was 'gay', not only a sign of the changing times, but also an indicator of the fact that the interviewer demands to *know* – to categorise things as one way or the other. To describe the bed sharing of Morecambe and Wise as 'queer', however, allows it to exist within a continuum that makes space for ambiguity and a broader range of sexual identities, practices, and performances, while also resisting the application of homogenised labels.

This chapter will consider some of the many ways in which comedy might be 'queer', where 'queer' refers to a fluid spectrum of identities, in order to show not only the way in which comedy creates a space for identities and practices alternative to the heteronormative mainstream, but also the extent to which it seeks to explore human sexuality beyond the impulse to categorise.

'NOBODY'S PERFECT': AS YOU LIKE IT AND SOME LIKE IT HOT

One of the most familiar motifs in the comic exploration of sexuality is the cross-dressing 'progress narrative'. According to Majorie Garber, these narratives require one or more characters to disguise their gender 'in order to get a job, escape repression, or gain artistic or political "freedom"' (Garber, 1992: 70). There are many examples of this in comedy, including the plays *Charley's Aunt* (1892) and *La Cage Aux Folles* (1978), the movies *Mrs. Doubtfire* (1993), *Tootsie, Victor/Victoria* (both 1982), and *Some Like It Hot* (1959), as well as the cross-dressing comedies of Shakespeare: *As You Like It, Twelfth Night*, and *The Merchant of Venice*. In *As You Like It,* cross-dressing allows the play to develop a heightened eroticism and an inclusive attitude towards sexuality, and even the title suggests a relaxed attitude to sex with the 'it' presumably an inclusive reference to all forms of desire. 'It' is a good word to use in relation to the sexual tensions of this play, which are at once indeterminate, elliptical, and absolutely central to the plot. *As You Like It* is the story of Rosalind and her companion Celia, forced by the usurper Duke Frederick to follow her father into exile into the Forest of Arden. Aware of the danger facing lone women travellers as 'Beauty provoketh thieves sooner than gold' (Shakespeare, 1989: 1.3.109), Rosalind decides to disguise herself as a man:

> Because that I am more than common tall,
> That I did suit me all points like a man,
> A gallant curtal-axe upon my thigh,
> A boar-spear in my hand, and in my heart,
> Lie there what hidden woman's fear there will.
> (Shakespeare, 1989: 1.3.114–118)

Taking up the props of masculinity and burying 'female' traits such as apprehension, Rosalind completes her transformation and adopts the suggestive name 'Ganymede'. The Shakespearean stage used boy actors in female roles exclusively, since women were forbidden from performing in public and did not take parts in plays in the public theatres until the Restoration. That all of

Shakespeare's female roles, even the most demanding tragic ones, were played by boys without reducing drama to farce, tells us that this convention makes Rosalind's gender transformation utterly convincing within the context of the play. But *As You Like It* is complicated by an additional layer of transformation. Rosalind's male disguise reminds us of the initial gender of the performer, highlighting the fact that his femaleness is a theatrical convention, with the effect of blurring gender distinctions while accentuating them thematically. This gender ambiguity appears to be at the centre of sexual fascination in the play, as instead of protecting her from unwanted attention, Rosalind's disguise makes the apparent youthful maleness of her character its central sexual object. The cross-dressing of *As You Like It* therefore encourages the boy actor to assume a heightened erotic presence by placing him in the playful and indeterminate world of comic identities. The key to this is the choice of the name 'Ganymede' with which Rosalind completes her disguise. In Greek mythology, Ganymede was a beautiful Trojan youth, so admired by Zeus he was taken as his lover. There is a deliberateness in Rosalind naming herself after 'Jove's own page' (Shakespeare, 1989: 1.3.124), as the choice introduces the idea of men as compelling sexual objects, usurping women in the traditional role of the desired one (an idea further underlined in the un-cross-dressed Celia's choice of pseudonym, 'Aliena', which pushes women further to the margins). The naming of Ganymede ensures that Rosalind will be at the heart of a series of crossed and interacting desiring relationships that centre specifically on the strange and alluring identity she has created for herself. Chief amongst these are two fascinations that might now be labelled as straightforwardly homosexual. First, the desire of Phoebe for Rosalind, displacing the shepherd Silvius, her appropriate and conventional mate; and second (and more importantly) the apparent fascination that Orlando has for Ganymede irrespective of his proclaimed love for Rosalind. Ganymede's interactions with those he fascinates are characterised by verbal sparring and witty rejoinders that Stephen Greenblatt explains as a stage version of sexual excitement. 'Dallying with words is the principal Shake-spearian representation of erotic heat', he writes. 'Hence his plots go out of their way to create not only obstacles in the lovers' path but occasions for friction between them' (Greenblatt, 1988: 90). The contest of Beatrice and Benedict in *Much Ado About Nothing* (1598) exemplifies this kind of verbal foreplay, and in the green-world of Arden the friction caused between man and boy appears to similarly condone alternative desiring partnerships outside the compulsory heterosexuality of the town. Given these circumstances, Stephen Orgel sees a radical sexual agenda at work in the play, calling Ganymede a 'dangerous alternative' to heterosexual norms and reproductive sexuality, since 'the idea of the boy displacing the woman appears in its most potentially threatening form, the catamite for whom Jove abandons his marriage bed' (Orgel, 1997: 57). Evidence for this can be found in the 'wooing scenes' of acts 3 and 4, in which Ganymede proposes to take Rosalind's place and invites Orlando to practise his seduction of Rosalind upon him: 'woo me, woo me, for now I am in a / holiday humour, and like enough to consent', she/he says (Shakespeare, 1989: 4.1.64–65). Orlando, wholeheartedly embracing the fantasy Ganymede has proposed, pleads with him:

ORL. Then love me, Rosalind.
ROS. Yes, faith, will I, Fridays and Saturdays and all.
ORL. And wilt thou have me?
ROS. Ay, and twenty such.
ORL. What sayst thou?
ROS. Are you not good?
ORL. I hope so.
ROS. Why then, can one desire too much of a good
      thing? (*to Celia*) Come, sister, you shall be the priest
      and marry us – Give me your hand Orlando. – What
      do you say sister?
ORL. (*to Celia*) Pray thee, marry us.

(Shakespeare, 1989: 4.1.107–118)

So happy is Orlando to accept Ganymede as Rosalind that he pleads with Celia to marry them and allow the boy to displace the woman in the marriage rite. That this was not acceptable in its day is demonstrated by the attitudes of early-modern opponents of the stage who condemned the erotic lure of theatre practice and considered the presence of the boy player to encourage homo-sexuality. John Rainolds, in *Th'overthrow of Stage-Playes* (1599), warned that the kisses of boy actors could so turn a man that he could be moved to infidelity: 'If they do but touch men only with their mouth, they put them to wonderful pain and make them mad, so beautiful boys by kissing does sting and pour secretly in a kind of poison' (quoted in Orgel, 1997: 28). Philip Stubbes's *Anatomy of Abuses* (1583) held that public performances, with their 'wanton gestures' and 'bawdy speeches', were a place for men to meet for the purpose of finding a sexual partner. After the play was done, 'everyone brings another homeward of their very friendly, and in their secret conclaves, covertly, they play the sodomites, or worse' (quoted in Orgel, 1997: 29). For Orgel, these anti-theatrical attacks offer three very important insights into the connection between sexuality and the early-modern stage. Although he emphasises the ideological extremity of opponents to theatre, he concludes that their arguments indicate, first, that 'the basic form of response to theatre is erotic; second, that erotically, theatre is uncontrollably exciting; and third, that the basic, essential form of erotic excitement in men is homosexual – that, indeed, women are only a cover for men' (Orgel, 1989: 17).

Billy Wilder's 1959 film, voted the best comedy of all time by the American Film Institute, brings the cross-dressing theme into the twentieth century. *Some Like It Hot* shares many similarities with *As You Like It*, not least the indeterminate and enticing 'it' of the title. The film restates the idea that men can adequately replace women, both as women and as sexual partners for men, and that femininity does not reside in biological gender or onto-logical identity, but in 'feminine' supplements to the body such as high heels, make-up, and brassières. The film tells the story of two depression-era musicians, Joe and Jerry, played by Tony Curtis and Jack Lemmon, who witness a mob killing and are forced to go into hiding. They dress as women, rename them-selves Josephine and Daphne, and join 'Sweet Sue's Society Syn-copators', an all-girl jazz band travelling on an engagement to Florida. Joe falls in love with the band's singer, Sugar, played by Marilyn Monroe, which necessitates the adoption of a further identity as 'Shell Jr.' in a ploy conceived in answer to Sugar's fantasy of marrying a rich man in glasses. Joe and Jerry, motivated by the threat of death, come to understand quickly that the authenticity of 'femaleness' resides in the quality of its performance. For example, when joining the band for the first time, they struggle with their disguises until they find an example to emulate in Marilyn Monroe:

JER. (*rubbing his ankle*) How can they walk on these things? How do they keep their balance?

JOE. Must be the way their weight is distributed. Come on.

As they proceed along the platform, a gust of wind sends their skirts billowing. Jerry stops again and pulls his skirt down.

JER. And it's so drafty. They must be catching colds all the time.

JOE. (*urging him on*) Quit stalling. We'll miss the train.

JER. I feel so naked. Like everybody's looking at me.

JOE. With those legs? Are you crazy?

JER. (*stopping in his tracks*) It's no use. We'll never get away with it, Joe.

JOE. The name is Josephine. And it was your idea in the first place.

... a member of the girls' band comes hurrying past them, carrying a valise and ukulele case. Her name is SUGAR ...

JER. Who are we kidding? Look at that – look how she moves – it's like jello on springs – they must have some sort of a built-in motor. I tell you it's a whole different sex.

(Wilder, 1959)

Simply wearing women's clothes seems to accentuate the men's sense of essential sexual differences, as well as foreground their view of women as sex objects. But once given insight into the tricks of the performance, 'jello on springs', accompanied by a close-up of Monroe's backside in motion, they copy it and are successfully assimilated into the band with absolutely no suspicions raised. The transvestism of the two leading men is, of course, foisted upon them, and we are continually reminded that their cross-dressing is a means to an end, not evidence of a latent fetish. Thus, Joe and Jerry's clothing is continually depicted as costume, complicated and unusual and always in need of adjustment, and therefore risible in its unnaturalness when contrasted with their authentic maleness. However, while a masculine authenticity is alluded to beneath the clothes, women themselves remain conspicuously facile. Monroe's Sugar is portrayed as a stereotype of a certain kind of woman. Singing 'I Wanna Be Loved By You', Monroe wears a tight dress that accentuates her bosom by appearing to be translucent. Amid the 'conscious heightening as well as dissolving of sexual stereotypes' that Bruce Babington and Peter William Evans see at work in this film, Monroe represents 'overflowing female excess' (Babington and Evans, 1989: 227–228), a figure of hyperbolic femininity that Molly Haskell describes as being 'as much in "drag"' as Joe and Jerry (quoted in Sikov, 1994: 142). During the song, which tells of passive availability and urges the lover to approach, so much is made of Monroe's bosom that, rather than guaranteeing hers as an authentic female body amongst the fakes, she appears as an unrealistic construct and a product of 'glamour', Hollywood, and girlie magazines. As Ed Sikov writes, 'If the film has a central deficiency, it is Wilder's inability to move Monroe's character beyond a sort of paralysed observation of her own image' (Sikov, 1994: 143). Even 'real' women seem to lack substance beyond the trappings of their gender.

Structurally, *Some Like It Hot* and *As You Like It* are close. Both feature the removal from the hostile and dangerous city: in Shakespeare's play it is the court under the tyrannical Duke Frederick, in Wilder's film a violent Chicago of gangsters, prohibition, unemployment, and hunger. Both the Forest of Arden and Miami Beach represent liberation from danger and the opportunity to explore alternative identities and romantic relationships. Both are then, in essence, green-world comedies, as both locations are associated with holiday and with respite from economic demands: as Rosalind says to Orlando, 'There's / no clock in the forest' (Shakespeare, 1989: 3.2.294–295). As green-world comedies, the queered desires of Miami and Arden are only to be considered within the context of temporarily loosened social conventions. They are queer under licence, as it were – a licence that is due to expire at the conclusion of the drama. As Majorie Garber argues, the fluctuation of playful identities is only a temporary measure, necessary to reconfirm heterosexual norms which remain fundamentally unaltered in spite of the cross-dressing interlude:

> The ideological patterns of this implication are clear: cross-dressing can be 'fun' or 'functional' so long as it occupies a liminal space and a temporary time period; after this carnivalization, however ... the cross-dresser is expected to resume life as he or she was, having, presumably, recognized the touch of 'femininity' or 'masculinity' in her or his otherwise 'male' or 'female' self.
>
> (Garber, 1992: 70)

Yet when we consider the endings of both narratives, we can see that they refuse to relinquish their hold on the alternative world absolutely, and that more than a 'touch' of the freer desiring relationships and gender identifications they have discovered lingers after the narrative ends. In the epilogue to *As You Like It*, the actor playing Rosalind comes out of character, addressing the audience with conventional pleas for leniency before saying to the men:

> If I were a woman I would kiss as many of you as had
> beards that pleased me, complexions that liked me, and
> breaths that I defied not. And I am sure as many as
> have good beards, or good faces, or sweet breaths will
> for my kind offer, when I make curtsy, bid me farewell.
>
> (Shakespeare, 1989: Epilogue, 16–20)

At the end of *Some Like It Hot*, Jerry, still disguised as Daphne, offers a series of reasons why he cannot marry Osgood Fielding III, the millionaire who has fervently pursued him, finally admitting 'Damn it, I'm a man.' Osgood's reply is the outrageously pragmatic comic line: 'Nobody's perfect.' Such a wonderfully reasonable response intimates that heterosexuality is not necessary for a perfectly good marriage. Rosalind, revealed finally as a boy actor offering to kiss the men, suggests that the sexuality of *As You Like It* is not contained entirely by the parameters of the fiction, but is 'diffuse, non-localized, and inclusive, extending to the audience an invitation to "come play"' (Traub, 1992: 142). Both endings suggest the possibility of the homoeroticism of the cross-dressed period continuing in the world after the issues that forced characters into disguise have been resolved. However, for the philosopher and gender theorist, Judith Butler, *Some Like It Hot* is a text filled with 'homophobia and homosexual panic':

> Indeed, one might argue that such films are functional in providing a ritualistic release for a heterosexual economy that must constantly police its own boundaries against the invasion of queerness and that this displaced production and resolution of homosexual panic actually fortifies the heterosexual regime in its self-perpetuating task.
>
> (Butler, 2005: 385)

But rather than serving the need to express homosexuality in order to contain it, Ed Sikov emphatically says of Jerry's situation, 'Osgood's final declaration is openly gay, there's no question about that. The line is meaningless otherwise' (Sikov, 1994: 146). Sikov, chiding critics who claim that '"Nobody's perfect" is not specifically about gay sexuality', points out their wish to 'steal what precious little mainstream cultural participation gay men and lesbians can claim for ourselves' (Sikov, 1994: 148).

Once again, the violation of social expectations poses the familiar problem of the carnivalesque: does transgression perform social anxiety in order to better contain it by letting off steam?; or does the trangressive performance possess a velocity of its own, sufficient to escape the gravitational pull of the power that hopes to contain it?

PERFORMING GENDER: DRAG AND TRANSVESTISM

The reluctantly cross-dressed protagonist of a progress narrative is a substantially different prospect from the female impersonator, or drag act, that has been a successful comic franchise since the mid-1800s. Here, drag is not donned as a means to achieve an end in the conventionally dressed world, but is the focus of the entire performance. The female impersonator derived in part from nineteenth-century circus acts that sought to enhance their box-office appeal by tricking their audiences into believing that daring acrobats and gymnasts were in fact dainty girls, as well as the tradition of men playing women's roles in minstrel shows. 'Putting on the drag' originally meant applying the brakes of a carriage, but once the word had entered homosexual slang through the 'molly-houses' or transvestite clubs of nineteenth-century London, it stood to mean the 'drag of a gown with a train' (Senelick, 2000: 302). Early drag acts conventionally concluded with the removal of the wig to reveal the close-cropped hair that acted as a guarantor of the performer's masculinity, a gesture that places great signifying emphasis on the coiffure, as in the finale of Ben Jonson's *Epicene*. In music hall, the term 'female impersonator' was commonly used to describe drag acts, a label that makes the performer's gender self-evident. For comic drag, whose best-known mainstream exponents are performers like Danny La Rue (1927–2009), Barry Humphries (1934–) as Dame Edna Everage, Paul O'Grady (1955–) as Lily Savage, and RuPaul (1960–), the intention is to parody types of femininity through a knowing masculine prism that acknowledges the nature of the travesty at all times. The question of what is being parodied is largely dependent on the performer, but generally drag allows the male comedian to exploit his attire to offer a deliberately provoking perspective on women. This amounts to a form of ventriloquism that explores women's attitudes to sex, women's conversation, and monologues intended to puncture idealised versions of femininity. In the tradition of pantomime dames, comic drag paints a picture of feminine grotesque, self-delusion, hyperbolised glamour, and sexual outrageousness that would be inappropriate in 'real' women. Danny La Rue, who was enormously successful in Britain in the 1970s, with his own nightclub, television series, and appearances at Royal Variety shows, assumed the persona of a raucous show-girl with lower-middle-class manners and a crass addiction to extraordinary outfits, high wigs, and sparkling accessories. La Rue's prime-time popularity and insistence on being a 'family act' meant that much of the sexual tension in drag was removed from his show. La Rue was keen to point out that what he parodied was artifice in women, especially a certain kind of woman he found vulgar. Laurence Senelick sees this as a contradiction, writing that La Rue creates an 'anodyne illusion' that mocks overly sexualised women, while simultaneously placing them at the centre of a family show (Senelick, 2000: 247). Lily Savage, his postmodern alternative, to whom glamour is distinctly foreign, is a 6' 2" peroxide blond from Birkenhead with a distinctly lower-class Liverpool accent, who was first unveiled in the gay cabaret of London's Vauxhall Tavern in 1985. Wearily smoking onstage, she is resigned to failure and petty brutality while acknowledging the free-market nature of sexuality in the underground economy. In both the financial success that putting on drag has brought Paul O'Grady, as well as Lily's own fictional history of low-grade prostitution, the characterisation of woman as a commodity is always thematically present.

How might we then think about the representation of gender through drag acts and female impersonators? Certainly the politics of drag have produced a number of theoretical perspectives that shed important light on its representation of gender, although it must also be acknowledged that these are almost exclusively concerned with the meaning of drag in gay and lesbian culture, where comedy is not always the primary focus of the act. Esther Newton, writing in 1979, argued that drag existed within a two-tier 'sartorial system' in which the gender identification of the performer was best understood in relation to the first two layers of their clothing. The top layer of clothing, visible on the outside, was a 'costume' and presumed to be part of an act or symbolic presentation on behalf of the wearer. The second layer of clothing, essentially underwear, hidden from view, reveals the true nature of the wearer's gender identification that 'anchors' their gender during the performance. Thus, Newton argued, drag 'poses an opposition between one sex-role sartorial system and the "self", whose identity has to be indicated in some way', because, 'when impersonators are performing, the oppositional play is between "appearance" which is female, and "reality", or "essence", which is male' (Newton, 1979: 101). Drag is, then, a parodic interplay between 'appearance' and 'essence', in which the performer retains their 'real' gender as a consequence of a guarantee of the authentic concealed body. Applying Newton's position to comic drag, we might conclude that its garish make-up, euphemistic sexual content, and parody of female behaviour amounts to mimicry and mockery of women by men who always confidently remain men, and whose appeal, in the case of Danny La Rue, depends on an awareness of that essential gender identity. Yet Newton's sartorial distinction remains questionable: how can one set of clothes be said to stand for gender authenticity while another represents quotation and parody? Mark Simpson, for example, has argued that drag can go beyond a 'mere carnival' parody of women and challenge the heart of suppositions about gender in society. Drag, he writes, can

> take the form of an *incitement to rebellion*. It can express a desire to revolt against the most tyrannical of laws, the 'natural' link between sex and gender. This drag-as-rebellion, strange to relate, can even represent a rejection of the denigration of women's bodies on the basis of lack.
>
> (quoted in Bruzzi, 1997: 165)

If this is the case, and we can think of drag as an interrogation of gender, one that breaks the link between biologically determined categories and socially constructed conceptions of sex, then female impersonation may constitute a rebuttal of prescriptive roles and an exploration of alternative genders and sexualities. As we have seen, there is a large body of work that drives the argument that comic inversion can be a political force, so why not extend it to include drag? If we accept this argument, then we would also be able to apply it, as some Shakespearean critics have done already, to the 'progress narrative'. In this revised version, Shakespearean cross-dressing is not simply explained by 'holiday humours', but is a politicised investigation of gender hierarchies that questions the inferiority of women at a time when the assumption of male superiority was overwhelming. Drag is the vehicle for this investigation because it focuses attention on the sartorial symbols of gender and recontextualises them in a way that might lead us to question their cultural power.

The most influential theorist of drag has been the American philosopher Judith Butler, whose work touches on cross-dressing by way of a larger argument concerning the fluidity of gender identities. Butler's position can be broadly characterised as 'anti-essentialist' in that she argues for a concept of gender that is not built on a foundation of biology or other predetermined categories, but one that is continually 'iterated' through the 'performances' of gender required by culture. Thus we make our gender by performing the expressions that are culturally characteristic of it. 'In this sense, gender is always a doing, though not a doing by a subject who might be said to preexist the deed', she writes, 'there is no gender identity behind the expressions of gender; that identity is performatively constituted by the very "expressions" that are said to be its results' (Butler, 1993: 25). It should be noted that 'gender identity' is not identical to biological sex, but rather the gender with which the subject identifies him or herself, irrespective of their anatomically prescribed or medically understood sexuality. Traditional feminist responses to drag and cross-dressing, claims Butler, have viewed it as either degrading to women, or as 'an uncritical appropriation of sex-role stereotyping from within the practice of heterosexuality' (Butler, 1993: 137). Rather than arguing that the politics of drag rely on a discrepancy between the biological sex of the performer and the gender that is being performed, Butler insists that there are three categories at work: 'anatomical gender, gender identity, and the gender that is being performed' (Butler, 1993: 137). As she writes,

> If the anatomy of the performer is already distinct from the gender of the performer, and both of those are distinct from gender of the performance, then the performance suggests a dissonance not only between sex and performance, but sex and gender and gender and performance.
>
> (Butler, 1993: 137)

This concept of drag is one in which the various categories that are confused, mixed, and invoked in cross-dressing demonstrate the non-essential nature of gender:

> In imitating gender, drag implicitly reveals the imitative structure of gender itself – as well as its contingency. Indeed, part of the pleasure, the giddiness of the performance is in the recognition of a radical contingency in the relation between sex and gender in the face of cultural configurations of causal unities that are regularly assumed to be natural and necessary.
>
> (Butler, 1993: 137–138)

Drag may therefore be said to reveal that gendered social discourse has no stable foundation or essence, even if the performer is unaware of the broader implications of their act. However, as Butler concludes, there is no simple test or rubric that determines whether acts of gender parody are subversive, or simply images that have been 'domesticated and recirculated as instruments of cultural hegemony' (Butler, 1993: 139).

While the politicisation of drag has not entered the world of comedy to the extent that it exists in the lesbian, gay, bisexual, transsexual, and queer communities, the themes of 'imitative' gender and gender contingency have been dealt with by performers like the US comedian Sandra Bernhard and the British comedian Eddie Izzard. Clearly neither of these performers wears drag in the conventional sense, but both use their performances to draw attention to the politics of sartorial choice and the gendered assumptions of dress. Both resist the application of prefabricated definitions to label their sexuality, preferring to use their comedy as a means of questioning the validity of labels. Bernhard, who refuses to allow either her performances or sexual orientation to be easily categorised, has been described by Camille Paglia as a 'drag queen ... [who] can defend herself without running to grievance committees. Whether lesbian or bisexual, she accepts and respects male lust without trying to censor it' (Paglia, 1994: 140). Izzard describes himself as a 'male lesbian transvestite', a convolution consistent with his routines that are not so much surreal, the usual epithet he attracts, as a cut and paste of the found objects of the media age. Izzard often wears women's clothes on stage, but his representation of sexuality follows much the same principle of casual choice and assemblage as his act, creating a gender role that does not conform to pre-existing definitions. Izzard says, 'People say, "Why don't you change your clothes at half-time?" Why? Do footballers do this? I'm not a drag act. This is not about the clothes, it's about the comedy and I just do whatever I want' (Izzard et al., 1998: 61).

CAMP: WILDE AND COWARD

So far, this chapter has highlighted themes that are very much focused on the external signifiers of gender – dress and deportment – but what of subtler, attitudinal resistances to heteronormative culture? One lens through which to view this kind of critique is through 'camp', the knowing elevation of style and debonair dismissal of gravity closely associated with queer sexualities. The influential American cultural critic Susan Sontag defined camp as 'a certain mode of aestheticism. It is one way of seeing the world as an aesthetic phenomenon ... not in terms of beauty but in terms of the degree of artifice, of stylization' (Sontag, 1982: 106). Published in 1964, Sontag's 'Notes on Camp' anticipates some postmodernist discussion of the triumph of style, but actually finds its origins in much older forms such as Mannerism and eighteenth-century persiflage – a witty, verbal excess. 'Camp sees everything in quotation marks', she writes, in order to 'understand Being-as-Playing-a-Role' (Sontag, 1982: 109).

Oscar Wilde's play, *The Importance of Being Earnest* (1859), fits perfectly into Sontag's criteria. As Wilde's Gwendolen says, 'in matters of grave importance, style, not sincerity, is the vital thing' (Wilde, 1980: 2.28–29). Wilde's own aesthetic beliefs held that art was essentially useless, but that its lack of utility was also the source of its beauty. That art existed only for its own sake made it independent of the world and, therefore, liberated from it, a liberation that left art free to concentrate on its beauty, and 'the sheer absoluteness of its detachment' (Leggatt, 1998: 34). This position is embodied in Algernon Moncrieff, the louche aristocrat at the centre of Wilde's play, whose total self-absorption places him in a perpetually ironised relationship to the society in which he lives, where contradictions form the foundation of knowledge: 'More than half of modern culture depends on what one shouldn't read', he says (Wilde, 1980: 1.131–132). His friend Jack Worthing enjoys land, income, and social position as a Justice of the Peace, but lacks a family history and therefore 'an assured basis for a recognized position in good society' (Wilde, 1980: 1.579–580). At the heart of the play is the plasticity of identity: Jack is 'Ernest in town and Jack in the country', while Algy is an enthusiastic 'Bunburyist', an author of fictional persons, who becomes Ernest in the country (Wilde, 1980: 1.168). In the twice-invented Ernest we have the perfect emblem of identity in Wilde's world: all surface and no content. Embodied twice in

Jack and Algy, Ernest is simultaneously two people and no-one at all. *The Importance of Being Earnest* is therefore a play about the multiplication of a central identity that is notable because of its absence. At face value, its anxieties concern the expectations of high society and the importance of conforming to them. From the manner in which the criteria are filled, however, changing names, adopting false identities, the fortunate coincidence of Miss Prism's retrospectively legitimising narrative, reminiscent of the recognition scene in Roman New Comedy, it is clear that authenticity is secondary to the maintenance of appearances and contorting oneself to fit the bill. While the title insists on the importance of honesty, the play itself resounds with inconsistent and contradictory pronouncements for the purposes of stylish effect. Gwendolen and Cecily's resolve to be scandalised, for example, is a performance of being scandalised, rather than the thing itself:

GWENDOLEN. Let us preserve a dignified silence.
CECILY. Certainly. It's the only thing to do now.

> *Enter* JACK *followed by* ALGERNON. *They whistle some dreadful popular air from a British Opera.*

GWENDOLEN. This dignified silence seems to produce an unpleasant effect.
CECILY. A most distasteful one.
GWENDOLEN. But we will not be the first to speak.
CECILY. Certainly not.
GWENDOLEN. Mr. Worthing, I have something very particular to ask you ...

(Wilde, 1980: 3.12–17)

In the twentieth century, Wilde's sophisticated style continued in the work of Noël Coward. Coward, 'a man who spent a life-time merchandising his deluxe persona', was a prolific writer of prose, drama, and over three hundred published songs, all of which were characterised by effortless wit and laissez-faire charm (Lahr, 1984: 22). Using comedy marked by irony, frivolity, detachment, and artifice, Coward has often been viewed as the successor to Wilde, a comparison he himself disliked, dismissing Wilde as 'a tiresome, affected sod', 'silly, conceited, inadequate', and 'a "beauty-lover"' (quoted in Eltis, 2008: 211). However, as with Wilde's aristocrats, Coward's characters clearly enjoy their own fictionality. The divorced and reunited couple of *Private Lives* (1930), for example, share flippancy as a philosophy of life and deploy it as a defence against reality:

AMANDA. Don't laugh at me, I'm serious.
ELYOT [*seriously*]. You musn't be serious, my dear one; it's just what they want.
AMANDA. Who's they?
ELYOT. All the futile moralists who try to make life unbearable. Laugh at them. Be flippant. Laugh at everything, all their sacred shibboleths. Flippancy brings out the acid in their damned sweetness and light.
AMANDA. If I laugh at everything, I must laugh at us too.
ELYOT. Certainly you must. We're figures of fun all right.

(Coward, 1999: 226–227)

In Wilde and Coward, then, camp wit is deployed as a means of refusing incorporation into a communal identity defined by the sobriety of the establishment. In both cases there is a celebration of individualism over the masses, an elitist appreciation of privilege over all that is dull and ordinary, and a belief that easy intelligence equals freedom from conformity. But while Wilde and Coward were both gay men, we run the risk of falling into anachronism if we insist on reading camp as the coded language of homosexuality. As Alan Sinfield has written in relation to Oscar Wilde, Wilde's public persona and self-portrayal was not identified as sexually 'deviant' until after his conviction for Gross Indecency in 1895:

To us, Wilde looks like the ultimate instance of the queer man, but that is because the trials established him, and his image, as this – in English-speaking countries at least – until the 1970s. Of course, Wilde didn't do this by himself or out of nothing, and other concepts of same-sex passion certainly coexisted in the early and mid-twentieth century. But at the trials the entire, vaguely disconcerting nexus of effeminacy, leisure, idleness, immorality, luxury, insouciance, decadence and aestheticism, which Wilde was perceived as instantiating, was transformed into a brilliantly precise image: the queer.

(Sinfield, 1999: 28)

MARRIAGE AGAIN

One of the most notable aspects of mainstream comedy in the late twentieth and early twenty-first centuries has been the incorporation of explicitly gay characters into syndicated sitcoms, especially in the USA. This is a group that has been significantly underrepresented in the past. In 2000, for example, when 10–13 per cent of the US population identified as gay, only 2 per cent of characters in US sitcoms could be identified as such (Fouts and Inch, 2005: 35). In 2011, by contrast, the Neilsen media research firm calculated that over a quarter of broadcast primetime shows could be considered 'LGBT-inclusive', with 3.9 per cent of characters in comedy and drama identified as LGBTQ (Neilsen, 2011). The evidence would suggest, therefore, that while American audiences have become more amenable to shows broaching queer content, explicitly 'out' characters remain somewhat marginalised.

Instead of proportionally representing queer characters, US television has preferred to feature one or two 'out' characters in prominent roles, one of the first of whom was the eponymous heroine of Ellen Degeneres's sitcom *Ellen* (1994–1998). For three years, Ellen was played as a romantically hapless heterosexual woman in her mid-thirties, until in 1997, she came out on television, a fictional revelation that coincided with Degeneres's coming out in real life. Controversy followed, a parental advisory label was attached to the show and the following year it was cancelled. But whereas the fictional Ellen openly grappled with her sexuality, the next high-profile example of an openly gay character, Will Truman in *Will and Grace* (1998–2005), never questioned his identity as a gay man. This show, based around the long-standing friendship of a male lawyer and a female interior designer, took homosexuality as one of the contextual parameters of their relationship rather than the focus of the show, and as such, managed to invoke much of gay culture without it becoming a matter of existential or ethical anxiety.

In 2009, the representation of mainstream homosexual characters evolved further thanks to *Modern Family* (2009–), a show that President Obama claimed was his family's favourite television programme. This sitcom features two gay men, Mitchell and Cameron, who have married and adopted one child and hope to adopt another. Critics have applauded *Modern Family* for its inclusivity and its embrace of marriage equality in America, and for showing gay parents as stable, loving, and attentive. Others have argued that placing Mitchell and Cameron within the confines of marriage is to place gay relationships within the framework of conventional monogamy, and in so doing, neutralise any potential for truly transformative political commentary that two such characters might be capable of.

Perhaps it is too much to expect US network television to be overtly radical, for while its comedy shows have undoubtedly provided a forum through which the nation can discuss its attitudes towards sexuality in general, it cannot escape its primary purpose as a medium owned and run for profit. With the increased visibility of the LBGTQ community on television comes an awareness of the spending power of the queer consumer. According to the research firm Experian Marketing Services, for example, gay men have the highest discretionary spending per capita, with the household income of gay male couples being 12 per cent higher than that of heterosexual couples. Similarly, Ellen Degeneres's recent appearance as a spokesperson for American Express credit cards offers another example of the way in which, as Marusya Bociurkiw has argued, 'gay lifestyle and economic lifestyle are completely interchangeable' (Bociurkiw, 2005: 180). Ultimately, there is little inherently queer about buying things, but perhaps this is the neutral ground on which mainstream culture is most willing to entertain alternative sexualities.

7

POLITICS AND SATIRE

If you're going to tell people the truth, you better make them laugh; otherwise they'll kill you.

George Bernard Shaw

The philosopher John Morreall believes that a resilient sense of humour provides an intrinsic defence against tyranny. 'The person with a sense of humour can never be fully dominated, even by a government which imprisons him', he writes, 'for his ability to laugh at what is incongruous in the political situation will put him above it to some extent, and will preserve a measure of his freedom – if not of movement, at least of thought' (Morreall, 1983: 101). A similar idea may be found in Lord Shaftesbury's *Sensus Communis* (1709), where humour offers a release from the frustrations of social justice, and a nation's appetite for comedy is formed in direct proportion to the degree of political oppression it experiences. Discussing the 'spiritual Tyranny' of Italy, he writes that:

> the greatest of Buffoons are the ITALIANS: and In their Writings, in their freer sort of Conversations, on their Theatres, and in their Streets, Buffoonery and Burlesque are in the highest vogue. 'Tis the

> only manner in which the poor cramp'd Wretches can discharge a
> free Thought ... The greater the Weight is, the bitterer will be the Satir.
> The higher the Slavery, the more exquisite the Buffoonery.
>
> (Shaftesbury, 1988: 141)

More recently, the puppet show *Top Goon: Diaries of a Little Dictator*, performed on YouTube by the dissident Syrian theatre group Masasit Mati, has shown the importance of satire to cultivating a culture of resistance to the repressive regime of the Syrian President, Bashar Al-Assad. Masasit Mati see satire as an essential part of the political struggle – of helping to break down psychological dependence on a ruler who has built his regime on a decades-old culture of personality, but also of keeping the resistance itself open to scrutiny. 'Given the cruelty the Syrian people face in our struggle for freedom', they write on their website,

> satire and black comedy allow us to voice our collective pain and grief
> while expressing our ultimate determination to live. Since the very
> beginning of the uprising, Masasit Mati's show has mocked Bashar
> al-Assad, portraying him not as a bloody dictator, but rather as child-
> ish, often insane, a puppet figure suitable for ridicule. We have sought
> to strip the carefully crafted image of the dictator as a god. But Assad
> is not the only target: All aspects of the revolution are examined and
> satirised, including the political and armed opposition. We believe
> there must be no red lines if we want to build a democratic and
> pluralistic Syrian society for the future.
>
> (Masasit Mati, 2011)

Perhaps the notion of humour as an inherent expression of freedom is over-romanticised, as it is possible to imagine circumstances or hardships where laughter offers no comfort. Nevertheless, humour has been policed or punished by many governments who see it as a form of subversion. In 1737, the fear of ridicule prompted Sir Robert Walpole to introduce the Licensing Act censoring the theatre and its satirical attacks on his government. In 1935, the Berlin cabaret comedian Werner Finck was imprisoned in a concentration camp for a sketch that parodied limitations imposed on freedom of speech under Nazism (London, 2000: 34). Hitler 'was so wary of the danger of humour to the Third Reich that he had special "joke courts" set up for, among other things, punishing people who named their dogs and horses "Adolph"' (Morreall, 1983: 102). In Soviet Russia, publishing satire that criticised the party or its officers was a crime punishable by imprisonment in labour camps. In the United States during the 1950s, the investigations of Senator Joseph McCarthy's House Committee on Un-American Activities, established to root out communist sympathisers and treasonous plots at home, drove humorists underground for fear of blacklisting or incarceration. In 1952, Charlie Chaplin's uncontroversial film *Limelight* was singled out for McCarthyite suppression after the millionaire Chaplin, who had always retained his British citizenship, was thought to hold too much sympathy for the working class. After leaving for Europe, Chaplin was refused re-entry to the USA until he had appeared in front of the Immigration Board of Inquiry to answer questions of a 'political nature and of moral turpitude'. He resettled in Switzerland and returned only once to receive an Oscar in 1972 (Boskin, 1997: 75–76).

Considering all this, we would still be inclined to agree with the British journalist Malcolm Muggeridge, who once wrote that 'humour is an aspect of freedom, without which it cannot exist at all.' Yet while we might wish to equate comedy with freedom of speech and pit laughter against the tyranny of paranoid regimes, it is equally the case that comedy can be used in the service of repression, what Christopher Wilson has called the 'cryptic conservative' (Wilson, 1979: 226). As we have seen, the denigration of difference found in racist and sexist comedy, for example, reinforces and validates a discourse of power that relies on the systematic humiliation of targeted groups to secure its own sense of identity. In Albert Cook's view 'comedy is approval, not disapproval, of present society; it is conservative, not liberal' (quoted in Carlson, 1991: 15). Cook overstates the case, but the question of what we laugh at, and how it is censored or condoned by authority, is a highly politicised one. The topic of this chapter, then, will be the ways in which comedy has been, and is used as a form of politic commentary, and the successes and limitations of political satire.

COMEDY AND THE STATE: *FROGS* AND *BRASS EYE*

From its earliest roots, comedy has engaged with politics and the state. Aristophanic comedy, for example, frequently defamed identifiable Athenian public figures and derided their policies. Each of Aristophanes's eleven surviving plays is broadly based on a political theme pertinent to Athenian institutions and democracy or individuals within the polis. Abuse that we would now consider libellous was a fundamental part of the comedy, with named officials, military officers, and prominent citizens all insulted in considerable detail. Given the level of communal participation in Greek drama and the huge attendances at the annual Dionysia, Aristophanic dissent would have been widely broadcast. This responsibility or function appears to have constituted part of the identity of the playwright, and textual evidence makes it clear that Aristophanes imagined himself as the conscience of the people, exposing corruption and political mismanagement and ridiculing the offenders. As the Chorus of *The Acharnians* says:

> He'll carry on impeaching
> Every abuse he sees, and give much valuable teaching,
> Making you wiser, happier men. There won't be any diddling
> Or flattery or bribes, or any other kind of fiddling,
> Nor will you drown in fulsome praises, such as all the rest
> Bestow on you: he thinks his job's to teach you what is best.
>
> (Aristophanes, 1973: 78)

In all likelihood, this passage was written in response to events of the previous year, when *The Babylonians*, a play now lost, resulted in Aristophanes's probable conviction for slandering the city in the presence of foreigners. This is probably the first textual reference of comedy claiming for itself the privilege of licence, or of operating somewhere beyond the law.

The nature of political commentary in Aristophanes tells us that his work was conceived as a deliberate intervention in affairs of state. At the beginning of his career, Athens was a powerful and democratic city under the leadership of the popular and charismatic Pericles (c.495–429 BC). Athens's success threatened its neighbour Sparta, and in 431 BC, the two cities entered into wars that would continue intermittently for twenty-six years and result in the eventual surrender and subjugation of Athens in 405 BC. Throughout this period, Aristophanes maintained consistently pacifist sentiments and opposed the hardships and loss of freedoms brought about by lengthy conflict. Towards the end of his career, condemnations and caricatures of politicians were coupled with a new nostalgia for pre-war Athens and a lament for the depletion of the ideals of democracy. In *Frogs*, written only a few months before the final surrender of the Athenians, the god Dionysus is found mourning the recent deaths of the tragic poets Euripides and Sophocles, and lamenting the absence of good writers in Athens. With his servant Xanthias, Dionysus disguises himself as Heracles and travels into Hades to recover Euripides and return him to the upper world. In the underworld he presides over a poetical contest between Euripides and the older poet Aeschylus, and on balance, the high-minded, old-fashioned verse of Aeschylus is preferred over the newer style of his opponent. *Frogs* therefore insists upon the importance of literature to the spiritual life of the nation and affirms conservative poetical values. We can see this as an assertion of the centrality of drama to political and cultural discourse, with comedy as the only literary form able to enlist fantasy and disregard boundaries as a means of retrieving lost ideals.

Even though Aristophanic comedy is immersed in political themes, it is not necessarily a vehicle for dissent and political change. Criticism is divided between those who read his comedy as a profound engagement with the issues of public life and those who see him as a professional comedian getting laughs from the humiliation of authority figures. To support this latter argument, critics point to the context of comic drama within the two annual dramatic festivals, the Lanaea and the Dionysia. Adopting an approach familiar from Bakhtin and New Historicism, the argument cites the loosening of manners and mores during festival time, and the ritualistic centrality of raillery and abuse in the *komos* as the principal motivation for apparently political humour. The insults of Aristophanes are therefore part of the same formula as phallic worship and farce, and their political relevance is secondary. In Stephen Halliwell's words, this 'is not an evasion of standards, but rather an institutionalised and culturally sanctioned exemption from them' (Halliwell, 1984: 19). According to this view, comedy is, by its very nature, as politically impotent as it is apparently permissive, a form of temporary release that reinforces the existing social order while doing nothing, ultimately, to change it.

In the modern day, the question of whether or not comic form might automatically disarm the political potential of satirical content has been raised by the scandal involving a British television programme named *Brass Eye*. This programme, co-written by and starring Chris Morris, was a parody of current-affairs shows that sought to satirise media sensationalism, lazy journalism, and the irresponsibility of tabloid practices in a jaded media market. To expose the culture of uninformed sound-bites and ubiquitous celebrity comment, it regularly featured politicians and media figures who were duped into condemning fictional issues and making on-camera appeals in support of invented campaigns. One particular episode, broadcast on Channel 4 on 26 July 2001, mocked the media's obsession with paedophilia, and featured (among others) the musician Phil Collins supporting a campaign called 'Nonce Sense', and the radio DJ Dr Fox seated in front of a dead shellfish, saying, 'Genetically, paedophiles have more genes in common with crabs than they do with you or me … it is scientific fact.' Reactions to the programme were fierce. The then Culture Secretary Tessa Jowell spoke directly to the head of Channel 4 to voice her concern and tried to elicit a guarantee that the programme would never be repeated. The Home Office minister Beverley Hughes branded the show 'unspeakably sick', and the Home Secretary David Blunkett called it 'not remotely funny', although both later admitted that they had not seen it. The *Daily Mail* columnist Simon Heffer described it as 'the most grievous breach of taste I have ever witnessed on TV, and a programme that only a small proportion of the psychologically sick could have found enjoyable' (*Daily Mail*, 28 July 2001). While upholding the channel's right to free speech, the Independent Television Commission forced Channel 4 to broadcast an apology two months later, after it became clear that *Brass Eye* was the most complained about television programme in British broadcasting history. Clearly, it was the opinion of many that comedy had no business dealing with such a topic.

This particular episode of *Brass Eye* was conceived in response to the reductive and hysterical treatment of the issue of paedophilia in the British media. The summer of 2000 had seen a series of riots involving anti-paedophile protestors distressed at the presence of men they believed to be abusers living freely in their neighbourhoods. Such actions were inspired in part by the (now defunct) *News of the World* newspaper which had been running a series of articles naming alleged offenders and including some details of their locations. As the target of the programme was the media, the issues surrounding paedophilia as such were not considered. This undoubtedly proved to be the most provocative feature of the programme, since, as a consequence, it appeared to lack any sentimentality for children, or reiterate any familiar expressions of the sanctity of childhood as a state of being. Nor did it temper its attack on publicity-hungry celebrities and politicians with an unambiguous statement in support of the victims of abuse. Many read these omissions as signs of a fatal ambiguity, but one suspects that demands for overt statements of authorial intent, or the refusal to permit one aspect of the issue to be separated from the others, would have been unnecessary had the programme treated a different subject. As co-writer David Quantick said, 'I think a lot of people complained because it had the word paedophilia in the title and that a lot of complaints seemed to be related to a show that didn't go out' (*Guardian*, 30 July 2001). Much of the opposition to the show now seems to have been sparked by its enunciation of a culturally volatile term that continues to provoke suspicion every time it is uttered outside a condemnatory discourse designed by the media. Yet for the representatives of the government to comment on the content of a comedy show demonstrates that not all issues are covered by a blanket licence to speak out of turn.

SATIRE

Brass Eye's defence was built entirely upon its self-identification as satire. While claiming that something is satirical does not exempt it from criticism, it does imply a parodic tone that should not be confused with a straightforward correspondence with an author's views. Satire exists throughout the media, and is by no means an exclusive effect of comedy, but it is the most directly political of comic forms and the one that has caused the majority of censorious government interventions. Satire aims to denounce folly and vice and to urge ethical and political reform through the subjection of ideas to humorous analysis. In the best instances, it takes its subject matter from the heart of political life or cultural anxiety, re-framing issues at an ironic distance that enables us to revisit fundamental questions that have been obscured by rhetoric, personal interests or *Realpolitik*. Michael Moore's satirical documentary on US gun laws, *Bowling for Columbine* (2002), for example, had an enormous impact on audiences and provoked fierce criticism from conservative groups, with the result that Moore was both cheered and booed when the film received an Oscar. As for fictional works, Stanley Kubrick's 1964 film, *Dr. Strangelove, or: How I Learned to Stop Worrying and Love the Bomb*, is an excellent example of how satire can ask a question that has been dismissed by the establishment as naive, but that nevertheless remains absolutely crucial to the future of humanity. Kubrick's film is the story of an insanely paranoid American general who initiates a nuclear strike on Russia to prevent them from stealing his bodily fluids. Russia launches a counter-strike, and even though both governments try to recall their planes, one gets through and drops a hydrogen bomb on the Russian base at Laputa, named after the floating island in Jonathan Swift's *Gulliver's Travels*, the inhabitants of which exist 'under continual disquietudes, never enjoying a moment's peace of mind', and whose 'disturbances proceed from causes which very little affect the rest of mortals' (Swift, 1985: 206). *Dr. Strangelove* therefore asks a perfectly reasonable but basic question: are our military leaders and their fail-safe systems competent enough to prevent a devastating nuclear accident? In the character of the psychotic ex-Nazi Strangelove, it asks if we can really trust the individuals who lurk behind the anonymity of government departments. In the wake of President John F. Kennedy's assassination, Columbia Pictures delayed releasing the film to avoid accusations of anti-Americanism, and when it went on general release, the following disclaimer appeared over the title sequence:

> It is the stated position of the United States Air Force that their safeguards would prevent the occurrence of such events as are depicted in this film. Furthermore, it should be noted that none of the characters portrayed in this film are meant to represent any real persons living or dead.
>
> (Kubrick, 1964)

The second half of this statement is not entirely true: President Merkin Muffley was based on Presidential candidate Adlai Stephenson, and the monstrous Strangelove is a concoction of various German scientists whom the USA had adopted in a Faustian bargain, among them the V2 rocket designer Werner von Braun. Still, the film's insistence on its fictionality reveals its acute sensitivity to the potential volatility of its satire.

Satire is derived from the Latin *satura*, which means 'medley', or 'hotch-potch', and also describes a type of dish, alluding to its origins in country festivals and at feasts. Satire is often categorised according to the influence of two ancient Roman writers, Horace (65–8 BC) and Juvenal (c. AD 60–c.136), popularly thought of as stylistically opposite. Horace is gentler, concerned with maintaining moral standards and wishing to improve the ethics of his contemporaries by suggesting a point of equilibrium between extremes. His tone is one of amusement but not scorn, appearing as a spokesperson for common sense, judicious balance, and 'telling the truth with a smile' (Horace, 1959: 34). Central to Horatian satire is a series of contrasts between the country and the city, ideal and practical ethics, and the demands of public and private life. In all these, Horace is a poet of moderation, reserving his censure for those who desire more than they need. Satire VI is typical of Horace's modesty and rejection of the ambition that 'pulls everyone forward, chained to the wheels / Of her gleaming chariot'. Addressing an imagined politician, whose own status is derived from his father's elevated position, Horace, the son of a freed slave, says:

> If nature arranged for us all
> After a specified time to begin life all over,

Choosing parents who suited our fancy, I'd stick with mine
And not go for persons distinguished in public life.
The mob would think me insane, but you, perhaps, wouldn't,
For being unwilling to shoulder a load I'm not used to.
If I took on this role, I'd straightaway need some more money,
Need to receive more callers and endure more visits,
Take this friend along or the other, and never go out
By myself or get out to the country ...
In this, and in thousands of other respects,
I am much better off than you, my dear Public Figure.

(Horace, 1959: 66–67)

This sense of balance reflects the poet's own relative investment in the status quo. Horace was a part of the literary circle gathered around the emperor Augustus's finance minister Maecenas, a privileged group devoted to the Latinisation of Greek poetic forms and the enhancement of Roman poetry that included Virgil, the poet of the *Aeneid* (19 BC). We can also detect the influence of Stoicism, an Athenian philosophical system widely adopted in Rome. Stoicism's chief ethical concern was that humanity should live according to the tenets of nature and reason. All animals have needs befitting their nature, such as the need for food, shelter, and a mate. But, as humans are possessed of reason, they can determine the quality of appropriate actions with greater accuracy and consistency than animals, allowing them to move beyond simply answering their needs, and enabling them to act in concert with nature's prescriptions. To act and understand in this way is to act virtuously. Thus, while we can see that Horace is not an explicitly philosophical poet, his satire is concerned with the spiritual well-being of the person, achieved through individual choice and the reconciliation of self with its place in society.

A century later, the satire of Juvenal suggested that Roman life had changed. Unlike Horace, Juvenal's work was not popular or widely read in his own lifetime – in fact, he was not really 'discovered' until two and a half centuries after his death. Juvenalian satire is the satire of *saeva indignatio*, or savage indignation, the bitter condemnation of venal and stupid humanity. Whereas Horace scolds deviation from an essentially benign human nature,

Juvenal starts from the position that vice is at its highest point and virtue has been virtually extinguished. 'When was there ever a time more rich in abundance of vices?', he asks in his First Satire, 'Wealth, in our hearts, is set in the veriest Holy of Holies' (Juvenal, 1958: 21). Juvenal's two most influential satires, Satires III and X, focus on city living and its corruptions. Satire III, 'Against the City of Rome', for example, makes it clear that hypocrisy is necessary for those who wish to prosper:

> What should I do in Rome? I am no good at lying.
> If a book's bad, I can't praise it, or go around ordering copies.
> I don't know the stars; I can't hire out as assassin
> When some young man wants his father knocked off for a price;
> ...
> I am no lookout for thieves, so I cannot expect a commission
> On some governor's staff. I'm a useless corpse, or a cripple.
> Who has a pull these days, except your yes men and stooges
> With blackmail in their hearts, yet smart enough to keep silent?
> (Juvenal, 1958: 35)

Juvenal enjoyed a particular vogue in the eighteenth century when English authors rediscovered satirical models as a powerful form of social commentary. The most influential of these was undoubtedly the Irish writer and divine Jonathan Swift (1667–1745). Swift's satire, although difficult to define absolutely, adopts the Juvenalian tone of bitter indignation, appalled by man's inhumanity and the greed and hypocrisy of political and religious factionalism. Swift's misanthropy is voiced through the techniques of irony and parody, deploying an urbane and calming narrative tone to investigate some of the darkest and most unsettling of topics, and using pre-existing literary modes to convey them. This is clearly the technique of *A Modest Proposal* (1729), a short text that outlines a plan to address 'the present deplorable state' of famine in Ireland by selling babies to be eaten as food (Swift, 1993: 2181). *A Modest Proposal* is a parody of the political treatises and pamphlets published in abundance at this time and ventriloquises the helpful tone of the concerned philanthropist. 'I shall now humbly propose my own thoughts, which

I hope will not be liable to the least objection', writes the narrator, before telling us that

> I have been assured by a very knowing American of my acquaintance in London, that a young healthy child well nursed is at a year old a most delicious, nourishing, and wholesome food, whether stewed, roasted, baked, or boiled; and I make no doubt that it will equally serve in a fricassee or a ragout.

(Swift, 1993: 2182)

The ethics of cannibalism and degradations of the Irish under colonial English rule are entirely flattened amid the logical computations and analyses of the humanitarian benefits outlined by the pamphleteer. Such appalling obliviousness to the variance between the 'modest' proposal and the consequences of selling one hundred thousand children a year for meat is typical of the cognitive dissonance Swift exploits in order to expose his targets to maximum contempt. Like Juvenal, and indeed like *Brass Eye*, Swift offers no counter-argument that can either be concretely identified with the authorial position or be considered socially constructive. This has made his satire appeal to widely disparate groups: both English and Irish nationalists have claimed them as his; the Protestant and Catholic churches see him as a defender of their faiths; Marxists read in his satire a withering critique of bourgeois capitalism; and 'despite his association with misogyny', Swift was celebrated as one of the 'Fathers of Feminism' during Women's History Month in 1996 (Kelly, 2002: 133). 'Satire', he wrote in the preface to *The Battle of the Books* (1704), 'is a sort of glass, wherein beholders do generally discover everybody's face but their own' (Swift, 1984: 104).

SATIRE AS DIS-ENGAGEMENT: STEPHEN COLBERT, *THE DAILY SHOW*, AND *HAVE I GOT NEWS FOR YOU*

Satire's appeal has traditionally rested in its ability to speak truth to power and to effect the resistance implied by George Orwell's proposition that 'every joke is a tiny revolution'. This is especially true in the modern day as politicians appear increasingly remote and sequestered from their electorates, interested only in performing for cameras and perfecting the arts of dissimulation. It was this perceived disengagement that made moments such as the White House Correspondents' Association Dinner in 2006 especially memorable. This was the year in which the American comedian Stephen Colbert stood on stage alongside President George W. Bush and delivered the comic address that is a part of this annual banquet to honour the press corps. In his persona as a right-wing news show host, the monstrous offspring of Rush Limbaugh and the Fox News Corporation, Colbert launched into exaggerated praise of the President, grounded in an absurd version of the Republican world view. 'I give people the truth unfiltered by rational argument', said Colbert, before going on to announce that

> I believe in this President. Now I know that there are some polls out there that say that this man has a 32% approval rating, but guys like us [*turning to President Bush*], we don't pay attention to the polls. We know that polls are just a collection of statistics that reflect what people are thinking in reality. And reality has a well-known liberal bias.

The performance was not well received. The audience looked tense, several Bush aides walked out, and First Lady Laura Bush was reportedly angry at the lack of respect shown to both her husband and to her own initiative to promote literacy. 'I've never been a fan of books', said Colbert, addressing the First Lady. 'I don't trust them. They're all facts, no heart. I mean, they're elitist, telling us what is and isn't true.'

Although some took umbrage, others appreciated the routine for its audacity as much as its humour, and for Colbert's ability to appear seemingly unawed by the Presidential presence or the obvious lack of warmth for his performance. Indeed, many people have seen satire of this kind as being one of the sole remaining avenues available for critiquing those who exercise power. In the UK, for example, the *Guardian* newspaper has described Ian Hislop, editor of the British satirical magazine *Private Eye* and for twenty-five years a panelist on the satirical news show *Have I Got News For You* (1990–), as the most influential political voice in Britain (Kettle,

2011). 'And what is Hislop's principal message?' asked the paper. 'Week in and week out, it is that most pretty much all politicians are corrupt, deluded, incompetent, second-rate and hypocritical' (Kettle, 2011).

That such performances exist at all is surely a sign of a healthy democracy, yet for the political scientist Steven Fielding, the success of *Have I Got News For You* is not evidence of the health of participatory democracy, but rather its opposite, the rise of a brand of comedy that has ceased to engage with politics altogether. 'Satire', he says, 'is meant to hold up an object to ridicule with the intention of provoking its reform: it is supposed to be comedy for a purpose. *Have I Got News for You* is comedy without a purpose' (Fielding, 2012). The problem, as Fielding sees it, is that such shows merely repeat the stereotypical commonplace that all politicians are opportunist, self-serving, and hypocritical. As Jonathan Coe has similarly argued in relation to satirical television, politicians have 'nothing to fear from public laughter at all':

> These days, every politician is a laughing-stock, and the laughter which occasionally used to illuminate the dark corners of the political world with dazzling, unexpected shafts of hilarity has become an unthinking reflex on our part, a tired Pavlovian reaction to situations that are too difficult or too depressing to think about clearly.
>
> (Coe, 2013: 31)

For all that it soothes our frustrations, satirical laughter may ultimately foreclose discussion and dispel the energy required to make positive change. In the USA, the success of Jon Stewart's *Daily Show* (1996–) has provoked similar concerns. 'Our lazy embrace of Stewart and Colbert', writes the American author, Steve Almond,

> is a testament to our own impoverished comic standards. We have come to accept coy mockery as genuine subversion and snarky mimesis as originality. It would be more accurate to describe our golden age of political comedy as the peak output of a lucrative corporate plantation whose chief export is a cheap and powerful opiate for progressive angst and rage.
>
> (Almond, 2012: 30)

In making the connection between political satire and an entertainment industry with no commitment to systemic political change, Almond draws our attention to the fact that performers like Colbert and Stewart provide a valuable service by packaging voter anger, acknowledging it, and offering a kind of non-threatening remedy that also brings them considerable rewards. Jon Stewart earns $16 million a year according to *Forbes.Com*, which would suggest that his production company, if not Stewart himself, has a considerable investment in maintaining the status quo.

THE END OF LAUGHTER?: THREE HOLOCAUST COMEDIES

The self-evidently inappropriate proximity of the word 'comedy' to 'Holocaust' begs an important question: are there times when comedy and politics must not mix? Like Eddie Waters in *Comedians*, our instincts tell us that comedy has no place in such appalling events, but still it persists. Several attempts have been made to treat Holocaust themes within a context that is either structurally or tonally comedic. The results are of course varied, but the interaction of two categories that common sense tells us are diametrically opposed can be extremely interesting, both in terms of what possible benefits, if any, comic elements bring to an understanding of history, and also where the practicable boundaries of comedy's much-vaunted freedom to flaunt taboos might lie. Allusions to the Holocaust have been used many times by Jewish comedians in order to indicate the limits of bad taste or wrong-headedness, suggesting that even thinking about it is fraught with guilt and difficulty. The comically abysmal musical 'Springtime for Hitler' at the heart of Mel Brooks's film *The Producers* (1968), devised to defraud an insurance company with a failed Broadway show, suffers a reversal when it turns out that the theatre-going public *love* Nazi-themed musicals. The fraudsters, the critics, and the Broadway audience are all shown to be appalling philistines. An episode of *Seinfeld* saw Jerry censured by his parents and his girlfriend's father after he was spotted kissing her during a screening of *Schindler's List* (1993). In *Annie Hall* (1977), Woody Allen's character Alvy refuses to see any movies other than the four-hour documentary on Nazi-occupied Paris, *The Sorrow and the Pity,* because 'everything else is such garbage' (Allen, 1977). With this comment he demeans the force of Marcel Ophül's film by placing it in the same category as the average Hollywood blockbuster, appreciable according to standard popular criticisms such as the credibility of its plot, the thrillingness of effects, and so on. In all of these examples, the Holocaust is used as the absolute signifier of seriousness contrasted against light-headed concern for entertainment, daily life, and diminutive but nagging desires. The Holocaust acts as a grave reminder against which the self-centredness of the over-privileged modern bourgeois is made utterly risible.

Other attempts at considering Holocaust themes in comedy have been horribly ill-conceived. The American comedian Jerry Lewis directed and starred in a 1972 film entitled *The Day the Clown Cried*, a story about a German circus clown, Helmut Doork, who is arrested for a drunken impersonation of Hitler and sent to Auschwitz. During his incarceration he befriends the children of the camp and performs for them with the hope of bringing some laughter into their lives. At the end of the film he tries to shield them from their fear by leading them to the gas chambers, while, the screenplay says, playing the harmonica like the 'pied piper'. That the film lacked judgement is borne out by the fact that it has never been released. Lewis's unfortunate project underlines the extreme difficulty of attempting to treat the subject of the Holocaust without reducing it to banal sentimentality or simply using it as a backdrop for clowning. The problems of the meeting of comedy with content of this kind are obvious. Not only is comedy generically and tonally unsuited to a treatment of the Holocaust, but there is a structural misfit too. Comedy concludes with a standardised happy ending, 'a conscious superimposition of a formal pattern on material that may until the very last moment whirl with turbulence', in Zvi Jagendorf's phrase, whereas here, such a conclusion would be both historically inaccurate and morally objectionable (Jagendorf, 1984: 43).

However, let us consider three films that have attempted to do exactly this with varying degrees of success: Charlie Chaplin's *The Great Dictator* (1940); Frank Beyer's *Jakob the Liar* (1974), based on the novel by East German writer Jurek Becker, and re-made in

America as a vehicle for Robin Williams in 1999; and Roberto Benigni's triple Oscar-winning *Life Is Beautiful* (1998). While each of these films has a different strategy for dealing with the jarring incompatibility of comic form and historical fact, none of them can resist the implied trajectory of comic narrative as a means of injecting into their stories some optimism and the possibility of future happiness, even if it exists far beyond the final scene. We see this in the equation of laughter with hope, and the implication that comedy is the representation of a caring and inclusive human spirit that cannot be extinguished by fascism.

In *The Great Dictator,* set in fictional Tomainia, Hitler look-alike Adenoid Hynkel has risen to power on anti-Semitic policies and by fomenting international unrest. The film contrasts Hynkel's rampant megalomania, revealed in a scene where he performs a delicate *pas de deux* with an inflatable world globe, with the parallel story of a humble Jewish barber who returns to the ghetto after several years in hospital suffering from amnesia. Chaplin plays both Hynkel and the Barber, and the stories move together in order to bring about a concluding scene in which the Barber, imprisoned for his religion, escapes from a concentration camp and is mistaken for Hynkel just as it is time for him to deliver a speech. Knowing that his life depends on maintaining the charade, the Barber launches into an impassioned six-minute plea that closes the movie. From his opening words, the speech is resolutely anti-dictatorial: 'I'm sorry, but I don't want to be an Emperor', he says, 'that's not my business. I don't want to rule or conquer anyone. I should like to help everyone if possible, Jew, gentile, black man, white. We all want to help one another, human beings are like that' (Chaplin, 1940). In response to Nazi militarism, which he associates with the profiteering of industrialised society, Chaplin asserts the redemptive qualities of nature and instinct, together with an idealisation of the power of human empathy:

> Greed has poisoned men's souls, has barricaded the world with hate, has goose-stepped us into misery and bloodshed. We have developed speed but we have shut ourselves in. Machinery that gives us abundance has left us in want. Our knowledge has made us cynical, our cleverness hard and unkind. We think too much and feel too little.

> More than machinery we need humanity. More than cleverness we need
> kindness and gentleness. Without these qualities, life will be violent
> and all will be lost.
>
> (Chaplin, 1940)

As Alan Dale writes, 'the Barber embodies a concept of insignif-
icance Chaplin associates with all kinds of worthiness – honesty,
hard work, courtesy, gallantry, the whole load' (Dale, 2000: 47).
In the concept of a society that can be saved by simplicity and
considerateness, the Jewish Barber's speech demonstrates a clear
continuity between Chaplin's critique of dehumanising labour in
Modern Times and what he perceived as the automation of Hitler's
fascism, 'unnatural men, machine men, with machine minds and
machine hearts' (Chaplin, 1940). Chaplin has abandoned the
structure of comedy and the business of slapstick by this point of
the film, as historical circumstances do not allow for a traditional
resolution. However, the implicit optimism of comedy strongly
influences the finale, as the Jewish Barber's speech is superimposed
over images of dignified Jewish families in pastoral exile. As sheaves
of corn blow in the wind with the promise of a new tomorrow,
Chaplin's political naivety seems utterly exposed. Such images
rang hollow for Theodor Adorno and Max Horkheimer, for
example, who, in their 1944 essay 'The Culture Industry', felt they
gave 'the lie to the anti-fascist plea for freedom' and served 'to
confirm the immutability of circumstances' rather than proposing a
radically new direction (Adorno and Horkheimer, 2001: 148–149).
This would not be the last time that anyone accused Chaplin of
inchoate sentimentalism.

Becker's *Jakob the Liar* was the first important fictional narrative
of the Jewish wartime experience to come from East Germany
(the former German Democratic Republic). The film tells the
story of the middle-aged Jakob, living in the ghetto and forced to
work in a freight yard. One night he is sent to the police station
where he accidentally overhears a radio report of the Russian army's
advance. Given hope by this news, he tells his friend Kowalski,
who pressures him to reveal how he could possibly have heard
a radio in the ghetto. Jakob tells him the truth, but Kowalski
refuses to believe that he had heard the broadcast as he feels that

Jakob would never have been allowed to leave the police station alive. Jakob then revises the story and claims that he has a radio hidden in his house, and soon, the entire ghetto is coming to him for news. The more he prevaricates, the more convinced they become that he has access to forbidden information (a perfect example of Bergson's 'reciprocal interference of series'). Faced with the choice of either giving his neighbours hope or telling them the truth, Jakob selects the former. In this, and Jakob's simulation of radio broadcasts to tell his niece fairy-tales, we are asked to condone his fiction as a gift that momentarily relieves suffering by extending the promise of a happy ending. There is no happy ending, of course, and the final scene contrasts the journey to the concentration camp with a fairy-tale projected onto the clouds, unhappily indicating the optimism and intangibility of fiction. For Sander L. Gilman, *Jakob the Liar* is one of the few successful humorous treatments of Holocaust material, because its comic aspects are expressions of the accidental rather than the precursors of absorption into a comic resolution. 'Accident', he writes,

> is the wellspring of comedy and laughter, not because it is the opposite of tragedy but because it is the instantiation of the random in life, over which one can only laugh or weep. Becker provides the ability to do both in *Jakob the Liar* and made it possible to use the elicitation of laughter as a means of presenting the unpresentable, not only in the Shoah, but the randomness of life.
>
> (Gilman, 2000: 304)

Gilman's view of Benigni's more recent film is quite different. *Life is Beautiful* ends with the liberation of the camps by the US army, and Joshua, the little boy who has been saved from brutality by his father's protective fiction, is hauled up onto a tank by a friendly soldier, just as his father had predicted. In the concluding *deus ex machina* that also enables Joshua to be reunited with his mother, Gilman accuses Benigni of reducing the topic to fit the demands of form, as 'Benigni's promise is that there are no accidents, that at the end of the comedy the gods in the machine will arrive to resolve the action and rescue those in danger' (Gilman, 2000: 304). In the ultimate imposition of comic form, the imperatives of fascist inhumanity are overridden: 'Benigni's laughter is proof that whatever else will happen the promise of the film, the rescue of the child, must take place. Our expectations are fulfilled, and we feel good about our laughter' (Gilman, 2000: 304).

The three Oscars and huge box office success of *Life is Beautiful* made it one of the most successful films in Italian history (Ezrahi, 2001: 292). For its supporters, Benigni has produced an important recognition of Italy's participation in the deportation of Jews, and told a fable of selfless love and the ability of the spirit to resist the most appalling oppression. The worst accusations levelled at the film insist that it is sanitised, fabricated, dishonest, and 'a whitewash of European guilt' (Ezrahi, 2001: 295). In his review published in the November 1998 issue of *Time* magazine, Richard Shickel argued that the comic frame-work of the film amounted to an insult to the living victims of the Holocaust, who 'inevitably grow fewer each year. The voices that would deny it ever took place remain strident. In this climate, turning even a small corner of this century's central horror into feel-good enter-tainment is abhorrent. Sentimentality is a kind of fascism too' (quoted in Flanzbaum, 2001: 281). A similar degree of outrage was expressed by David Denby in *The New Yorker*, who accused Benigni of wanting 'the authority of the Holocaust without the actuality' and of 'feeling relieved and happy that *Life is Beautiful* is a benign form of Holocaust denial' (quoted in Flanzbaum, 2001: 282). It is easy to see comic structure as a primary cause of this distaste, coupled with the fact that it was devised and performed by a non-Jewish comedian, laying the film open to accusations of careless optimism and inauthenticity. Rather than seeking to define some truth of the Holocaust and Italy's part in it, the film provides only easy comic solutions and a belief in the Christianised conception of absolution, 'the comic as artificial human construct of the universe *as it should be*' (Ezrahi, 2001: 307). Ruth Ben-Ghiat argues that Benigni's film also tries to deflect some of the attention away from the Holocaust as a specifically Jewish tragedy through 'the inclusion of a self-sacrificing Christian wife [who] affirms that Jews have no monopoly in Italy on the state of victimhood, even as they remain the most acceptable public symbols of fascism's inhumanity' (Ben-Ghiat, 2001: 263). In response to these criticisms, however, several writers have argued that the way in which Holocaust history has come to be policed ensures that any treatment of it can be instantly condemned as facile, with the result that a number of otherwise valid narratives are dismissed out of hand. Hilene Flanzbaum, for example, points to a contradiction amongst those who reject Benigni's film, because they occupy 'a paradoxical and infinite regress in which critics feel obliged to repeat that the Holocaust cannot ever be truly represented, while at the same time, these very same critics vigorously complain each time an individual representation insufficiently portrays the event' (Flanzbaum, 2001: 284). For her, *Life Is Beautiful* 'acknowledges at the start that it is a myth, and in so doing, it clearly – and I believe, more honestly than films that claim historical veracity – accepts its limitations as a work of art' (Flanzbaum, 2001: 283). As long as we understand that the film is a fictional construct, Benigni's treatment is justified precisely because it does not claim to be an authentic history, but does other work by placing the issues in an entirely new and unusual context that has the virtue of reaching a very wide audience. While not satisfied that the film is entirely innocent of all the accusations levelled at it, Flanzbaum concludes that 'Benigni accomplishes a great deal when he defamiliarizes the Holocaust enough to make such viewers feel it all over again' (Flanzbaum, 2001: 283).

Perhaps the question of comedy and politics might be reduced to questions of effect and efficacy. When laughter is directed with aggression, it can be an extremely powerful tool, representing its targets in purely negative terms and reinforcing prejudice. Comedy that seeks to do the same to tyrannical or prejudicial ideologies, however, often has to relinquish a reasonable base for its arguments before it enters the arena. Parody and satire are good for demolishing dogma but not for constructively offering alternatives to it. The alternative comedy of the 1980s found itself censoring guilty forms to the extent that it struggled to find material and had to replace blacks and women with red-haired people and Margaret Thatcher. Holocaust comedies exist within such a complicated terrain of history, representation, politics, and prejudice that they become instantly suspect, with the result that both comedy and politics lose their immediacy and productions become debatable at best, and insulting at worst. Perhaps it is true that comedy has nothing to offer politics when the project requires something more than simple derision. Maybe the limited usefulness of comedy in politics is a function of laughter's association with ridicule. Let us then turn our attention to the question of laughter, what it is, and how it is used.

8

LAUGHTER

> Perhaps even if nothing else today has any future, our *laughter* may
> yet have a future.
>
> Friedrich Nietzsche

Satisfactory explanations of laughter have always been notoriously
elusive. As Henri Bergson put it, 'this little problem ... has a
knack of baffling every effort, of slipping away only to bob up
again, a pert challenge flung at philosophical speculation' (Bergson,
1980: 61). Across the centuries, laughter has been variously
understood as vice or cowardice, as delight caused by surprise, the
product of defamiliarisation, a means of averting anti-social conflict,
or an extra-linguistic bark signalling the limits of understanding.
Aristotle, noting that laughter is exclusive to human beings,
believed that an infant could not be considered truly human until
it had laughed its first laugh at forty days old. By acknowledging
laughter as essentially human, every discussion of it also tends to
contain an idea of what being human means. A further theme
seemingly unifies all theories of laughter: they all take it to be
the manifestation of a perfectly serious urge, process, or function,
as in Dutch historian Johann Huizinga's theory of the serious

importance of play. Laughter is never just fun, as in all accounts of it the human being is using their laughter to serve a social, psychological, or physiological need. This chapter will survey a number of the most prominent theories of laughter in order to show how this idea, so closely associated with comedy, has been used as a means of understanding human identity.

CHRISTIAN LAUGHTER

In the Book of Genesis, God tells Abraham that his wife Sarah will give birth to a son despite the fact that she is ninety years of age. Sarah understandably laughs at the very thought of it, but later, when the prophecy comes true, she laughs again, this time in wonder. But despite this instance of laughter as a means of acknowledging a marvel beyond the ken of human experience, early Christianity was generally hostile to laughter. Nowhere does the New Testament mention Christ laughing, although he twice wept, and evidence for his sense of humour is scant. Instead, the early church generally equated levity and mirth with foolishness and ignorance. Ecclesiastes states that

> The heart of the wise is in the house of mourning; but the heart of fools is in the house of mirth. It is better to hear the rebuke of the wise, than for a man to hear the song of fools. For as the crackling of thorns under a pot, so is the laughter of the fool: this also is vanity.
>
> (Ecclesiastes, 7.4–6)

Early Christian converts in Rome founded their principles of conduct in opposition to the luxurious and debauched lives of their pagan masters. Christian theology actively rewarded simplicity and poverty, and found virtue in privation and self-control. The abrogation of the body and the rigid imposition of pious abstinence made physical pleasure suspicious. In Philippa Pullar's words, 'the body *had* to be broken; it had to be abused and maltreated, its reactions, sensations and natural functions became to the Christians a real and terrible neurosis' (Pullar, 2001: 37). The contrast between Roman and Christian attitudes to laughter is apparent in the story of St Genesius, a pagan Roman actor and now the patron saint of comedians. During a performance for the Emperor Diocletian that parodied the Christian baptism, Genesius received an angelic visitation that delivered an admonition. His laughter quickly turned to mortification and servility as he asked forgiveness of his newly discovered God. Diocletian, who was expecting a laugh, had him stretched, beheaded, and burnt (Jacobson, 1997: 163–164). Laughter, then, was a vulgar eruption of the body that contained the indecent excess of paganism and was impudent, raucous, and ill-disciplined: 'Sorrow is better than laughter: for by the sadness of the countenance the heart is made better' (Ecclesiastes, 7.3). As we have seen in Chapter 3, governing the body requires the regulation and the repression of certain corporeal traits. In early Christianity, it was conventional to understand the human subject as fundamentally torn between the animalistic urges of the flesh and the sanctity of a pious soul. The earliest ascetic condemnation of laughter, authored in the second century by Clement of Alexandria, conceded that laughter was human, but urged Christians to restrain it as they might similar bestial instincts:

> For, in a word, whatever things are natural to men we must not eradicate from them, but rather impose on them limits and suitable times. For man is not to laugh on all occasions because he is a laughing animal, any more than the horse neighs on all occasions because he is a neighing animal. But as rational beings, we are to regulate ourselves suitably, harmoniously relaxing the austerity and over-tension of our serious pursuits, not inharmoniously breaking them up altogether.
>
> (Clement of Alexandria, 1983: 250)

In the process of determining pious deportment, laughter became subject to the rules of appropriate behaviour and the rational ordinances of self-control that kept base instincts in check. Clement was particularly wary of the susceptibility of women to laughter, equating their mirth with sexual immorality: 'the discordant relaxation of countenance in the case of women is called a giggle, and is meretricious laughter' (Clement of Alexandria, 1983: 250). Ascetic control of the body was clearly troubled by occasions that might convulse, distort, and overthrow it, and in women the repercussions might be damnable. Similarly, early monastic life held laughing to be one of its greatest crimes. As Jerry Palmer writes:

> In the earliest monastic regulations (in the fifth century) laughter is condemned as the grossest breach of the rule of silence, and later it is considered a breach of the rule of humility; it is also considered the greatest dirtying of the mouth, which should be a filter for good and evil to enter and leave the body; therefore it must be prevented.
>
> (Palmer, 1994: 44)

Both examples, of female reserve and monastic silence, are indicative of the belief that 'the more the body was closed against the world, the more the soul was opened up to God' (Gilhus, 1997: 67).

While the early church made significant attempts to banish and condemn laughter, the medieval period saw ecclesiastical authorities drawing it into the liturgical calendar and distinguishing between good laughter and bad. The enigmatic question of whether or not Jesus had laughed in his early life enjoyed a vogue in ecclesiastical cirlces, so much that in the thirteenth century, the University of Paris organised an annual conference on the subject (Le Goff, 1997: 43). In Chapter 2, we saw how medieval culture made the figure of folly into a universal symbol of human ignorance. Similarly in medieval morality plays the role of Vice was given to a clown to better underline the need for folly to be overcome before Mankind can proceed to Grace. 'If there were no devils to expel, there would be no comedy to enjoy', writes Howard Jacobson, adding that, during the medieval period 'hell remained a locus for hilarity' (Jacobson, 1997: 151). Stage Hellmouths would repeatedly provide the entrance for the most amusing comic entertainers, a vestige of which can be seen in the devils tumbling out of the arras and chasing the clowns in Christopher Marlowe's play, *Doctor Faustus* (1594). Jacobson also lists a number of *Ioculatores Domini*, jokers and jesters of God, canonised holy men, including St Francis of Assisi, who used humour in their proselytising (Jacobson, 1997: 166). Religious festivals, such as the Feast of Fools, are further examples of the reconciliation of laughter with religion. While Pope Innocent III (1198–1216) issued a decree condemning the Feast of Fools, in pragmatic terms the incorporation of laughter into worship was a necessity if the church were to extend its authority over areas of folk-belief and folk practices, including the still-thriving Roman Saturnalia that it had so far failed to assimilate. The moral equation of laughter with vice remained, but it was now utilised in ritual as an instructive counterpoint to official discourse that emphasised human failings and therefore the necessity of spiritual intervention. In rituals of this kind, laughter serves joyfully to instruct humility and the distance between the human and the divine. Laughter in the medieval period therefore expressed human folly and postlapsarian weakness, a liturgically important rite of exorcism. Enid Welsford argues that the Feast of Fools should not be thought of as a decline into idiocy, so much as a demonstration of a subtle intelligence that understood the incompatible tensions between riot and ritual as fundamental aspects of human existence (Welsford, 1935: 202). Medieval laughter was part of creation, it had an exegetical purpose that could find the truth of the gospel in the pious and the grotesque, rather than through a rigid, contrasting system of truth and its opposite.

In addition to the metaphysical implications of laughter, there was a tradition in early-modern medicine that stressed its healthful benefits. Influenced by Hippocrates (c.460–357 BC), the most celebrated physician of antiquity, and Democritus (b. c.460 BC), the 'laughing philosopher', both of whom had encouraged the cultivation of a sense of humour as a defence against illness and depression, medical men such as Laurent Joubert (1529–1582), and, of course Rabelais himself, saw laughter as a means of maintaining the body's humoral balance. Joubert, whose *Treatise on Laughter* (1560) presents itself as a scientific investigation, writes that 'being joyful and ready to laugh indicates a good nature and purity of blood, [and] thus contributes to the health of the body and the mind' (Joubert, 1980: 126). After recounting three detailed stories about the laughter-provoking actions of monkeys at the bedside of the dangerously ill, he concludes that 'the dignity and excellence of laughter is ... very great inasmuch as it reinforces the spirit so much that it can suddenly change the state of the patient, and from his deathbed render him curable' (Joubert, 1980: 128).

Mikhail Bakhtin, apparently inspired by the restorative function attributed to laughter by early-modern science, extends its
implications into the political arena by crediting it with the
ability to triumph over oppression: 'festive folk laughter presents
an element of victory not only over supernatural awe, of the
sacred over death; it also means the defeat of power, of earthly
kings, of the earthly upper classes, of all that oppresses and
restricts' (Bakhtin, 1984: 92). Largely silenced by an official culture that consolidates its power through seriousness, Bakhtin's
laughter is the popular voice of the people, not only alleviating
the tensions of official ideology, but cutting right through them
and denying their influence. As we shall see below, this conception of laughter as an extra-linguistic challenge to systems of
order is a notion that enjoys some popularity in the criticism of
the present day.

SUPERIORITY AND INCONGRUITY THEORIES

The superiority theory of laughter states that human beings are
moved to laugh when presented with a person or situation they
feel themselves to be intellectually, morally, or physically above.
Bakhtin's argument claims that by the sixteenth century a reor-
ganisation of intellectual categories under the auspices of
Humanism continued to separate laughter from official culture.
This led to a starker demarcation of the serious and the comic
where 'that which is important and essential cannot be comical',
and 'the essential truth about the world and man cannot be told
in the language of laughter' (Bakhtin, 1984: 67). Laughter was
removed from its position in philosophy and turned into scorn,
becoming 'a light amusement or a form of salutary social punishment of corrupt and low persons' (Bakhtin, 1984: 67). We can
certainly see that the concept of laughter changes in the sixteenth
and seventeenth centuries, in a way that imbues it with an ethical
significance. Sir Philip Sidney, for example, remarked that
laughter 'hath only a scornful tickling' (Sidney, 1991: 68). This
attitude is developed further in studies of rhetoric in the period.
Thomas Wilson's *The Arte of Rhetoricke* (1567) provides a perfect

example of the Humanist conception of laughter. 'The occasion of laughter', he writes,

> and the meane that maketh us merrie ... is the fondnes, the filthiness, the deformitie, and al suche evil behaviour, as we se to bee in each other. For we laugh always at those thinges, which either onely, or chiefly touche handsomely, and wittely, some speciall fault, or fond behavior in some one body or some one thing.
>
> (Wilson, 1567: f.69, verso)

Laughter is used in rhetoric as a means of besting one's opponent. This idea is borrowed directly from Cicero (103–43 BC), the father and codifier of oratorical arts and hero of the Humanists, who writes:

> It clearly becomes an orator to raise laughter ... merriment naturally wins goodwill for its author; and everyone admires acuteness, which is often concentrated in a single word, uttered generally in repelling, though sometimes in delivering, an attack; and it shatters or obstructs or makes light of an opponent, or alarms or repulses him; and it shows the orator himself to be a man of finish, accomplishment and taste.
>
> (Cicero, 1984: 28)

Fritz Gaf writes that Roman laughter was mainly intended 'to correct deviance – in a socially acceptable way' (Gaf, 1997: 31). The importance of rhetoric in Humanism may therefore have had the effect of replacing medieval conceptions of redemptive, inclusive laughter with the idea of it as a weapon used in verbal conflict and directed specifically against failure or weaknesses. Thinking of laughter as a weapon would therefore allow us to think of it as an ethically determined tool, one that can be applied to both good and bad ends. Certainly mockery and ridicule in Tudor and Stuart England were prevalent means of consolidating social norms. Michael Bristol tells us that

> ridicule is a recognized element in law enforcement, in the punishment of insubordination and in the everyday feeling of superiority enjoyed by nobles in respect to their servants. Laughter is also an important element in the strategies of social appeasement used by servants in

> respect of their masters. Self-abjection and self-ridicule are significant
> elements in an elaborate system of deferential gesture and compliment.
>
> (Bristol, 1985: 126)

From this idea, it is not far to 'superiority theory', one of the three most durable explanations of laughter in Western culture. By far the most famous representative of superiority theory is the seventeenth-century English philosopher Thomas Hobbes (1588–1679). In truth, Hobbes had little to say about laughter, but what he did say is quoted in almost every discussion of the subject, even though his ambiguity towards it is clear when he calls laughter the signal of a 'passion that hath no name' (Hobbes, 1840: 45). 'Laughter', he wrote in *Human Nature* (1650), 'is nothing else but a sudden glory arising from some sudden conception of some eminency in ourselves, by comparison with the infirmity of others, or with our own formerly' (Hobbes, 1840: 46). For Hobbes, laughter is always antagonistic and conflictual, establishing a hierarchy at the moment of pleasure. In *Leviathan* (1660), he makes his ethical objection to this clear when he states that 'much laughter at the defects of others is a sign of Pusillanimity' (Hobbes, 1991: 43). Even laughter that is not immediately directed at an 'inferior' person actually present is structured according to this principle: 'Laughter without offense, must be at absurdities and infirmities abstracted from persons, and when all the company may laugh together' (Hobbes, 1840: 46–47). Clearly, there are types of humour that depend on a feeling of superiority for their operation. Racist and sexist jokes, as we have seen, presume an ethnic, gendered, and intellectual advantage on the part of the teller and his or her audience. Yet it is also possible to see that much laughter does not arise from a feeling of pre-eminence, even one that is suppressed or inverted. Like the early Christian commentators, Hobbes's definition belongs to the tradition that understands laughter operating within a moral framework that sees laughers as self-regarding and uncharitable. Superiority theory even became an edict of manners in eighteenth-century 'men of quality' who refused to laugh on grounds of breeding. In one of his comprehensive letters, Lord Chesterfield (1694–1773) warns his son that he should be

never heard to laugh while you live. Frequent and loud laughter is the
characteristic of folly and ill manners ... In my mind nothing so illib-
eral, and so ill-bred as audible laughter ... how low and unbecoming a
thing laughter is. Not to mention the disagreeable noise it makes,
and the shocking distortion of the face it occasions.

(Stanhope, 1929: 49)

Here we find the Christian disapprobation of laughter and its fear
of bodily disorder overridden by a class consciousness that sees
laughter as the enemy of social distinctions. According to Samuel
Johnson, neither Jonathan Swift nor Alexander Pope could be
induced to laugh, and Lord Froth in Congreve's *The Double Dealer*
(1694) states, 'There is nothing more unbecoming a Man of
Quality than to laugh; Jesu, 'tis such a vulgar expression of the
passion! Everybody can laugh' (Congreve, 1973: 7). The class-based
rejection of laughter penetrated further than the fear of appearing
vulgar. Addison claimed that laughter 'slackens and unbraces the
Mind, weakens the Faculties, and causes a Kind of Remissness,
and Dissolution in all the powers of the soul' (Addison and Steele,
1979, vol. 2: 237–238). That every important household used to
keep a jester is conclusive proof that 'everyone diverts himself with
some person or other that is below him in Point of Understanding,
and triumphs in the Superiority of his Genius, whilst he has such
objects of derision in his eyes' (Addison and Steele, 1979, vol. 1:
142–143). Superiority theory was therefore confirmed by the
superior members of society refraining from laughing.

The continuity of superiority theory, and a general disdain for
laughter in elite circles, was eventually challenged in the eighteenth century by analyses of humour that indicated the importance of pleasure in laughter over mockery and derision.
Superiority theory operates in the absence of a joke and focuses on
physical defects, personal misfortunes, and social inequality; as
such its view of humour is dictated by grotesque and burlesque
forms. The new emphasis of eighteenth-century laughter-studies
highlighted the linguistic formulae of humour, the operation of
verbal triggers and the juxtaposition of elements in the production of comic effects. Francis Hutcheson (1694–1746), professor
of Philosophy at the University of Glasgow, was an early and

effective challenger to the Hobbesian position. Writing in *The Dublin Journal* in 1726, Hutcheson attacked the malevolent theory of laughter, remarking that when we laugh there is a 'great fund of pleasantry' (Hutcheson, 1750: 7). Hutcheson was keen to prove that laughter and a sense of the ridiculous 'is plainly of considerable moment in human society' and 'is exceeding useful to abate our concerns or resentment' in matters of small affront or inappropriate conduct (Hutcheson, 1750: 32). Indeed, he found 'that nature has given us a sense of the ridiculous as an avenue to pleasure and a remedy for sorrow' (Trave, 1960: 69). A new generation of writers began to praise the corrective, admonitory aspects of comedy over its corrosive qualities. Shaftesbury's *Sensus Communis* finds humour a 'lenitive Remedy against Vice, and a kind of Specifick against Superstition and Melancholy Delusion' (Shaftesbury, 1988: 188). In addition, Hutcheson makes the elegant point that if laughter were only prompted by a feeling of pre-eminence, then it would surely be easier to elicit. 'Strange!', he writes, 'that none of the Hobbists banish canary birds and squirrels, and lap-dogs and pugs, and cats out of their houses, and substitute in their places asses, and owls, and snails, and oysters to be merry upon' (Hutcheson, 1750: 12). In other words, if one can be moved to laughter by confirmation of one's superiority, then anytime one felt like laughing one need only look upon a snail.

The idea that most clearly represents a rejection of superiority theory is Hutcheson's belief that the risible emanated from a juxtaposition of incompatible contrasts. By the means of a discussion of great men on the toilet he explains that the ludicrous is generated by the combination of high and low in a single scene: 'the jest is increased by the dignity, gravity, or modesty of the person', he writes, 'which shows that it is this contrast, or opposition of ideas and dignity and meanness, which is the occasion of laughter' (Hutcheson, 1750: 21). In the image of the great man otherwise occupied, greatness and gravity collide with lowering bodily urgency. Henry Fielding makes a similar point in his preface to the novel *Joseph Andrews* (1742). The unfortunate, deformed, or disproportionate are not humorous in themselves, he writes, but may become so if they adopt an affectation:

Surely he hath a very ill-framed Mind, who can look on Ugliness, Infirmity, or Poverty, as ridiculous in themselves: nor do I believe any Man
living who meets a dirty Fellow riding through the Streets in a Cart, is
struck with an Idea of the Ridiculous from it; but if he should see the same
Figure descend from his Coach and Six, or bolt from his Chair with
his Hat under his Arm, he would then begin to laugh, and with justice.

(Fielding, 1980: 7)

Pursuing the clash of incompatible ideas, James Beattie (1735–
1803), professor of Moral Philosophy and Logic at the University
of Aberdeen, writes in his essay 'On Laughter and Ludicrous
Composition':

Laughter arises from the view of two or more inconsistent, unsuitable,
or incongruous parts or circumstances, considered as united in one
complex object or assemblage, or as acquiring a sort of mutual relation
from the peculiar manner in which the mind takes notice of them.

(Beattie, 1776: 347)

While Beattie was not the first to use the words 'incongruous' or
'incongruity' in relation to humour (that honour remains to Mark
Akenside's *Pleasures of Imagination* [1744]), his definition of
laughter's trigger is entirely representative of the shift in dominance from superiority to incongruity theories in the eighteenth
century, and is the key to humour upheld by philosophers such as
Kant and Schopenhauer. The new focus on incongruity appears to
be historically appropriate to the eighteenth century where alea-
tory wit and linguistic invention were culturally privileged skills.
Addison, who while disapproving of laughter celebrated wit,
gives an account of the latter as follows:

That every resemblance of Ideas is not that which we call Wit, unless it
be such an one that gives *Delight* and *Surprize* to the Reader: These two
Properties seem essential to Wit, more particularly the last of them.
In order therefore that the Resemblance in the Ideas be Wit, it is
necessary that the Ideas should not lie too near one another in the
Nature of things; for where the Likeness is obvious, it gives no Surprize.

(Addison and Steele, 1979, vol. 1: 189)

What is apparent in this description is the similarity between Addison's definition and Hutcheson's and Beattie's discussions of laughter's triggers. Wit, according to Addison, resides in the inventive drawing together of apparently distant ideas for the amusement and intellectual thrill of the listener. Again, we see the importance of crossing ideational boundaries and the bringing of something into a taxonomy to which it is not considered to belong. As incongruity plays with taxonomies and hierarchies it suggests that these hierarchies are permeable and fluid rather than rigid and permanent. The collision or juxtaposition of the great with the low, or the humble adopting the airs of the elite, take their humour from a displacement of order that simultaneously acknowledges order and reveals its absurdity. Pleasure in wit also does this, as it recognises the role of chance in the production of meaning, and the ability of language to make meanings outside the realm of practical sense. However, critics of incongruity theory point out that it over-privileges structural aspects in the production of laughter as if the formula of juxtaposition alone were the trigger. As John Lippitt writes, 'even if, in any given example of humour, it is possible to identify an element of incongruity, it is not necessarily this incongruity itself which is the predominant reason for amusement. To put all the emphasis on a factor such as incongruity is to stress form or structure at the expense of content' (Lippitt, 1992: 200). Presumably, then, there has to be a reason why some things are funny and others are not, which leads us on to explanations rooted in culture and the unconscious.

RELIEF THEORY: FREUD AND SPENCER

The successor to incongruity theory was in some respects a continued and internalised version of it. Nineteenth- and early-twentieth-century considerations of laughter, particularly those of Herbert Spencer and Sigmund Freud, saw the triggers of laughter not so much as a recognition of incongruity within scenarios or linguistic formulae, but as a symptom of division and struggle within the self, recognition, as it were, of incongruous selfhood. This is known as 'release' or 'relief' theory. The impact of Freud's 'discovery' of the unconscious is clearly of great relevance to an understanding of the process that recognises conflicted impulses within subjectivity as a cause of laughter. From this principle, Freud theorised that humour works because it appeals to unconscious thoughts that remain largely hidden in the majority of our social interactions. This would explain the concept of a relative and individuated 'sense of humour' not shared by all, as individual psyches are wont to find different topics or ideas humorously appealing based on the different experiences that have helped to shape them.

The mechanics of Freud's theory of laughter are not entirely his, but rather based in part on the work of Herbert Spencer (1820–1903), the father of evolutionary philosophy. Spencer attributed laughter to a physiological cause, proposing the flow of 'nerve force', internal energy that is generated by cerebral activity and which circulates in the body until it is discharged by muscular action, such as conversation, or respiration. On occasion, nervous energy will be displaced from its proper outlet and redirect itself in short bursts of activity such as heavy breathing, jumping up and down, or rubbing one's hands with glee. Laughter, like the release of pressure from a steam valve, is a manifestation of the internal redirection of nervous energy. This was not an entirely new idea. The anonymous author of *An Essay on Laughter* (1769) describes the physiological effect as a *'laughter-struggle'* (Anon., 1769: 75), an internal battle between the mind and the muscles. Spencer holds that 'laughter naturally results when consciousness is unawares transferred from great things to small', when an anticipated sequence of thoughts is bathetically interrupted with the result that the accumulated nervous energy of one emotion now needs to be re-channelled and provided with an alternative outlet (Spencer, 1860: 400). Spencer imagines internal channels along which nervous energy flows. The grander or more serious the emotion, the more the channels dilate. If a sequence of ideas were to then take a ludicrous turn, the channels become restricted and the surplus of energy expends itself: 'the excess must therefore discharge itself in some other direction; and ... there results an efflux through the motor nerves to various classes of the muscles, producing the half convulsive actions we call laughter' (Spencer, 1860: 400). Laughter, then, is always the product of a lowering of anticipated ideas, although these can have healthful effects: 'The heart and stomach must come in for a fair share of discharge'. He adds '... there seems to be a good physiological basis for the popular notion that laughter facilitates the digestion' (Spencer, 1860: 401).

While Spencer's hydraulic explanation of laughter may not have aged well, it is worth considering for the influence it has exerted on Freud's analysis of the question in his 1905 study, *Jokes and Their Relation to the Unconscious*. Freud's theory is in general agreement with Spencer's model of laughter as re-directed internal energy, although he modifies it beyond a biological explanation and explains the need for energetic redirection as the circumvention of internal prohibitions put in place by the superego. Jokes in Freud can be used as a means of making public statements about taboo topics: 'a purpose being satisfied whose satisfaction would otherwise not have taken place' (Freud, 2001: 117). Freud's discussion of laughter occurs within the context of laughter as a response to jokes only, and two types of joke in particular that he identifies as 'innocent' and 'tendentious'. The innocent joke is essentially a pun or word game and appeals because of its technique and formal qualities, its play on words or transposition of concepts, as in Freud's example: 'Not only did he not believe in ghosts; he wasn't even frightened of them' (Freud, 2001: 92). As for the tendentious joke, says Freud, 'there are only two purposes that it may serve, and these two can themselves be subsumed under a single heading. It is either a *hostile* joke (serving the purpose of aggression, satire, or defence), or an *obscene* joke (serving the purpose of exposure)' (Freud, 2001: 97). The need for these jokes is a response to social expectations, as the norms of etiquette usually prevent us from directly insulting others or broaching taboo subjects. By touching on these difficult topics, the joke does important work, as it alleviates the inhibition of the joker and addresses the taboo while also keeping it in place. Laughing is the audible signal that the energy required for 'cathexis', the accumulation of energy around an idea, has been lifted and can now be dispersed in a pleasurable fashion. The joker, says Freud,

> has saved his psychological expenditure ... We should say that his pleasure corresponds to this economy. Our insight into the

mechanism of laughter leads us rather to the introduction of the proscribed idea by means of an auditory perception, the cathectic energy used for the inhibition has now suddenly become superfluous and has been lifted, and is therefore now ready to be discharged by laughter.

(Freud, 2001: 148–149)

Laughter, then, is the smack of anti-social thoughts colliding with a censorious brick wall: 'in laughter', writes Freud, 'the conditions are present under which a sum of psychical energy which has hitherto been used for cathexis is allowed discharge' (Freud, 2001: 148). Like Spencer, Freud's concept of laughter fits into an internal economy, a functional system that retains the equilibrium of the subject by disposing of waste in a socially acceptable way, and so preserving mental health.

LAUGHTER AT THE LIMIT

Milan Kundera's novel, *The Book of Laughter and Forgetting* (1980), contains a scene in which two students wearing cardboard horns begin to giggle uncontrollably during a class discussion of Eugene Ionesco's play *Rhinoceros*. Their teacher joins in:

The three women danced and laughed, the cardboard noses jiggled, and the class looked at them in mute horror. But by now the three dancing women were unaware of the others, they were concentrating entirely on themselves and on their sensual pleasure. Suddenly Madame Raphael stamped her foot harder and rose a few centimetres above the floor and then, with the next step, was no longer touching the ground. She pulled her two companions after her, and in a moment all three were revolving above the floor and rising slowly in a spiral. When their hair touched the ceiling, it started little by little to open. They rose higher and higher through that opening, their cardboard noses were no longer visible, and now there were only three pairs of shoes passing through the gaping hole, but these too finally vanished, while from on high, the dumbfounded students heard the fading, radiant laughter of the three archangels.

(Kundera, 1996: 104)

Kundera's novel, set predominantly in communist Czechoslovakia, deals with personal relationships and asks if anything can remain private in an intrusive system. Weighed down by alienation and misunderstandings, laughter is the sound that accompanies freedom, a fantasy of weightlessness and unobstructed movement. This is laughter as an expression of the sublime: joyful, angelic, transcendent, desperate, exhausted, overwhelmed, substituting for speech when there is nothing left to be said. This moment evokes the laughter of Sarah in the Bible, a laughter of wonder and insight beyond words, which is in turn representative of the ways in which many writers have conceived of laughter in the late twentieth and early twenty-first centuries. This is not to say that these theories have adopted Kundera's depiction of a radiant laughter that transports one to a paradise far from the reach of oppressive law, but it has configured laughter as a trope that expresses a sense of the beyond, of something outside language and cognition as it is organised in the quotidian.

Following a theme established in the work of Friedrich Nietzsche, what Simon Critchley has called 'the golden laughter of tragic affirmation' (Critchley, 2002: 105), poststructuralist laughter acts like a sonar, reaching out and signalling the limit of everything that can be said and understood. This laughter is not an expression of pleasure, superiority, or release; nor is it nonsense, the worthless opposite of intelligibility. Rather, laughter acts as a powerful recognition of the end of understanding in language and of the subject's failure to grasp it. Georges Bataille has written of laughter as 'that place where nothing counts anymore – neither the "object", nor the "subject"' (quoted in Borch-Jacobsen, 1987: 741). Following Bataille closely, Mikkel Borch-Jacobsen speaks of laughter as the end of identity and absolute finitude: 'it is the *presentation*, necessarily pathetic and miniscule, of NOTHING ... NOTHING is the impossible, the impossible to present, and thus its presentation can be nothing other than a comedy, risible and ridiculous' (Borch-Jacobsen, 1987: 756). While not entirely unlike Bakhtin's soaring laughter of liberation, this formulation of laughter neither rejuvenates nor serves as a palliative against oppressive seriousness. This is not laughter as a release from oppression, but laughter that encounters the limits of all conceptual formulae and returns to acknowledge the finitude of its own existence. Critchley offers this useful explanation:

> Laughter is an acknowledgement of finitude, precisely not a manic affirmation of finitude in the solitary, neurotic laughter of the mountain tops (all too present in imitators of Nietzsche, although administered with liberal doses of irony by Nietzsche himself), but as an affirmation that finitude cannot be affirmed because it cannot be grasped ... Laughter returns us to that limited condition of our finitude, the shabby and degenerating state of our upper and lower bodily strata, and it is here that the comic allows the windows to fly open onto our tragic condition.
>
> (Critchley, 1997: 159)

What appears to be the intangible, impermanent, extra-linguistic nature of laughter has appealed to some writers on deconstruction. The self-reflexive structure of deconstructive readings, their interest in 'play', effective repetitions, aporia (the expression of doubt), and linguistic and etymological puns have been understood as an innovative and necessary incorporation of a type of laughter in work that engages with the foundational discourses of philosophy, discourses from which laughter has previously been excluded. Jean-Luc Nancy sees the utility of a concept of laughter to deconstruction:

> Laughter is neither a presence nor an absence, it is the giving of a presence in its own disappearance. Not given, but giving, and thus suspended on the edge of its own presentation ... laughter is the giving of an infinite variety of possible faces and meanings. It is, in a word, the repetition of this offer.
>
> (Nancy, 1987: 729)

Understood this way, laughter is a form of the Derridean concept of *différance*, a way of thinking of language as a structure of infinite referral and deferral, in which there are no fully meaningful terms, only traces of them. In a piece that specifically focuses on the work of French philosopher of language Jacques Derrida (1930–2004), Nancy continues the thematisation of laughter as a trope that can be used to interrogate the problem of the absent or

deferred presence of full meaning that is a key theme in deconstructive work. Deconstruction argues that the centre or core of
meaning, the plentiful 'originary' truth that validates all thought
and understanding, whether it be envisaged as a theological or
philosophical concept, can never be revealed through language
but only ever be alluded to and infinitely deferred. For Nancy,
this absent centre can be reconceived as a laugh. 'The origin is
laughing', he writes. 'There is a transcendental laugh':

> What is a transcendental laugh? It is not the obverse of the sign or
> value accorded to serious matters, which thinking, necessarily,
> reclaims. It is knowledge of a condition of possibility which gives noth-
> ing to know. There is nothing comic about it: it is neither nonsense nor
> irony. This laugh does not laugh *at* anything. It laughs at nothing, for
> nothing. It signifies nothing, without ever being absurd. It laughs at
> being the peal of its laughter, we might say. Which is not to say that it
> is unserious or that it is painless. It is beyond all opposition of
> serious and non-serious, of pain and pleasure. Or rather, it is at the
> juncture of these oppositions, at the limit of which they share and
> which itself is only the limit of each one of these terms, the limit of
> their signification.
>
> (Nancy, 1992: 41)

Laughter comes to symbolise the absent origin that has no full
significance of its own, but which is constitutive of conceptual
attempts to positively structure systems of meaning. What is note-
worthy in this formulation is the extraction of the comic from its
understanding of laughter. Instead of thinking of laughter as the
opposite of the serious, Nancy asks it to represent a fundamental
contradiction that affronts modes of understanding grounded in
reason. As such, laughter is a kind of metaphysical contradiction
encountered at the boundary of reason.

The French feminist critic Hélène Cixous offers us a similar
image of laughter in her famous essay 'The Laugh of the Medusa',
a title that evokes an idea of mythical female monstrosity and
'outsidedness', which deals with the acts of definition that
constitute the formulation of gender distinctions in language.
Cixous calls for a redefinition of gender distinctions through a

revolution in signification, a re-deployment of language capable of countering the domination of language by patriarchy, a language that can 'break up the "truth" with laughter' (Cixous, 1976: 888). The laugh of the Medusa is the revolutionary call of the woman outside patriarchal definitions; this laughter rejects phallocentric identification, and is forging a new language:

> Too bad for them if they fall apart upon discovering that women aren't men, or that the mother doesn't have one. But isn't this fear convenient for them? Wouldn't the worst be, isn't the worst, in truth, that women aren't castrated, that they only have to stop listening to the Sirens (for the Sirens were men) for history to change its meaning? You only have to look at the Medusa straight on to see her. And she's not deadly. She's beautiful, and she's laughing.
>
> (Cixous, 1976: 885)

As Frances Gray has written, 'for Cixous, the laughter of the Medusa destroys all hierarchies by rendering nonsensical the aggression between father and son that is their basis; in destroying hierarchy it will remove all difference between margin and centre. Women will not be outsiders, because the concept of the "outside" or "inside" will become meaningless' (Gray, 1994: 37). This is laughter as a radical commentary that refuses to work inside the significatory system established by the oppressor, busy about the work of dismantling patriarchal structures of knowledge.

The Marxist critics Theodor Adorno and Max Horkheimer, writing in 1944, held a radically different view of the uses of laughter. For them, 'Fun is a medicinal bath' (Adorno and Horkheimer, 2001: 140). While the poststructuralist theory of Cixous and Derrida might treat laughter as a trope of some allegorical significance, Adorno and Horkheimer see it only as an empty reminder of a previously satisfying experience. The 'culture industry', they argue, referring to mainstream art and media under capitalism, manipulates laughter and uses it as a placebo which it feeds to the population of the 'false society' through television and film in order to divert them from reflecting on their inauthentic existence. The mass-market debasement of art reduces content to prudish titillation, and, having dispensed with complex aesthetic challenges, mass-market culture resorts to humour as a means of obscuring the vacuity it peddles at the expense of critical thought. The laughter of the culture industry is therefore a kind of infantilised false consciousness, attached to images in films that allude to the gratification of desires, such as kissing or the possibility of sexual intercourse. By framing these scenes as vicarious thrills, the culture industry substitutes genuine pleasure and experience for a humorous alternative so that 'jovial denial takes the place of the pain found in ecstasy and in asceticism' (Adorno and Horkheimer, 2001: 141). Laughter is offered instead of satisfaction; it is a means of rendering all desires and ambition beyond those provided by capitalism as ludicrous and stupid propositions, as 'The supreme law is that they shall not satisfy their desires at any price; they must laugh and be content with laughter' (Adorno and Horkheimer, 2001: 141). In conclusion we may say that theoretical treatments of laughter have been attracted to its intangibility and association with a level of somatic existence beyond that mediated by language, an existence that therefore lends laughter the air of an extra-linguistic recognition of inauthenticity.

CONCLUSION

In the early 1820s, a patient called on the London surgeon John Abertheny seeking a cure for his depression. Having examined the man, Abertheny prescribed no medication, but merely 'relaxation and amusement':

> 'But where shall I find what you require?' said the patient.
>
> 'In genial companionship,' was the reply; 'perhaps sometimes at the theatre;– go and see Grimaldi.'
>
> 'Alas!' replied the patient, 'that is of no avail to me; I am Grimaldi.'
>
> (Goodwin, 1887: 14)

Joseph Grimaldi was a superstar of the Regency theatre, a clown who raised the status of the pantomime from a humble afterthought to the centrepiece of the theatrical calendar. His clowning was legendary, and he was said to be so funny that he once made a sailor laugh so hard that it cured him of being deaf and dumb. Yet however amusing Grimaldi was thought to be onstage, it was believed that his private life was wracked with unhappiness and melancholy. As such, Grimaldi has become the blueprint for a now-familiar figure, the concept of the weeping clown, the comedian who uses laughter to conceal their pain.

How have we arrived at this idea that laughter is the close cousin of pain, and that our comedy is as expressive of anguish as it is of joy? Such thoughts are at work behind the most disquieting double act of twentieth-century drama, the bleak couple of Vladimir and Estragon, the tragic clowns of Samuel Beckett's *Waiting for Godot*. Nonsense and quips are the only forms of language that allow them to communicate truly the full and fixed banality of their lives. A traditional belief of the Hopi Indians of North East Arizona sees clowning as fundamental to identity, as they hold that they are all descended from an original clown youth and clown maiden. For them 'Clowning symbolizes the sacredness of humanity in the strict sense – that there is something sacred in being a finite and mortal being separated from god' (Loftin, 1991: 112). By embracing the identity of their first parents, the Hopi acknowledge the distance between their daily lives and their idea of spiritual perfection, finding religious value in the knowledge that they are flawed. A similar idea motivates Dante's definition of his *Commedia* as a comedy.

These anecdotes confirm the great suspicion that incidences of comedy and humour always harbour a deeper, serious impulse, whether they be manifestations of psychological darkness, or a spiritual recognition of human imperfection. When we consider the ways in which comedy is used for hostile and aggressive purposes, or as a means of deriding others and labelling their behaviour unacceptable, perhaps these impulses are not so hidden. From Donatus to George Meredith, comedy is employed as a form of castigation, a means of imposing normative values on those who deviate from agreed standards of citizenship within communities whose membership is well defined. Traditional finales like the marriage are indicative of the conservative and conformist roots of much comedy, reinforcing the homogeneity of the community after a period of uncertainty. Instances of comedy that openly deride ethnic, gender, or physical attributes are acts of aggression that indicate a fear of difference and a desire to present oneself as more roundly human than those in the target group. While Hobbes's superiority theory of laughter has been largely discarded, his view that it amounts to 'pusillanimity', or cowardice, represents the first ethics of humour to couple the urge to laugh with a responsibility to think through laughter's moral implications. In this we can see that comedy is a troubled form, attending to social anxieties and imposing a fictional logic on ill-fitting or contested world views. How else might we explain the constant worrying or fetishising of questions of identity and place, and aspects of existence like the fragility of the body, the obsession with reproduction and scatology, and continual tests of the properties of the outside world?

We must also emphasise the fact that comedy is contradictory and it frequently works in a way that is apparently antithetical to the maintenance of the status quo. Through joking and scenarios, or states of being such as folly or tricksterism, comedy opens up the possibility of an additional dimension of understanding, one in which language or perception are not rational meaning-oriented systems but have unpredictable applications. Take the joke, '"Doctor, doctor, I feel like a bridge". "What's come over you?" "Two trucks and a motorbike".' In this admittedly weak example, the punch-line explores the possibility of retrospectively reading the set-up against the grain of conventional sense, most obviously in the question 'What's come over you?', which is both a proverbial enquiry about one's health, and, we discover, a literal request to ascertain the volume of traffic that has passed over the patient. While the humorous effect of this joke is negligible, it shows for us the fact that jokes are often a formally structured means of revealing the susceptibility of language to alternative interpretations, the importance of contextual referents in meaning, and the co-existence of viable interpretations. Medieval concepts of folly understood this and fashioned from it a theological truth, that humanity was perpetually looking at the world with doubled vision and a refined understanding of its own simplicity. From this perspective, traditional endings like marriages are a practical way of restoring reason and closing off nonsense, acting as a barrier between the field of potentially radical interpretive alternatives that comedy opens up, and the rest of the world that needs to make sense if it is to carry on working.

Finally, we return to the difficult question of genre. Comedy's lowly status as an object of study is a product of its populism, its association with the lower bodily stratum, and its problematic resistance to generic definition. While the generic label continues to represent a meaningful and practicable brand, priming us for certain kinds of action and alerting us to a different type of discourse, the deracinated nature of comic effect and the permeability of generic boundaries mean that we can no longer be satisfied by the Aristotelian concepts of form that ground most understandings of what comedy is. Traditional generic definitions belonged to the theatre, and as alternative media evolved over the course of the twentieth century, different types of comedy emerged to mingle with other modes of narrative. Reading comedy, then, is not a matter of reading form, but of reading tone. As such, it cannot be neatly separated out from all that it touches, and neither should it be.

GLOSSARY

Bathos a descent from an elevated discourse to a ludicrous one, a sense of deflation.

Burlesque in the British theatrical tradition, a satirical play that parodies contemporary or well-known dramas, beginning in the Restoration period with the Duke of Buckingham's play *The Rehearsal* (1671), lampooning the heroic drama of Dryden. Burlesque comedies were at the height of their popularity in the Victorian period, and some burlesque revues ran into the twentieth century. In American theatrical parlance, a burlesque is a sex-themed comedy and variety revue with its origins in the second half of the nineteenth century, often featuring striptease.

Camp Susan Sontag defines camp as a 'way of seeing the world as an aesthetic phenomenon ... not in terms of beauty but in terms of the degree of artifice, of stylization' (Sontag, 1982: 106). Camp refers to a certain kitsch or trashy aesthetic, an elevation of elements of pop culture to a status beyond that deserved by its content according to traditional categories of taste.

Carnival the period of feasting immediately prior to Lent, but for Mikhail Bakhtin and others, a conceptual category that describes the potential of popular literary and festive forms to disrupt the dominant order, express dissent, and provide a framework for the celebration of unsanctioned or 'unofficial' modes of being. 'Carnivalesque' refers to texts, events, or practices that epitomise the spirit of Carnival, often associated with the gratification of bodily desires, but possessing the potential to be read as an expression of the voice of the plebeian class.

City comedy a popular form of drama in the Jacobean and Caroline theatre and associated with playwrights such as Ben Jonson, Thomas Middleton, John Marston, and Philip Massinger. City comedy is based on the principles of Roman New Comedy, but brings its satiric eye to bear on the financial dealings and sexual mores of a newly emergent mercantile class, active in the burgeoning city of London in the first half of the seventeenth century.

Commedia dell'arte a form of improvised comedy first recorded in Italy in 1545, and flourishing from the sixteenth to the early eighteenth centuries.

Commedia dell'arte is notable for its use of masks, each one representing the distended features of a familiar stock character. These stock characters are then placed in stock scenarios and expected to respond accordingly, the actors improvising the specific action and dialogue at the moment of performance.

Commedia erudita 'erudite', or learned comedy, counterpart to *commedia dell'arte*, and written for the Humanist courts of Italian Renaissance princes. Most plays were closely based on the Roman New Comedy of Plautus and Terence and intended for educated audiences.

Deconstruction a school of thought associated with the French philosopher Jacques Derrida. Deconstruction's principal interest lies in unravelling the 'metaphysics of presence' that are said to authorise key philosophical ideas and dominant discourses. Deconstructive analysis engages in a detailed reading of the ways in which concepts are structured through language, an unstable and volatile medium, examining the extent to which the transcendental claims of such ideas are undermined by their existence within the medium.

Drag most commonly a form of female impersonation, although drag can of course be female to male. Drag differs from the transvestism of the Shakespearean stage inasmuch as the drag act is not involved in a narrative that requires cross-dressing, and, even though no direct reference is made to the actual gender of the performer, the audience derives amusement from their knowledge that the woman is, in fact, a man.

Farce a form of comedy that relies principally on physical humour, horseplay, and awkward social situations to generate laughter. The origins of farce can be traced back as far as the ancient Roman *fabula*, the generic name for a variety of comic entertainments, but was particularly popular in medieval France. In the nineteenth century, one-act farces often accompanied the performance of five-act tragedies, while in modern usage, the term is generally applied to comedies that feature a series of contorted and overlapping intrigues, such as a series of adulterous couples in close quarters and in imminent danger of being found out.

Historicism a critical practice that claims that one only understands the nature of a literary or other creative work fully when it is returned to the original context of its production. Historicist readings of comedy, therefore, seek to relate comic forms to the social, cultural, and political movements of their day in an effort to show the investment and interrelatedness of one beside the other.

Humours the humours – blood, phlegm, black bile, and choler – were four fluids believed to be essential to human health. The humoral system was developed by Galen in the first century AD, and remained influential in medicine through the medieval and Renaissance periods. The dominance of one fluid over another was believed to affect the personality, and so the comedy of the humours, associated largely with the work of Ben Jonson, used the humoral system as a basis for characterisation.

Materialism a belief that ideas and societies develop as a result of their material conditions and environments, in opposition to idealism, which holds that ideas or concepts come first and are acted upon to develop material conditions. Materialism is especially interested in class and economic relationships as a determining factor in human interaction. This term is associated with Marxist and other forms of socialist thinking.

Meta-narrative any narrative that claims to be able to explain all aspects of existence within its own terms, Christianity for example.

Modernism a literary and artistic movement of the first half of the twentieth century that experimented with various modes of aesthetic representation, rejecting the figural or realist genres of the nineteenth century.

New Comedy the term applied to the comedy of the Greek dramatist Menander (c.342–c.291 BC), and used to differentiate his work from that of his predecessor Aristophanes (see 'Old Comedy'). New Comedy uses stock characters and situations and is usually set around the affairs and intrigues of a middle-class household. Plots revolve around intrigues of sex and money and conclude with the restoration of harmonious relationships. The Roman dramatists Plautus (c.254–184 BC) and Terence (c.190 or 180–159 BC) used Greek prototypes in the composition of their own New Comedy, and New Comedy forms inspired the English city comedies of the seventeenth century.

New Historicism like 'historicism', a critical school that believes in the reconstruction of context as an essential aspect of understanding literary texts. The 'new' in 'New Historicism' comes from its attempts to problematise the idea of history, pointing out that textual accounts of the historical past are themselves texts and therefore susceptible to the same principles of inclusion and exclusion, elision and omission as any other form and not necessarily imbued with any inherent authority. New Historicism came into being largely through the work of American literary critics in the 1980s.

Old Comedy represented solely by the works of Greek playwright Aristophanes (c.448–380 BC), Old Comedy represents the first recognisably comic narrative in Western literature. Characterised by loose plotting, fantastic situations, and scatological and slanderous humour, Old Comedy is thought to be derived in part from forms of ancient worship, especially in honour of the god Dionysus.

Pantomime used in the seventeenth century to describe a story told in dance, the British pantomime developed as an offshoot of Harlequin plays, themselves a variant of *commedia dell'arte* performances. Pantomime was developed in the eighteenth and nineteenth centuries using classic fairy-tale plots as a loose framework for a broader range of elements including songs, music hall routines, trick scenery, audience participation, acrobatics, slapstick, costume changes, and romance. A further convention of pantomime is its use of young women in the lead male role (the 'principal boy') and older men playing the parts of mature women, such as Cinderella's ugly sisters (known as 'pantomime dames'). Pantomime is traditionally associated with Christmas and is still a popular part of the British Christmas season.

Postmodernism a controversial and much-debated term, now largely understood to refer to creative or critical practices that reject totalising meta-narratives and celebrate complexity, self-reflexivity, fragmentation, doubt, ambiguity, relativism, and pastiche. The term received its earliest use in relation to architecture, particularly architectural styles that eschewed the monumentalist and technocratic aesthetics of Modernism, appearing instead to favour process over product and the witty quotation and incorporation of numerous architectural forms rather than subordination to one monolithic concept of the new. Postmodernist effects in literature and art generally draw attention to the concepts of form and artifice, rather than hiding them, and reject notions of transparency or intentionality in interpretation. Postmodernism has been viewed as many things, including a reaction against the idea of history as 'progress', an idea it credits in part with the development of ideologies that have led to fascism and Stalinism.

Poststructuralism a broad umbrella term that encompasses the work of a variety of thinkers and theorists, many of whom rose to prominence as a result of the student unrest of Paris in 1968. Poststructuralism is most readily associated with the work of Roland Barthes, Michel Foucault, Julia Kristeva, Jacques Lacan, Jacques Derrida, and others of that era, and represents a furthering of the debates begun by structuralist thinkers (hence the 'post'), who had posited the idea that communication operates according to a structurally organised system of signs. The poststructuralist generation retained this interest in the centrality of language to psychological and social organisation, but dispensed with the systematic approach of structuralism, pursuing its investigations in a number of different areas, including literature, politics, and psychoanalysis.

Queer originally a pejorative slur aimed at homosexuals, 'queer' has been appropriated by gender theorists and many in the lesbian, gay, bisexual, and transgender communities as a means of describing the continuum of human sexuality and the fluid permutations that constitute it beyond the confines of heterosexual normativity.

Satire a literary form that aims to criticise or censure people and ideas through the use of humour. Satire can take many forms but is generally measured according to its degree of viciousness.

Slapstick physical humour associated with the early-twentieth-century silent-film era and performers such as Charlie Chaplin, Buster Keaton, and Harold Lloyd, but still employed in much contemporary comedy. Slapstick involves falls, blows, mishaps, and accidents and demands considerable skill from its performers.

Travesty while a 'travesty' can refer to something that has been made ludicrous, it also means to alter the dress or appearance of a person, and can also refer to cross-dressing. The travesty of dress is a common theme in comedy.

BIBLIOGRAPHY

Addison, Joseph, and Steele, Sir Richard (1979), *The Spectator*, ed. Gregory Smith, 4 vols, London: Dent.

Adorno, Theodor (1996), 'Chaplin Times Two', trans. John MacKay, *Yale Journal of Criticism*, 9.1: 57–61.

Adorno, Theodor, and Horkheimer, Max (2001), *Dialectic of Enlightenment*, trans. John Cumming, New York: Continuum.

Allen, Woody (dir.) (1977), *Annie Hall*, starring Woody Allen, Diane Keaton: MGM Studios.

Almond, Steve (2012), 'The Jokes On You: Presenting *The Daily Show* and *The Colbert Report*', *The Baffler*, 20: 30–39.

Andrews, Maggie (1998), 'Butterflies and Caustic Asides: Housewives, Comedy and the Feminist Movement', in *Because I Tell a Joke or Two: Comedy, Politics and Social Difference*, ed. Stephen Wagg, London and New York: Routledge, pp.50–64.

Anon. (1769), *An Essay on Laughter, Wherein are Displayed its Natural and Moral Causes, With the Arts of Exciting It*, London.

Apte, Mahadev L. (1985), *Humor and Laughter: An Anthropological Approach*, Ithaca and London: Cornell University Press.

Aristophanes (1973), *Lysistrata, The Acharnians, The Clouds*, trans. Alan H. Somerstein, Harmondsworth: Penguin.

Aristotle (1996), *Poetics*, trans. Malcolm Heath, Harmondsworth: Penguin.

Austen, Jane (1987), *Emma*, ed. Ronald Blythe, Harmondsworth: Penguin.

Babington, Bruce, and Evans, Peter William (1989), *Affairs to Remember: The Hollywood Comedy of the Sexes*, Manchester and New York: Manchester University Press.

Bakhtin, Mikhail (1968), *Rabelais and His World*, trans. Helene Iswolsky, Cambridge, MA: MIT Press.

——(1984), *Rabelais and His World*, trans. Helene Iswolsky, Cambridge, MA: MIT Press.

Baldick, Chris (1987), *The Social Mission of English Criticism, 1848–1932*, Oxford: Clarendon.

——(1996), *Criticism and Literary Theory, 1890–Present*, London and New York: Longman.

Banks, Morwenna, and Swift, Amanda (1987), *Joke's On Us: Women in Comedy from Music Hall to the Present Day*, London: HarperCollins.

Banta, Martha (2003), *Barbaric Intercourse: Caricature and the Culture of Conduct, 1841–1936*, Chicago and London: University of Chicago Press.

Barber, C.L. (1963), *Shakespeare's Festive Comedy: A Study of Dramatic Form and its Relation to Social Custom*, Cleveland and New York: Meridian.

Barr, Roseanne (2011), 'And I Should Know', *New York Magazine*. Web. 24 June 2013.

Barreca, Regina (1991), *They Used to Call Me Snow White, But I Drifted: Women's Strategic Use of Humor*, New York: Viking.

Barton, Anne (1985), 'Falstaff and the Comic Community', in *'Shakespeare's Rough Magic': Renaissance Essays in Honor of C.L.Barber*, ed. Peter Erickson and Coppélia Kahn, Newark: University of Delaware Press, pp.131–148.

Baudelaire, Charles (1992), 'Of the Essence of Laughter, and Generally of the Comic in the Plastic Arts', in *Selected Writings on Art and Literature*, trans. P.E. Charvet, Harmondsworth: Penguin, pp.140–161.

Beattie, James (1776), 'On Laughter and Ludicrous Composition', in *Essays*, Edinburgh, pp.319–486.

Ben-Ghiat, Ruth (2001), 'The Secret Histories of Roberto Benigni's *Life is Beautiful*', *Yale Journal of Criticism*, 14.1: 253–266.

Berger, Peter L. (1997), *Redeeming Laughter: The Comic Dimension of Human Experience*, New York and Berlin: Walter de Gruyter.

Bergson, Henri (1980), 'Laughter: An Essay on the Meaning of the Comic', in *Comedy*, ed. Wylie Sypher, Baltimore and London: Johns Hopkins University Press, pp.59–190.

Black, Lewis (2003), *Rules of Enragement*, Comedy Central Records. Audio.

Bociurkiw, Marusya (2005), 'It's Not About the Sex: Racialization and Queerness in *Ellen* and *The Ellen Degeneres Show*', *Canadian Woman Studies* (Winter/Spring): 176–181.

Borch-Jacobsen, Mikkel (1987), 'The Laughter of Being', *MLN*, 102.4 (September): 737–760.

Borenstein, Eliot (2008), 'Our Borats, Our Selves: Yokels and Cosmopolitans on the Global Stage', *Slavic Review*, 67.1 (Spring): 1–7.

Boskin, Joseph (1997), *Rebellious Laughter: People's Humor in American Culture*, Syracuse: Syracuse University Press.

Bracewell, Michael (1998), *England is Mine: Pop Life in Albion from Wilde to Goldie*, London: Flamingo.

Bradley, A. C. (1929), 'Coriolanus', in *Miscellany*, London: Macmillan, pp.73–104.

Bristol, Michael (1985), *Carnival and Theater: Plebeian Culture and the Structure of Authority in Renaissance England*, New York: Methuen.

Bruns, John (2009), *Loopholes: Reading Comically*, Brunswick, NJ: Transaction.

Bruzzi, Stella (1997), *Undressing Cinema: Clothing and Identity in the Movies*, London and New York: Routledge.

Burney, Frances (1998), *Evelina, Or the History of A Young Lady's Entrance into the World*, ed. Stewart J. Cooke, New York and London: Norton.

Burns, Edward (1987), *Restoration Comedy: Crises of Desire and Identity*, Basingstoke: Macmillan.

Butler, Judith (1993), *Bodies that Matter: On the Discursive Limits of 'Sex'*, London and New York: Routledge.

——(2005), 'Gender is Burning: Questions of Appropriation and Subversion', in *Theory in Contemporary Art Since 1985*, ed. Zoya Kokur and Simon Leung, Malden: Blackwell, pp.166–181.

Carlson, Susan (1991), *Women and Comedy: Rewriting the British Theatrical Tradition*, Ann Arbor: University of Michigan Press.

Carpio, Glenda (2008), *Laughing Fit to Kill: Black Humor in the Fictions of Slavery*, Oxford: Oxford University Press.

Castiglione, Baldesar (1986), *The Book of the Courtier*, trans. George Bull, Harmondsworth: Penguin.

Cavell, Stanley (1979), *The World Viewed: Reflections on the Ontology of Film*, Cambridge, MA and London: Harvard University Press.

Chambers, Deborah (2005), 'Comedies of Sexual Morality and Female Singlehood', in *Beyond a Joke: The Limits of Humour*, ed. Sharon Lockyer and Michael Pickering, Basingstoke: Macmillan, pp.162–179.

Chapelle, Dave (2006), 'His First TV Interview: Why Dave Chapelle Walked Away from $50 Million', *The Oprah Winfrey Show*, ABC, Harpo Productions, Chicago. 3 February, television.

Chaplin, Charles (dir.) (1940), *The Great Dictator*, starring Charlie Chaplin, Paulette Goddard: Charles Chaplin Productions.

Chapman, Graham, Cleese, John, Gilliam, Terry, Idle, Eric, Jones, Terry, and Palin, Michael (1998), *Monty Python's Flying Circus: Just the Words*, 2 vols, London: Methuen.

Charney, Maurice (1978), *Comedy High and Low: An Introduction to the Experience of Comedy*, New York: Oxford University Press.

Cicero (1984), 'On the Orator's Use of Laughter', in D. J. Palmer (ed.) *Comedy: Developments in Criticism*, Basingstoke: Macmillan, pp.28–29.

Cixous, Hélène (1976), 'The Laugh of the Medusa', trans. Keith Cohen and Paula Cohen, *Signs*, 1.4 (Summer): 875–893.

Clare, Janet (1990), *'Art Made Tongue-Tied by Authority': Elizabethan and Jacobean Dramatic Censorship*, Manchester: Manchester University Press.

Clement of Alexandria (1983), *The Instructor*, in *The Ante-Nicene Fathers: Translations of the Writings of the Fathers Down to A.D.325*, ed. Alexander Roberts and James Donaldson, et al., 10 vols, Grand Rapids: Eerdmans, vol. 2, pp.207–296.

Coe, Jonathan (2013), 'Sinking Giggling Into the Sea', *The London Review of Books*, 35.14: 30–31.

Congreve, William (1973), *The Double Dealer*, London: Scolar.

——(1997a), 'Amendments of Mr. Collier's False and Imperfect Citations', in *Restoration and Eighteenth-Century Comedy*, ed. Scott McMillin, 2nd edn, New York and London: Norton, pp.513–516.

——(1997b), *The Way of the World*, in *Restoration and Eighteenth-Century Comedy*, ed. Scott McMillin, 2nd edn, New York and London: Norton, pp.251–319.

——(1997c), 'Concerning Humour in Comedy', in *Restoration and Eighteenth-Century Comedy*, ed. Scott McMillin, 2nd edn, New York and London: Norton, pp. 474–480.

Cook, William (1994), *Ha Bloody Ha: Comedians Talking*, London: Fourth Estate.

Cornford, Francis Macdonald (1914), *The Origins of Attic Comedy*, London: Edward Arnold.

Coward, Noël (1999), *Three Plays: Blithe Spirit, Hay Fever, Private Lives*, New York: Vintage.

Critchley, Simon (1997), *Very Little ... Almost Nothing: Death, Philosophy, Literature*, London: Routledge.

——(2002), *On Humour*, London: Routledge.

Dale, Alan (2000), *Comedy is a Man in Trouble: Slapstick in American Movies*, Minneapolis and London: University of Minnesota Press.

Daniell, David (1997), 'Shakespeare and the Traditions of Comedy', in *The Cambridge Companion to Shakespeare Studies*, ed. Stanley Wells, Cambridge: Cambridge University Press, pp.101–121.

Dante (1984), 'Epistle to Can Grande', in *Comedy: Developments in Criticism*, ed. D. J. Palmer, Basingstoke: Macmillan, p.31.

Davies, Christie (1982), 'Ethnic Jokes, Moral Values and Social Boundaries', *The British Journal of Sociology*, 33.2: 383–403.

De Man, Paul (1983), *Blindness and Insight: Essays in the Rhetoric of Contemporary Criticism*, 2nd edn, London: Routledge.

Dennis, Muriel White (1922), *The Training School of Popularity: The Letters of Jane Willard to Peggy MacIntryre, Her Adorée in High School*, New York: George H. Doren Co.

DiBattista, Maria (2001), *Fast-Talking Dames*, New Haven and London: Yale University Press.

Dickens, Charles (1968), *Memoirs of Joseph Grimaldi*, ed. Richard Findlater, London: MacGibbon and Kee.

Dollimore, Jonathan (1984), *Radical Tragedy: Religion, Ideology and Power in the Drama of Shakespeare and his Contemporaries*, Brighton: Harvester.

Double, Oliver (1997), *Stand-Up: On Being a Comedian*, London: Methuen.

Douglas, Mary (1975), *Implicit Meanings: Essays in Anthropology*, London: Routledge and Kegan Paul.

Dratch, Rachel (2012), *Girl Walks Into a Bar ... : Comedy Calamities, Dating Disasters, and a Midlife Miracle*, New York: Gotham.

Eco, Umberto (1983), *The Name of the Rose*, trans. William Weaver, San Diego et al.: Harcourt Brace Jovanovich.

Elias, Norbert (1978), *The Civilizing Process: The History of Manners*, trans. Edmund Jephcott, New York: Urizen.

Eltis, Sos (2008), 'Bringing Out the Acid: Noël Coward, Harold Pinter, Ivy Compton-Burnett and the Uses of Camp', *Modern Drama*, 51.2 (Summer): 211–233.

Erasmus (1993), *Praise of Folly*, trans. Betty Radice, rev. A. T. H. Levi, Harmondsworth: Penguin.

Ezrahi, Sidra DeKoven (2001), 'After Such Knowledge, What Laughter?', *Yale Journal of Criticism*, 14.1: 287–313.

Feig, Paul (dir.) (2011), *Bridesmaids*, starring Kristen Wiig, Maya Rudolph: Universal Pictures.

Ferris, Lesley (1990), *Acting Women: Images of Women in Theatre*, Basingstoke: Macmillan.

Fey, Tina (2011), *Bossypants*, New York: Little Brown.

Fielding, Helen (1996), *Bridget Jones' s Diary*, London: Picador.

Fielding, Henry (1980), *Joseph Andrews* and *Shamela*, ed. Douglas Brooks-Davis, Oxford: Oxford University Press.

Fielding, Steven (2012), 'Does the Political Studies Association Know the Meaning of Satire?', *Political Apparitions: Politics and the Representation of Politics*, 9 December. Web. 16 July 2013.

Fischer, Lucy (1991), 'Sometimes I Feel Like a Motherless Child: Comedy and Matricide', in *Comedy/Cinema/Theory*, ed. Andrew Horton, Berkeley et al.: University of California Press, pp.60–78.

Flanzbaum, Hilene (2001), '"But Wasn't it Terrific?": A Defense of Liking *Life is Beautiful*', *Yale Journal of Criticism*, 14.1: 273–286.

Fouts, Gregory, and Inch, Rebecca (2005), 'Homosexuality in TV Situation Comedies: Characters and Comments', *Journal of Homosexuality*, 49.1: 35–45.

Freud, Sigmund (2001), *Jokes and Their Relation to the Unconscious, The Standard Edition of the Complete Works of Sigmund Freud*, ed. James Strachey, 24 vols, London: Vintage, vol.8.

Friend, Tad (2002), 'What's So Funny? A Scientific Attempt to Discover Why We Laugh', *The New Yorker*, 11 November, pp.78–93.

Frye, Northrop (1953), 'Characterization in Shakespearian Comedy', *Shakespeare Quarterly*, 4.3: 271–277.

——(1990) *The Anatomy of Criticism: Four Essays*, Harmondsworth: Penguin.

Gaf, Fritz (1997), 'Cicero, Plautus and Roman Laughter', in *A Cultural History of Humour From Antiquity to the Present Day*, ed. Jan Bremmer and Herman Roodenburg, Cambridge: Polity, pp.29–39.

Garber, Majorie (1992), *Vested Interests: Cross-Dressing and Cultural Anxiety*, New York and London: Routledge.

Garner Jr, Stanton B. (1999), *Trevor Griffiths: Politics, Drama, History*, Ann Arbor: University of Michigan Press.

Gates Jr, Henry Louis (1988), *The Signifying Monkey: A Theory of African American Literary Criticism*, New York and Oxford: Oxford University Press.

Gilhus, Ingvild Saelid (1997), *Laughing Gods, Weeping Virgins: Laughter in the History of Religion*, London: Routledge.

Gill, Pat (1994), *Interpreting Ladies: Women, Wit, and Morality in the Restoration Comedy of Manners*, Athens: University of Georgia Press.

Gilman, Sander L. (2000), 'Is Life Beautiful? Can the Shoah be Funny? Some Thoughts on Recent and Older Films', *Critical Inquiry*, 26 (Winter): 279–308.

Goldman, Andrew (2011), 'There is No Escaping Whitney Cummings', *The New York Times Magazine*. Web. 10 July 2013.

Goodwin, Thomas (1887), *Sketches and Impressions: Musical, Theatrical, and Social, 1799–1885*, New York: Putnam.

Gray, Frances (1994), *Women and Laughter*, Basingstoke: Macmillan.

Greenblatt, Stephen (1985), 'Invisible Bullets: Renaissance Authority and Its Subversion, *Henry IV* and *Henry V*', in *Political Shakespeare: New Essays in*

Cultural Materialism, ed. Jonathan Dollimore and Alan Sinfield, Manchester: Manchester University Press, pp.18–47.

——(1988), *Shakespearean Negotiations: The Circulation of Social Energy in Renaissance England*, Berkeley: University of California Press.

Griffiths, Trevor (1979), *Comedians*, London: Faber and Faber.

Gurevich, Aaron (1997), 'Bakhtin and his Theory of Carnival', in *A Cultural History of Humour from Antiquity to the Present Day*, ed. Jan Bremmer and Herman Roodenburg, Cambridge: Polity, pp.54–60.

Hallam, Julia (2005), 'Remembering *Butterflies*: the Comic Art of Housework', in *Popular Television Drama: Critical Perspectives*, ed. Jonathan Bignell and Stephen Lacey, Manchester: Manchester University Press, pp.34–50.

Halliwell, Stephen (1984), 'Aristophanic Satire', in *English Satire and the Satiric Tradition*, ed. Claude Rawson, Oxford: Blackwell, pp.6–20.

Hanoosh, Michele (1992), *Baudelaire and Caricature: From the Comic to an Art of Modernity*, University Park: Pennsylvania State University Press.

Harris, Jonathan Gil (1998), 'Puck/Robin Goodfellow', in *Fools and Jesters in Literature, Art, and History: A Bio-Bibliographical Sourcebook*, ed. Viki K. Janik, Westport, CT and London: Greenwood, pp.351–362.

Hegel, G. W. F. (1998), *Hegel's Aesthetics*, trans. T. M. Knox, 2 vols, Oxford: Oxford University Press.

Herrick, Marvin T. (1950), *Comic Theory in the Sixteenth Century*, Urbana: University of Illinois Press.

Hitchens, Christopher (2007), 'Why Women Aren't Funny', *Vanity Fair*. Web. 25 June 2013.

Hobbes, Thomas (1840), *Human Nature*, in *The English Works of Thomas Hobbes*, ed. W. Molesworth, 11 vols, London: John Bohn, vol.4, pp.1–77.

——(1991), *Leviathan*, ed. Richard Tuck, Cambridge: Cambridge University Press.

Holpuch, Amanda (2012), 'Daniel Tosh Apologises for Rape Joke as Fellow Comedians Defend Topic', the *Guardian*, 11 July. Web. 21 February 2014.

Holt, Jim (2008), *Stop Me If You've Heard This: A History and Philosophy of Jokes*, New York: Norton.

Horace (1959), *The Satires and Epistles of Horace*, trans. Smith Palmer Bovie, Chicago: University of Chicago Press.

Horowitz, Susan (1997), *Queens of Comedy: Lucille Ball, Phyllis Diller, Carol Burnett, Joan Rivers and the New Generation of Funny Women*, Amsterdam: OPA.

Horton, Andrew (1991), 'Introduction', in *Comedy/Cinema/Theory*, ed. Andrew Horton, Berkeley et al.: University of California Press.

Howells, Richard (2006), '"Is It Because I Is Black": Race, Humour and the Polysemiology of Ali G.', *Historical Journal of Film, Radio and Television*, 26.2 (June): 155–177.

Howitt, Dennis and Owusu-Bempah, Kwame (2005), 'Race and Ethnicity in Popular Humour', in *Beyond a Joke: The Limits of Humour*, ed. Sharon Lockyer and Michael Pickering, Basingstoke: Palgrave, pp.45–62.

Hutcheson, Francis (1750), *Reflections Upon Laughter and Remarks Upon the Fable of the Bees*, Glasgow.

Hynes, William J., and Doty, William G., eds (1993), *Mythical Trickster Figures: Contours, Contexts and Criticisms*, Tuscaloosa and London: University of Alabama Press.

Hynes, William J., and Steele, Thomas J. (1993), 'Saint Peter: Apostle Transfigured into Trickster', in *Mythical Trickster Figures: Contours, Contexts and Criticisms*, ed. William J. Hynes and William G. Doty, Tuscaloosa and London: University of Alabama Press, pp.159–173.

Izzard, Eddie, with Quantick, David and Double, Steve (1998), *Dressed to Kill*, London: Virgin.

Jacobson, Howard (1997), *Seriously Funny: From the Ridiculous to the Sublime*, Harmondsworth: Viking.

Jagendorf, Zvi (1984), *The Happy End of Comedy: Jonson, Molière, and Shakespeare*, Newark: University of Delaware Press.

Janko, Richard (1984), *Aristotle on Comedy: Towards a Reconstruction of 'Poetics II'*, London: Duckworth.

Jardine, Lisa (1983), *Still Harping on Daughters: Women and Drama in the Age of Shakespeare*, New York: Columbia University Press.

Jayamanne, Laleen (2001), *Towards Cinema and Its Double: Cross-Cultural Mimesis*, Bloomington and Indianapolis: University of Indiana Press.

Jonson, Ben (1920), *Every Man Out of His Humour*, Oxford: Malone Society.

——(1979), *The Alchemist*, in *Ben Jonson's Plays and Masques*, ed. Robert M. Adams, New York and London: Norton.

Joubert, Laurent (1980), *Treatise on Laughter*, trans. Gregory David De Rocher, Tuscaloosa: University of Alabama Press.

Jung, C.G. (1959), 'On the Psychology of the Trickster Figure', in *The Archetypes and the Collective Unconscious: The Collected Works of C.G. Jung*, ed. Herbert Read, Michael Fordham and Gerhard Adler, 19 vols, vol. 9, pt 1, pp.255–272.

Juvenal (1958), *The Satires of Juvenal*, trans. Rolfe Humphries, Bloomington and London: Indiana University Press.

Kelly, Ann Cline (2002), *Jonathan Swift and Popular Culture: Myth, Media and the Man*, New York: Palgrave.

Kettle, Martin (2011), 'Heard the One about the Corrupt, Lying Politician?', the *Guardian*, 25 August. Web. 16 July 2013.

Knoedelseder, William (2009), *I'm Dying Up Here: Heartbreak and High Times in Stand-Up Comedy's Golden Era*, New York: Public Affairs.

Konstan, David (1983), *Roman Comedy*, Ithaca and London: Cornell University Press.

——(1995), *Greek Comedy and Ideology*, Oxford: Oxford University Press.

Kristeva, Julia (1982), *Powers of Horror: An Essay on Abjection*, trans. Leon S. Roudiez, New York: Columbia University Press.

Kubrick, Stanley (dir.) (1964), *Dr. Strangelove or: How I Stopped Worrying and Learned to Love the Bomb*, starring Peter Sellers, George C. Scott: Columbia-Tri Star Studios.

Kundera, Milan (1996), *The Book of Laughter and Forgetting*, trans. Aaron Asher, London: Faber and Faber.

Kyffin, Maurice (1588), *Andria: The First Comedie of Terence, in English*, London.

Lahr, John (1984), *Automatic Vaudeville: Essays on Star Turns*, New York: Knopf.

Landay, Lori (1998), *Madcaps, Screwballs, and Con Women: The Female Trickster in American Culture*, Philadelphia: University of Philadelphia Press.

Langer, Susanne (1953), *Feeling and Form*, London: Routledge and Kegan Paul.

Laroque, François (1993), *Shakespeare's Festive World: Elizabethan Seasonal Entertainment and the Professional Stage*, Cambridge: Cambridge University Press.

Le Goff, Jacques (1997), 'Laughter in the Middle Ages', in *A Cultural History of Humour from Antiquity to the Present Day*, ed. Jan Bremmer and Herman Roodenburg, Cambridge: Polity, pp.40–53.

Leavis, F. R. (1972 [1948]) *The Great Tradition*, Harmondsworth: Penguin.

Leggatt, Alexander (1973), *Citizen Comedy in the Age of Shakespeare*, Toronto: University of Toronto Press.

——(1998), *English Stage Comedy, 1490–1990*, New York and London: Routledge.

——(1999), *Introduction to English Renaissance Comedy*, Manchester: Manchester University Press.

Legman, G. (1975), *Rationale of the Dirty Joke*, 2 vols, New York: Breaking Point.

Lehrer, Brian (2006), 'Borat: Equal Opportunity Insults', *The Brian Lehrer Show*, WNYC, 15 November, radio.

Levin, Harry (1987), *Playboys and Killjoys: An Essay on the Theory and Practice of Comedy*, New York and Oxford: Oxford University Press.

Lévi-Strauss, Claude (1963), *Structural Anthropology*, trans. Claire Jacobson and Brooke Grundfest Schoepf, New York and London: Basic.

Lewisohn, Mark (1998), *The Radio Times Guide to TV Comedy*, London: BBC.

Limon, John (2000), *Stand-Up Comedy in Theory, or Abjection in America*, Durham and London: Duke University Press.

Lippitt, John (1992), 'Humour', in *A Companion to Aesthetics*, ed. David E. Cooper, Oxford: Blackwell, pp.199–203.

Lockyer, Sharon (2011), 'From Toothpick Legs to Dropping Vaginas: Gender and Sexuality in Joan Rivers' Stand-Up Comedy Performance', *Comedy Studies*, 2.12: 113–123.

Loftin, John D. (1991), *Religion and Hopi Life in the Twentieth Century*, Bloomington and Indianapolis: Indianapolis University Press.

London, John (2000), 'Introduction', in *Theatre Under the Nazis*, ed. John London, Manchester: Manchester University Press, pp.1–53.

Lyttleton, Darryl (2006), *Black Comedians on Black Comedy: How African-Americans Taught Us to Laugh*, New York: Applause.

Manning, Bernard (1993), *Bernard Manning Ungagged*, Castle Communications, DVD.

Marshall, George (dir.) (1932), *Their First Mistake*, starring Stan Laurel, Oliver Hardy, Hal Roach Studios.

Martin, Robert Bernard (1974), *The Triumph of Wit: A Study of Victorian Comic Theory*, Oxford: Clarendon.

Masasit Mati (2011), 'The Goal of Top Goon', *masasitmati.org*, Web.

Mayer, David, III (1969), *Harlequin in His Element: The English Pantomime 1806–1836*, Cambridge, MA: Harvard University Press.

McCluskey, Audrey Thomas (2008), 'Introduction', in *Richard Pryor: The Life and Legacy of a 'Crazy' Black Man*, ed. Audrey Thomas McCluskey, Bloomington and Indianapolis: University of Indiana Press, pp.1–19.

Medhurst, Andy (2007), *A National Joke: Popular Comedy and English Cultural Identities*, London and New York: Routledge.

Merchant, Moelwyn W. (1972), *Comedy*, London: Methuen.

Meredith, George (1980), 'An Essay on Comedy', in *Comedy*, ed. Wylie Sypher, Baltimore and London: Johns Hopkins University Press, pp.1–57.

Middleton, Thomas, and Dekker, Thomas (1994), *The Roaring Girl*, ed. Paul Mulholland, Manchester: Manchester University Press.

Morreall, John (1983), *Taking Laughter Seriously*, Albany: SUNY Press.

——(1987), 'A New Theory of Laughter', in *The Philosophy of Laughter and Humor*, ed. John Morreall, Albany: State University of New York Press, pp.128–138.

Mullaney, Steven (1988), *The Place of the Stage: License, Play and Power in Renaissance England*, Chicago: University of Chicago Press.

Nancy, Jean-Luc (1987), 'Wild Laughter in the Throat of Death', *Modern Language Notes*, 102.4 (September): 719–736.

——(1992), 'Elliptical Sense', in *Derrida: A Critical Reader*, ed. David Wood, Oxford: Blackwell, pp.36–51.

Neal, Steve, and Krutnik, Frank (1990), *Popular Film and Television Comedy*, London: Routledge.

Neilsen (2011), 'The New Mainstream: 28% of TV Warching spent on LGBT-inclusive shows'. http://www.nielsen.com/us/en/newswire/2011/the-new-mainstream-28-of-tv-watching-spent-on-lgbt-inclusive-shows.html

Newman, Karen (1991), *Fashioning Femininity and English Renaissance Drama*, Chicago: University of Chicago Press.

Newton, Esther (1979), *Mother Camp: Female Impersonators in America*, Chicago and London: University of Chicago Press.

Nussbaum, Emily (2011), 'Crass Warfare: Raunch and Ridicule on "Whitney" and "2 Broke Girls"', *The New Yorker*. Web. 24 June 2013.

Olson, Kirby (2001), *Comedy After Postmodernism: Rereading Comedy from Edward Lear to Charles Willeford*, Texas: Texas Tech University Press.

Orgel, Stephen (1989), 'Nobody's Perfect: Or Why Did the English Stage Take Boys for Women?', *The South Atlantic Quarterly*, 88.1 (Winter): 7–29.

——(1994), 'The Comedian as the Character C', in *English Comedy*, ed. Michael Cordner, Peter Holland and John Kerrigan, Cambridge: Cambridge University Press.

——(1997), *Impersonations: The Performance of Gender in Shakespeare's England*, Cambridge: Cambridge University Press.

Paglia, Camille (1994), *Vamps and Tramps: New Essays*, New York: Vintage.

——(2013), 'Joan Rivers Turns 80!', *Hollywood Reporter*, 419.22 (21 June): 104.

Palmer, D. J. (1984), *Comedy: Developments in Criticism*, Basingstoke: Macmillan.

Palmer, Jerry (1994), *Taking Humour Seriously*, London: Routledge.

Paster, Gail Kern (1993), *The Body Embarrassed: Drama and the Disciplines of Shame in Early Modern England*, Ithaca: Cornell University Press.

Perks, Lisa Glebatis (2008), 'A Sketch Comedy of Errors: *Chapelle's Show*, Stereotypes, and Viewers', unpublished Doctoral Dissertation, University of Texas, Austin.

Plato (1951), *The Symposium*, trans. Walter Hamilton, Harmondsworth: Penguin.

——(1994), *Republic*, trans. Robin Waterfield, Oxford and New York: Oxford University Press.

Plautus, Titus Maccius (1984), *The Pot of Gold and Other Plays*, trans. E. F. Watling, Harmondsworth: Penguin.

Plessner, Helmuth (1970), *Laughing and Crying*, trans. James Spencer Churchill and Majorie Grene, Evanston: Northwestern University Press.

Pope, Alexander (2012), *The Rape of the Lock*, in *The Norton Anthology of English Literature*, ed. Stephen Greenblatt et al., London and New York: W.W. Norton, pp.2686–2704.

Porter, Lorraine (1998), 'Tarts, Tampons and Tyrants: Women and Representation in British Comedy', in *Because I Tell a Joke or Two: Comedy, Politics and Social Difference*, ed. Stephen Wagg, London and New York: Routledge, pp.65–93.

Pozner, Jennifer L. (2012), 'Louis C.K. on Daniel Tosh's Rape Joke: Are Comedy and Feminism Enemies?', *The Daily Beast*, 18 July. Web. 21 February 2014.

Pullar, Philipa (2001), *Consuming Passions: A History of English Food and Appetite*, Harmondsworth: Penguin.

Purdie, Susan (1993), *Comedy: The Mastery of Discourse*, London: Harvester Wheatsheaf.

Rabelais, François (1955), *Gargantua* and *Pantagruel*, trans. J. M. Cohen, Harmondsworth: Penguin.

Rhodes, Neil (1980), *Elizabethan Grotesque*, London et al.: Routledge and Kegan Paul.

Rivers, Joan (2004), *Live at the Apollo*, prod. Alan Hardcastle, BBC One, television.

——(2012), 'Why Johnny Carson Never Spoke to Me Again', *The Hollywood Reporter*. Web. 25 June 2013.

Rountree, Wendy Alexia (2011), '"Faking the Funk": A Journey Towards Authentic Blackness', in *Authentic Blackness/'Real' Blackness: Essays on the Meaning of Blackness in Literature and Culture*, ed. Martin Japtok and Jerry Rafiki Jenkins, New York: Peter Lang, pp.101–108.

Rowe, Kathleen (1995), *The Unruly Woman: Gender and the Genres of Laughter*, Austin: University of Texas Press.

Rowse, A. L. (1976), *The Case Books of Simon Forman: Sex and Society in Shakespeare's Age*, London: Picador.

Ruggiers, Paul G. (1977), *Versions of Medieval Comedy*, Norman: University of Oklahoma Press.

Sacks, Mike (2009), *And Here's The Kicker: Conversations with 21 Top Humor Writers on their Craft*, Cincinnati, OH: Writer's Digest Books.

Sanborn, Kate (1885), *The Wit of Women*, New York: Funk and Wagnalls.

Sayle, Alexei (1988), *Alexei Sayle Live at the Comic Strip*, MCI Spoken Word.

Segal, Erich (2001), *The Death of Comedy*, Cambridge, MA and London: Harvard University Press.

Senelick, Laurence (2000), *The Changing Room: Sex, Drag, and Theatre*, London and New York: Routledge.

Shaftesbury, Anthony Ashley Cooper, Lord (1988), *An Old Spelling Edition of Shaftesbury's* Letter Concerning Human Understanding *and* Sensus Communis: An Essay on the Freedom of Wit and Humour, ed. Richard B. Wolf, New York and London: Garland.

Shakespeare, William (1989), *The Complete Works*, ed. Stanley Wells and Gary Taylor, Oxford: Oxford University Press.

——(1998), *Julius Caesar*, ed. Arthur Humphreys, Oxford: Oxford University Press.

Shanzer, Danuta (2002), 'Laughter and Humour in the Early Medieval West', in *Humour History and Politics in the Late Middle Ages*, ed. Guy Halsall, Cambridge: Cambridge University Press.

Sidney, Sir Philip (1991), *A Defence of Poetry*, ed. J. A. Van Dorsten, Oxford: Oxford University Press.

Sikov, Ed (1994), *Laughing Hysterically: American Screen Comedy of the 1950s*, New York: Columbia University Press.

Silk, M. S. (2000), *Aristophanes and the Definition of Comedy*, Oxford: Oxford University Press.

Silverman, Sarah (2005), *Sarah Silverman: Jesus is Magic*, dir. Liam Lynch: Roadside Attractions, DVD.

——(2010), *The Bedwetter: Stories of Courage, Redemption and Pee*, New York: HarperCollins.

Simpson, Tyrone R. (2008), 'When Keeping It Real Goes Wrong: Pryor, Chapelle, and the Comedic Politics of the Post-Soul', in *Richard Pryor: The Life and Legacy of a 'Crazy' Black Man*, ed. Audrey Thomas McCluskey, Bloomington and Indianapolis: University of Indiana Press, pp.106–138.

Sinfield, Alan (1999), *Out On Stage: Lesbian and Gay Theatre in the Twentieth Century*, New Haven: Yale.

Sontag, Susan (1982), 'Notes on Camp', in *A Susan Sontag Reader*, New York: Farrar/Strauss/Giroux, pp.105–119.

Spencer, Herbert (1860), 'The Physiology of Laughter', *Macmillan's Magazine*, 5 (March): 395–402.

Stallybrass, Peter, and White, Allon (1986), *The Politics and Poetics of Transgression*, London: Methuen.

Stanhope, W. (Lord Chesterfield) (1929), *Lord Chesterfield's Letters to His Son and Others*, London: Dent.

Stanley, Alessandra (2008), 'Who Says Women Aren't Funny?', *Vanity Fair*. Web. 8 July 2013.

Stuart, Roxana (1993), 'Duelling en Travestie: Cross-Dressed Swordfighters in Three Jacobean Comedies', *Theatre Studies*, 38: 29–34.

Swift, Jonathan (1984), *A Tale of a Tub and Other Works*, ed. Angus Ross and David Wooley, Oxford: Oxford University Press.

——(1985), *Gulliver's Travels*, ed. Peter Dixon and John Chalker, Harmondsworth: Penguin.

——(1993), *A Modest Proposal*, in *The Norton Anthology of English Literature*, ed. M. H. Abrams et al., 6th edn, 2 vols, New York and London: Norton, vol. 1, pp.2181–2187.

———(2012), 'The Lady's Dressing Room', in *The Norton Anthology of English Literature*, ed. Stephen Greenblatt et al., London and New York: W.W. Norton, pp.2767–2770.

Synott, Anthony (1993), *The Body Social: Symbolism, Self, and Society*, London: Routledge.

Taaffee, Lauren K. (1993), *Aristophanes and Women*, London and New York: Routledge.

Tatischeff, Sophie (1989), *In the Footsteps of M. Hulot*, Criterion Collection, DVD.

Taylor, Juval, and Austen, Jake (2012), *Darkest America: Black Minstrelsy From Slavery to Hip Hop*, New York: Norton.

Tillman, Aaron (2009), '"Through the Rube Goldberg Crazy Straw": Ethnic Mobility and Narcissistic Fantasy in *Sarah Silverman: Jesus Is Magic*', *Studies in American Humor*, 3.20: 58–84.

Traub, Valerie (1992), *Desire and Anxiety: Circulations of Sexuality in Shakespearean Drama*, London and New York: Routledge.

Trave, Stuart M. (1960), *The Amiable Humorist: A Study in Comic Theory and Criticism in the Eighteenth and Early Nineteenth Centuries*, Chicago and London: University of Chicago Press.

Udall, Nicholas (1984), *Ralph Roister Doister*, in *Four Tudor Comedies*, ed. William Tydeman, Harmondsworth: Penguin.

Vitruvius (1999), *Ten Books on Architecture*, trans. Ingrid D. Rowland, Cambridge: Cambridge University Press.

Viveros, Joy (2011), 'Black Authenticity, *Racial Drag*, and the Case of Dave Chapelle', in *Authentic Blackness/'Real' Blackness: Essays on the Meaning of Blackness in Literature and Culture*, ed. Martin Japtok and Jerry Rafiki Jenkins, New York: Peter Lang, pp. 140–153.

Wagg, Stephen (1998), '"At Ease Corporal": Social Class and the Situation Comedy in British Television from the 1950s to the 1990s', in *Because I Tell a Joke or Two: Comedy, Politics and Social Difference*, ed. Stephen Wagg, London and New York: Routledge, pp.1–31.

Watkins, Mel (1999), *On the Real Side: A History of African American Comedy*, Chicago: Lawrence Hill.

Weaver, Simon (2011), *The Rhetoric of Racist Humour: US, UK and Global Race Joking*, Farnham: Ashgate.

Welsford, Enid (1935), *The Fool: His Social and Literary History*, London: Faber and Faber.

Wilde, Oscar (1980), *The Importance of Being Earnest*, ed. Russell Jackson, London: Ernest Benn.

Wilder, Billy (dir.) (1959), *Some Like It Hot*, starring Tony Curtis, Jack Lemmon, Marilyn Monroe: MGM Studios.

Williams, John A., and Williams, Dennis A. (2008), 'The Politics of Being Black: From *If I Stop I'll Die: The Comedy and Tragedy of Richard Pryor*', in *Richard Pryor: The Life and Legacy of a 'Crazy' Black Man*, ed. Audrey Thomas McCluskey, Bloomington and Indianapolis: University of Indiana Press, pp.154–170.

Williams, Robert I. (1993), *Comic Practice/Comic Response*, London and Toronto: Associated University Press.

Wilson, Christopher P. (1979), *Jokes: Form, Content and Function*, London et al.: Academic Press.

Wilson, Thomas (1567), *The Arte of Rhetorike*, London.

Witke, Charles (1970), *Latin Satire: The Structure of Persuasion*, Leiden: E.J. Brill.

Wycherley, William (1996), *The Country Wife and Other Plays*, ed. Peter Dixon, Oxford: Oxford University Press.

Zinoman, Jason (2011), 'Female Comedians, Breaking the Taste-Taboo Ceiling', *The New York Times*. Web. 25 June 2013.

Zupančič, Alenka (2008), *The Odd One In: On Comedy*, Cambridge, MA: MIT Press.

INDEX